MW01631461

As the Executive Director of the Mexican Fine Arts Center Museum, it is a pleasure and honor to present *Frida Kahlo, Diego Rivera and 20th Century Mexican Art: The Jacques and Natasha Gelman Collection*. Regarded as one of the world's greatest private collections, the Gelman Collection pays tribute to the vast artistic vision of Jacques and Natasha Gelman and demonstrates the broad scope and power that has come to distinguish 20th Century Mexican Art internationally.

Whenever a museum presents such a noteworthy exhibition such as this one, there are always a great number of individuals and institutions that need to be thanked – this exhibition is no exception. Let me begin by thanking Robert Littman and Magda Carranza de Akle, and everyone at the Vergel Foundation for making this exhibition possible. I want to thank Berta Cea of the U.S. Embassy in Mexico City and locally to the Consul General of Mexico, Carlos Manuel Sada Solana and Luz del Amo, Cultural Attaché. I would also like to thank all of our funders: major support was provided by Kraft Foods, the Northern Trust Company, ComEd, and the Joyce Foundation. Other support was provided by la Secretaría de Relaciones Exteriores de México, CONACULTA, INBA, and the Instituto de Mexico, Chicago. Local support was provided by the Chicago Park District, the Illinois Arts Council, and the Chicago Department of Cultural Affairs. Media support was made possible by CBS 2 Chicago, Univision Chicago, Chicago Public Radio, and Exito Newspaper. Transportation was provided by American Airlines and accommodations by Lenox Suites. This exhibition was also supported by numerous padrinos and I want to express my sincere gratitude for their assistance.

I also extend a big "abrazo" to both the Board and Staff of The Mexican Fine Arts Center Museum who have all enthusiastically embraced this exhibition. Everyone on the museum's staff has worked so diligently to organize this exhibition, but special mention must be given to the following staff members – Cesáreo Moreno, Director of Visual Arts; Rebecca D. Meyers, Permanent Collections Director and Registrar; Angelina Villanueva, Graphic Arts Director; Eva Penar, Marketing/Media Director; Silvia Cisneros, Business Director; Lydia Huante, Education Director; Raquel Rios, Gift Shop Manager; Raquel Aguiñaga, Visual Arts Assistant Director; Oscar Sanchez, Preparator; and Ignacio Guzman, Building Operations Consultant. I also want to thank Juana Guzman, the Museum's Associate Executive Director and our Administration Office Manager Rachel Blanco. The *Frida Kahlo, Diego Rivera and 20th Century Mexican Art: The Jacques and Natasha Gelman Collection* is the inaugural exhibition for the Museum's new Development Director, Randy Adamsick, and I want to welcome him to our museum family.

In its effort to preserve and stimulate awareness of Mexico's rich culture, the Mexican Fine Arts Center Museum has earned its reputation as the nation's leading Latino arts institution. By presenting this magnificent exhibition, the museum affirms its commitment and dedication to showcasing the best of Mexican art and culture.

Carlos Tortolero
Executive Director

FRIDA KAHLO • DIEGO RIVERA

AND 20TH CENTURY MEXICAN ART

The Jacques and Natasha Gelman Collection

January 24 - April 27 2003

Emilio Baz Viaud (1918-1991)

Lola Alvarez Bravo (1905-1993)

Manuel Alvarez Bravo (1902-2002)

Leonora Carrington (1917-)

Elena Climent (1955-)

Miguel Covarrubias (1904-1957)

Gunther Gerzso (1915-2000)

María Izquierdo (1902-1955)

Frida Kahlo (1907-1954)

Agustín Lazo (1897-1971)

Carlos Mérida (1891-1984)

José Clemente Orozco (1883-1949)

Carlos Orozco Romero (1898-1984)

Diego Rivera (1886-1957)

Jesús Reyes Ferreira (1882-1977)

David Álfaro Siqueiros (1896-1974)

Juan Soriano (1920-)

Rufino Tamayo (1899-1991)

Francisco Toledo (1940-)

Angel Zárraga (1886-1946)

Nahum Zenil (1947-)

Contents | Contenido

Natasha Gelman died peacefully the morning of the fourth of May 1998, in her house in Cuernavaca where, on that very morning she, as on every morning, would have seen the peak of Popocatépetl from her bedroom window and faced on the wall in front of her a selection of self portraits by Frida Kahlo. She was eighty-six years old.

During the fifteen years of my life in Mexico, my friendship with both Natasha and her husband Jacques was a determining factor to my cultural transition. After Jacques' death in 1986, Natasha and I increasingly shared time together, as I lived only an hour away in Mexico City. During my last visit with her, the weekend before she died, we went for lunch to her favorite restaurant, a converted seventeenth-century manor house whose façade hides a tropical paradise with luscious gardens and wandering troops of white peacocks and yellow tufted herons. Natasha asked for her usual table adjacent to the entrance where she could analyze and succinctly comment on the manner and character of those clients entering and leaving. That perceptiveness and direct observation pretty much sums up the actual way the Gelmans collected: without hesitation and without regard to the opinion of others—and always on target.

Natasha and Jacques Gelman acquired the canvases of Frida Kahlo and her husband, Diego Rivera, when there were only a handful of collectors in Mexico. And when the Gelmans became enthusiastic about an artist's work, they reinforced their convictions (as well as the artist's financial well-being) by buying in depth the work of those so favored. It just so happened these artists came to be the most famous of their generation.

Natasha's great beauty was documented by the portraits her adoring husband commissioned by these same artists. One could fill a whole gallery just with these portraits. Her last portrait, painted by the Spanish artist Rafael Cidoncha demonstrates, a half a century later, that she had not lost any of her brilliance, charm, or vitality.

Natasha Gelman had a very clear idea and mission of what was needed to complete and strengthen the collection housed in Mexico and New York on Jacques' death. Not only did she use her connaissance to complete what works she felt were needed in the collection of School of Paris painting and sculpture which went to The Metropolitan Museum of Art on her death, but she concentrated an equal amount of energy in keeping her Mexican collection up to date. This collection was placed throughout the rooms of her house in Cuernavaca. One can take for example the late addition to the collection of an important oil by Francisco Toledo as well as the work of even more contemporary artists such as Adolfo Riestra, Sergio Hernandez, Elena Climent, and Paula Santiago.

This collection is still a work in progress, as it was for Natasha and Jacques Gelman during their lifetimes. In the year since her death, ten new works have been added both by contemporary and modern Mexican painters, and the collection will continue to grow as both Jacques and Natasha would have wished, encouraging and supporting Mexican artists of succeeding generations.

Robert R. Littman

Natasha Gelman se extinguió apaciblemente el 4 de mayo de 1998 en su casa de Cuernavaca donde, incluso esa mañana, ella había podido ver la cima del Popocatépetl por su ventana y frente a ella, en la pared de su cuarto, una selección de autorretratos de Frida Kahlo.
Tenía 86 años.

Durante los quince años que yo viví en México, los lazos de amistad que me ligaron a ella así como a su marido, Jacques Gelman, no habían cesado de reforzarse. Después de la muerte de él, mis encuentros con ella se hicieron más frecuentes aún. En mi última visita—yo vivo en la ciudad de México, a una hora de Cuernavaca en automóvil—fuimos a comer a su restaurante preferido, cuya austera fachada del siglo XVII esconde un paraíso tropical en el que deambulan escuadrones de pavorreales indolentes. Natasha pidió su mesa habitual, aquella desde la cual podía cómodamente analizar a los clients que entraban y salían. Los más — o más bien menos—afortunados tenían derecho a un comentario, no siempre cariñoso, pero breve y penetrante. Esa misma Mirada aguda, esas mismas observaciones directas y justas, caracterizaban el modo de actuar de los coleccionistas Gelman. Sin vacilaciones, ni preocupaciones por la opinión ajena.

Natasha y Jacques Gelman le compraron telas a Frida Kahlo y a su marido, Diego Rivera, cuando casi no había coleccionistas en México y sus obras apenas se vendían. Y, cuando los Gelman se entusiasmaban por un artista, se esforzaban por apuntalar su convicción (y el bienestar económico del artista) comprándole numerosas obras de calidad para hacer estallar la fuerza de su talento. Resultó que estos artistas llegaron a ser los más famosos de su generación.

De una gran belleza, Natasha Gelman—envalentonada por su marido que la adoraba—comisionaba retratos por los artistas. Se podría completar una sala entera de retratos de ella ejecutados por todos los grandes maestros mexicanos de su generación, Rivera, Kahlo, Siqueiros, Tamayo. El último de sus retratos pintado por el joven artista español Rafael Cidoncha, demuestra que medio siglo más tarde, ella no había perdido nada de su brillo, encanto ó vitalidad.

Natasha Gelman tenía una idea muy precisa de las lagunas de su colección y de las obras necesarias para completarla. Se empeñó tanto en la parte "escuela de París" de la colección, hasta hace poco colgada en su departamento newyorkino y actualment legada al Metropolitan Museum of Art, como en la parte mexicana de este excepcional conjunto, que la rodearía en su residencia de Cuernavaca hasta su muerte. Así, por ejemplo, ella enriqueció la colección con una importante tela de Francisco Toledo y adquirió obras de artistas más jóvenes como Adolfo Riesta, Sergio Hernández, Elena Climent y Paula Santiago.

Esta colección continúa siendo una obra en proceso, como lo fue para Natasha y Jacques Gelman durante sus vidas. En el año a partir de su muerte, se han añadido diez nuevas obras de pintores mexicanos tanto contemporáneos como modernos, y la colección continuara creciendo como lo hubieran deseado Jacques y Natasha, impulsando y apoyando a los artistas mexicanos de generaciones futuras.

Robert R. Littman

Emilio Baz Viaud
(1918-1991)

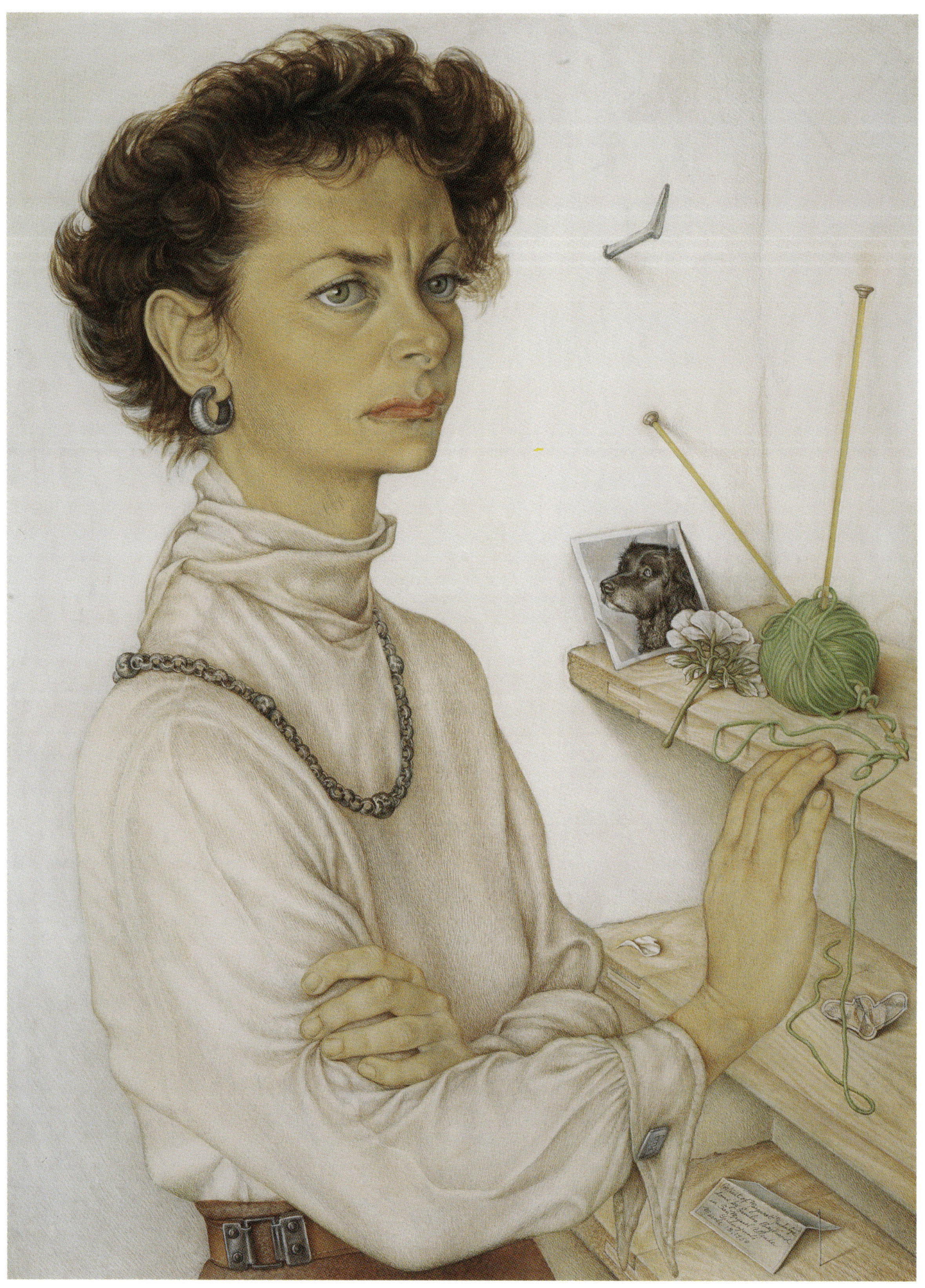

Emilio Baz Viaud
Portrait of Margot Mac Inteyre / *Retrato de Margot Mac Inteyre*, 1950, Watercolor and dry brush on cardboard / *Acuarela y pincel seco sobre cartulina*, 91.5 x 61 cm, 35 3/4" x 24"

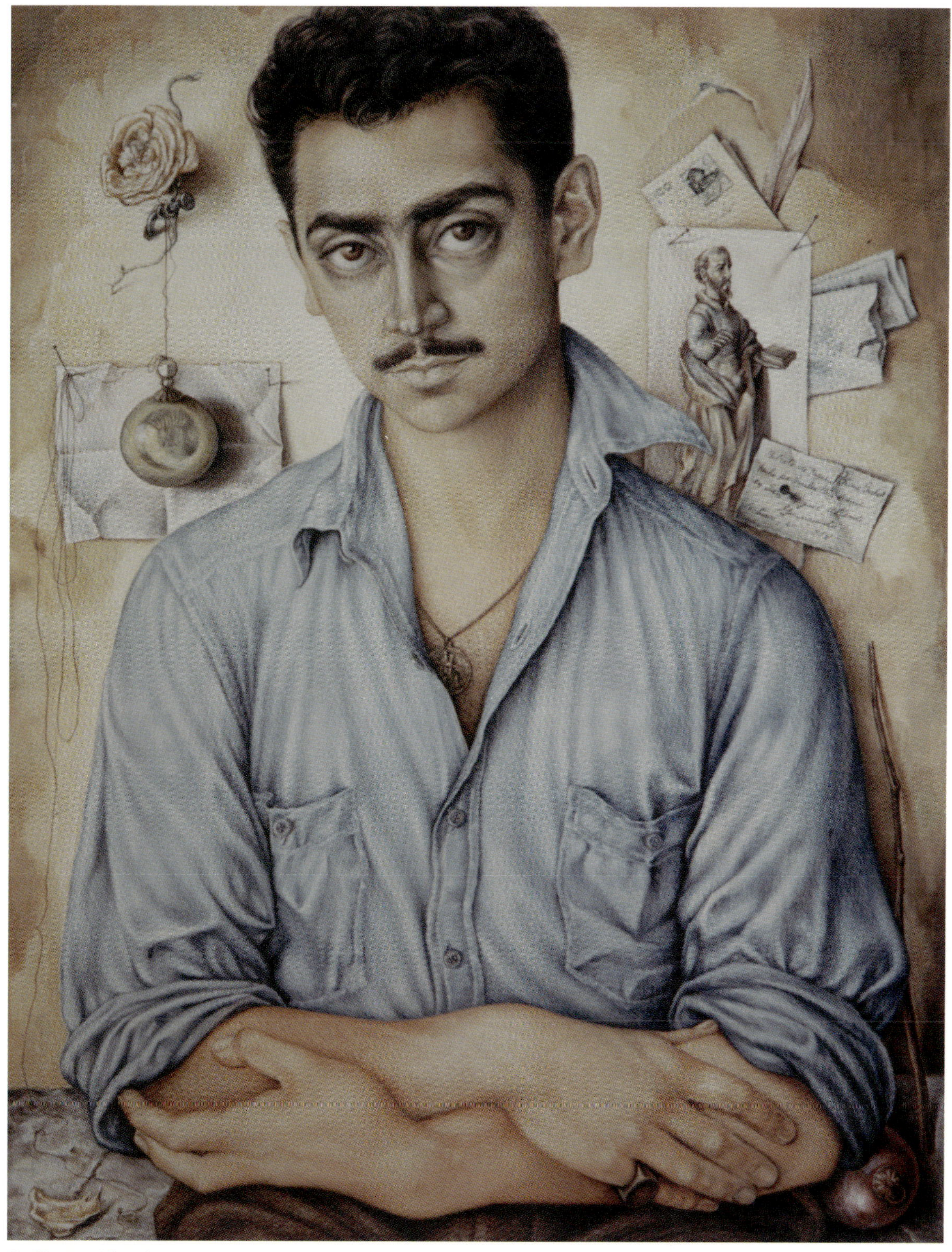

Emilio Baz Viaud
Portrait of Nazario Chimez Barket / *Retrato de Nazario Chimez Barket*, 1952, Watercolor and dry brush on cardboard / *Acuarela y pincel seco sobre cartulina*, 74 x 53 cm, 29 1/8" x 20 7/8"

Lola Alvarez Bravo
(1905-1993)

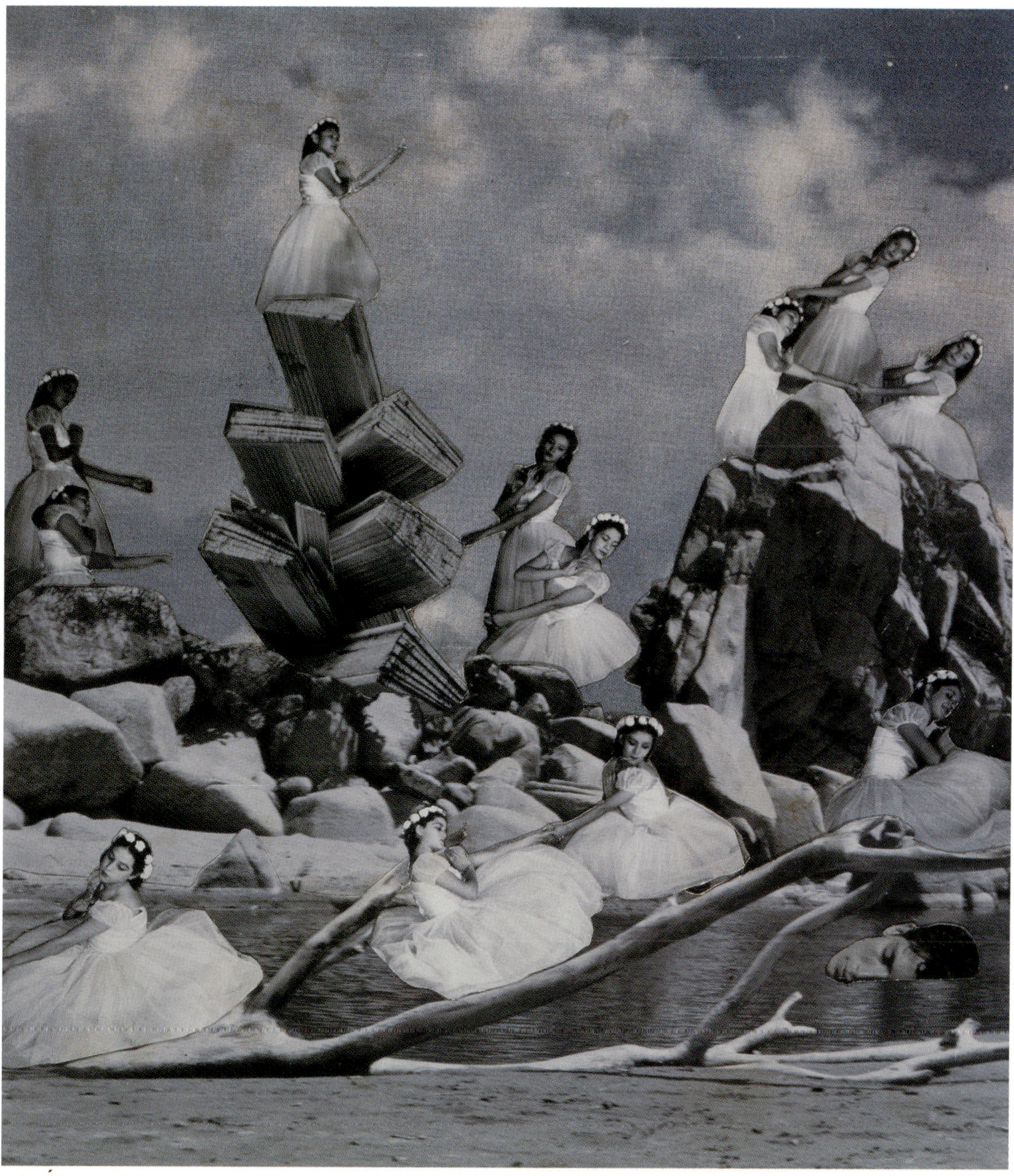

Lola Álvarez Bravo
The Dream of the Drowned / *El sueño del ahogado*, ca. 1945, Photo-collage (gelatin silver print, offset and ink) / *Fotocollage (plata gelatina, offset y tinta)*, 26 x 22 cm, 10 1/4" x 81 1/16"

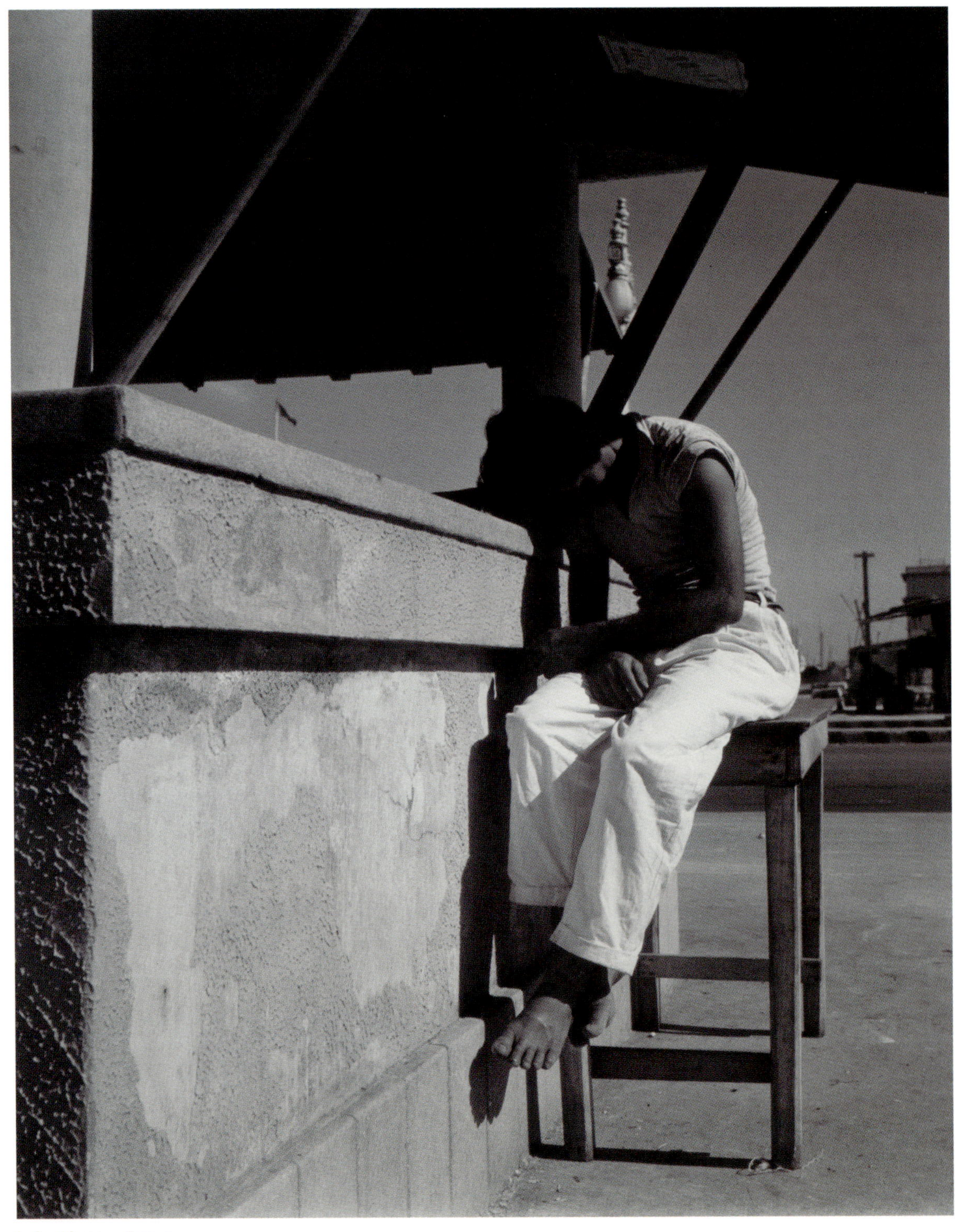

Lola Alvarez Bravo
The Hangover / *La cruda*, 1945, Veracruz, Mexico, Gelatin silver print / *Plata gelatina*, 25.4 x 20.32 cm, 8" x 10"

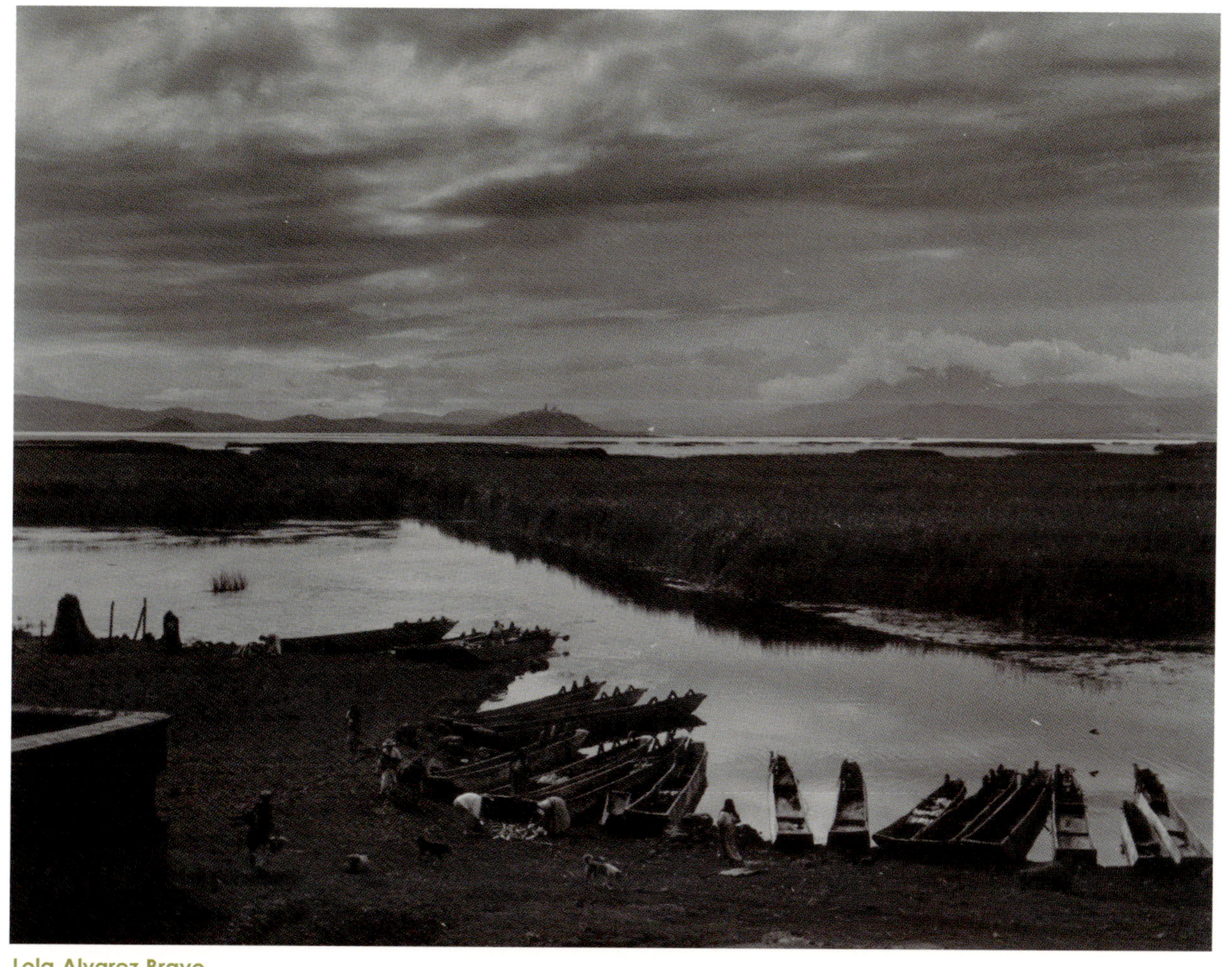

Lola Alvarez Bravo
Erongarícuaro, 1945, Michoacán, Mexico, Gelatin silver print / *Plata gelatina*, 17.78 x 24.13 cm, 7" x 9$^{1/2}$"

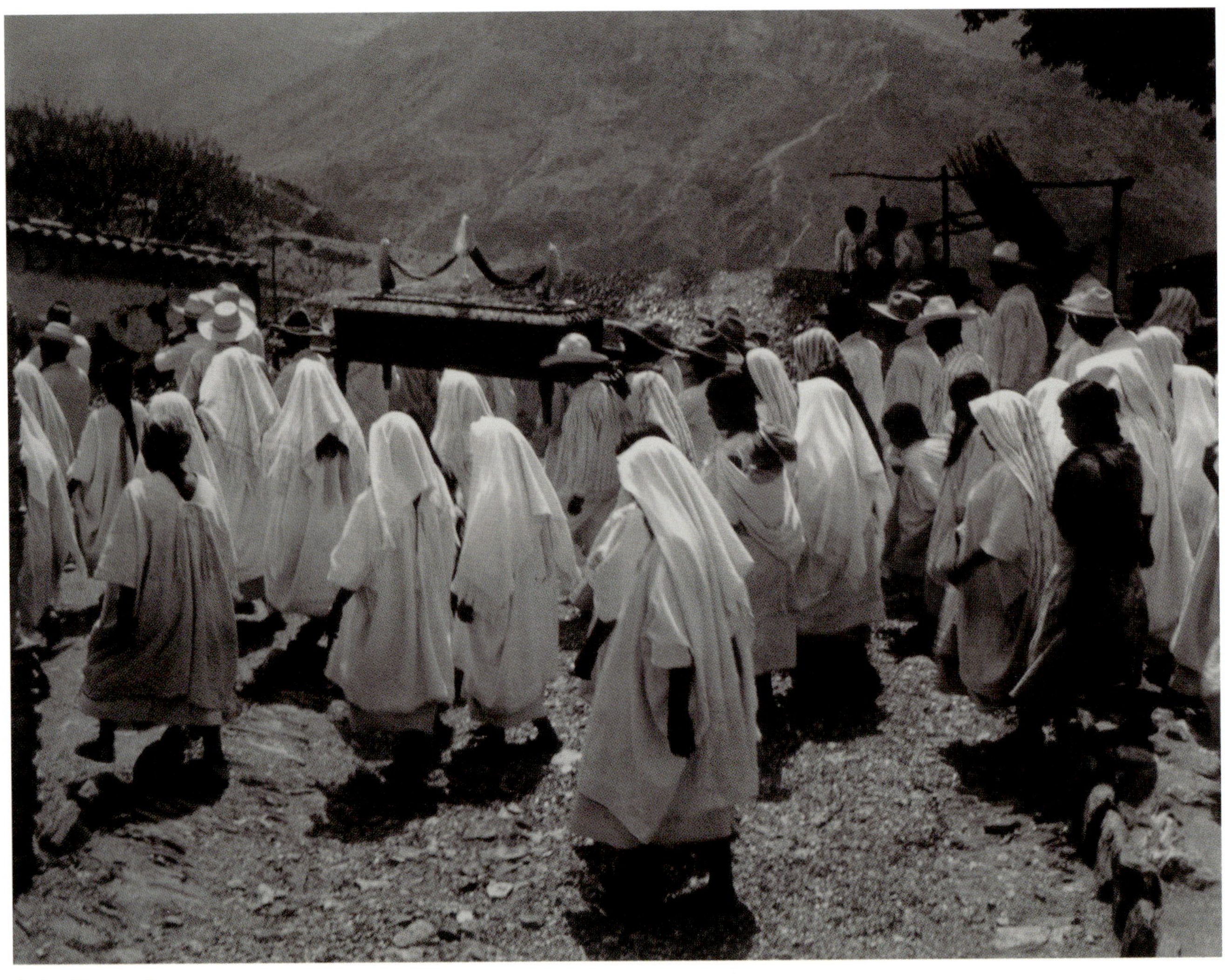

Lola Alvarez Bravo
Burial at Yalalag / *Entierro en Yalalag*, 1946, Oaxaca, Mexico, Gelatin silver print / *Plata gelatina*, 17.78 x 24.13 cm, 7" x 9$^{1/2}$"

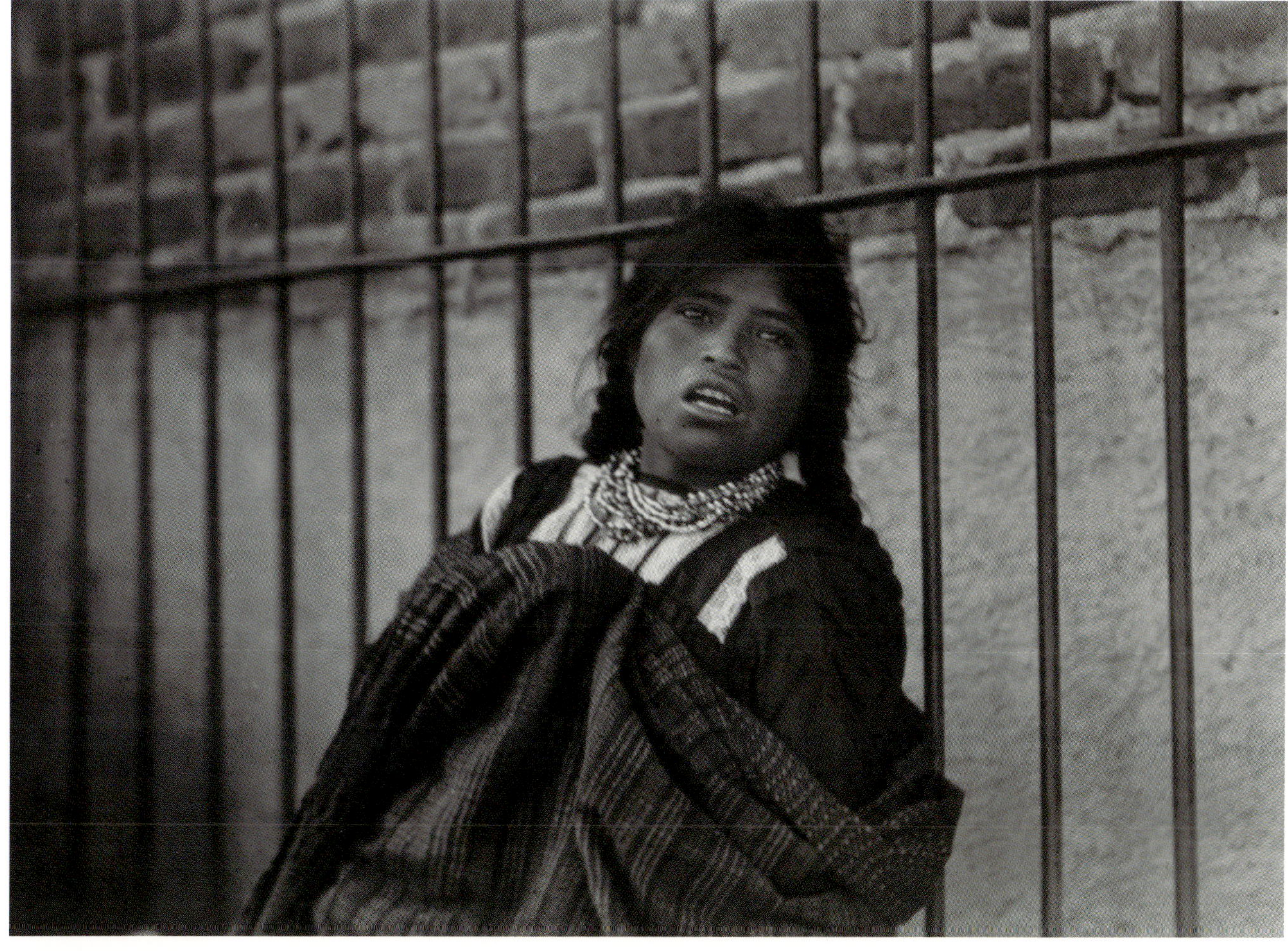

Lola Alvarez Bravo
Other People's Guilt / *Por culpas afines*, 1948, Mexico City, Mexico, Gelatin silver print / *Plata gelatina*, 17.78 x 22.86 cm, 7" x 9"

Manuel Alvarez Bravo

(1902-2002)

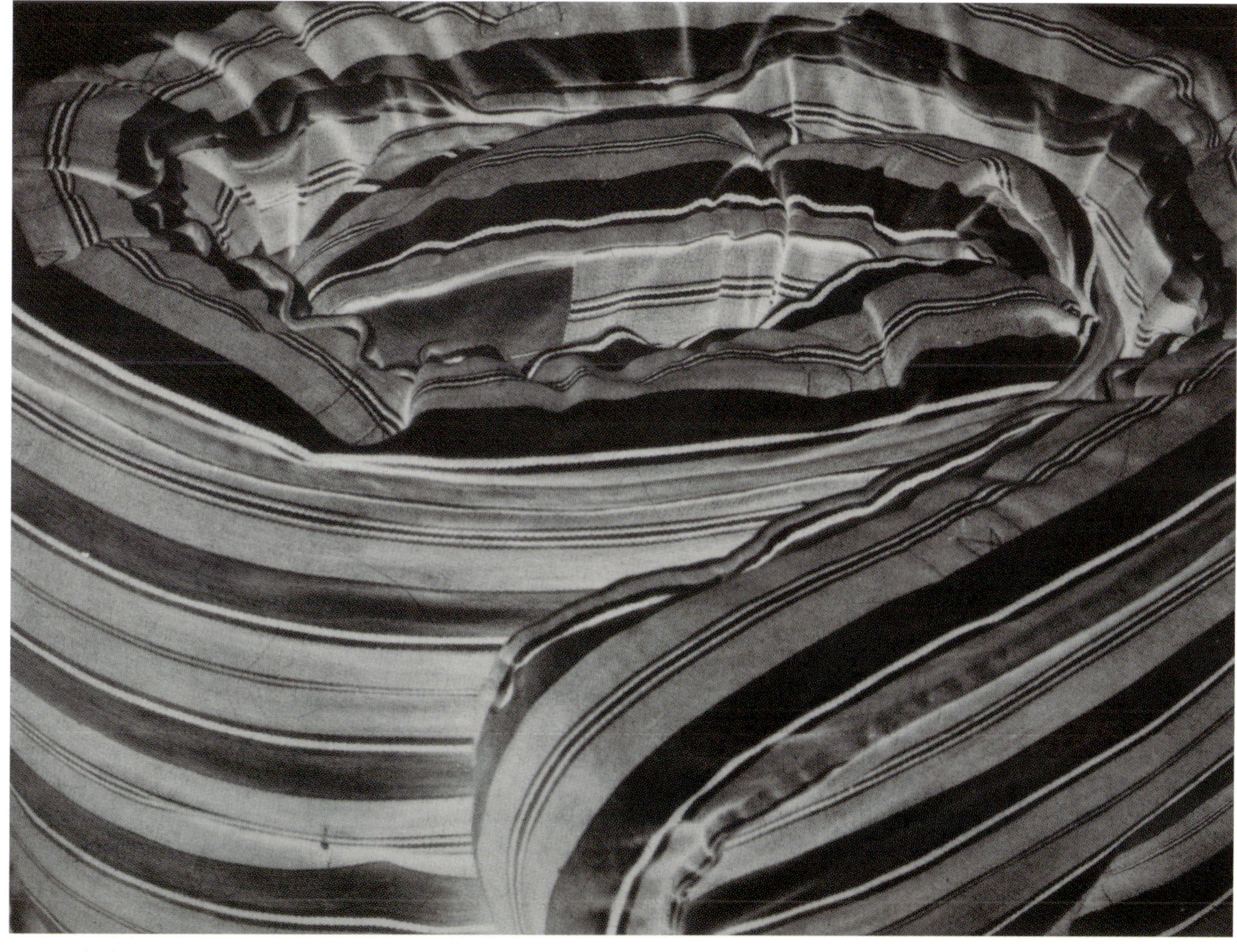

Manuel Alvarez Bravo
Mattress / *Colchón,* 1927, Platinum print / *Platino*, 20.32 x 25.4 cm, 8" x 10"

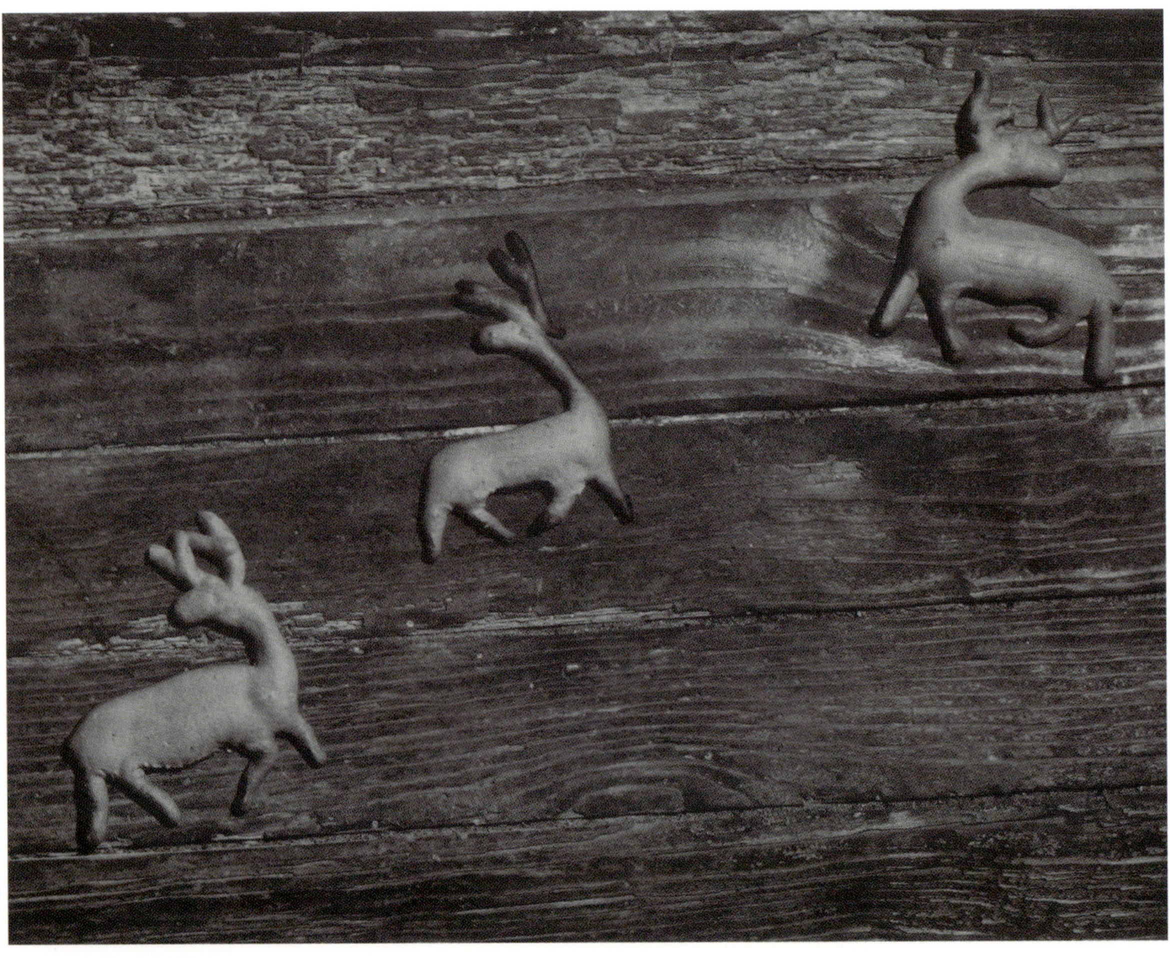

Manuel Alvarez Bravo
Our Daily Bread / *Pan nuestro,* 1929, Platinum print / *Platino*, 20.32 x 25.4 cm, 8" x 10"

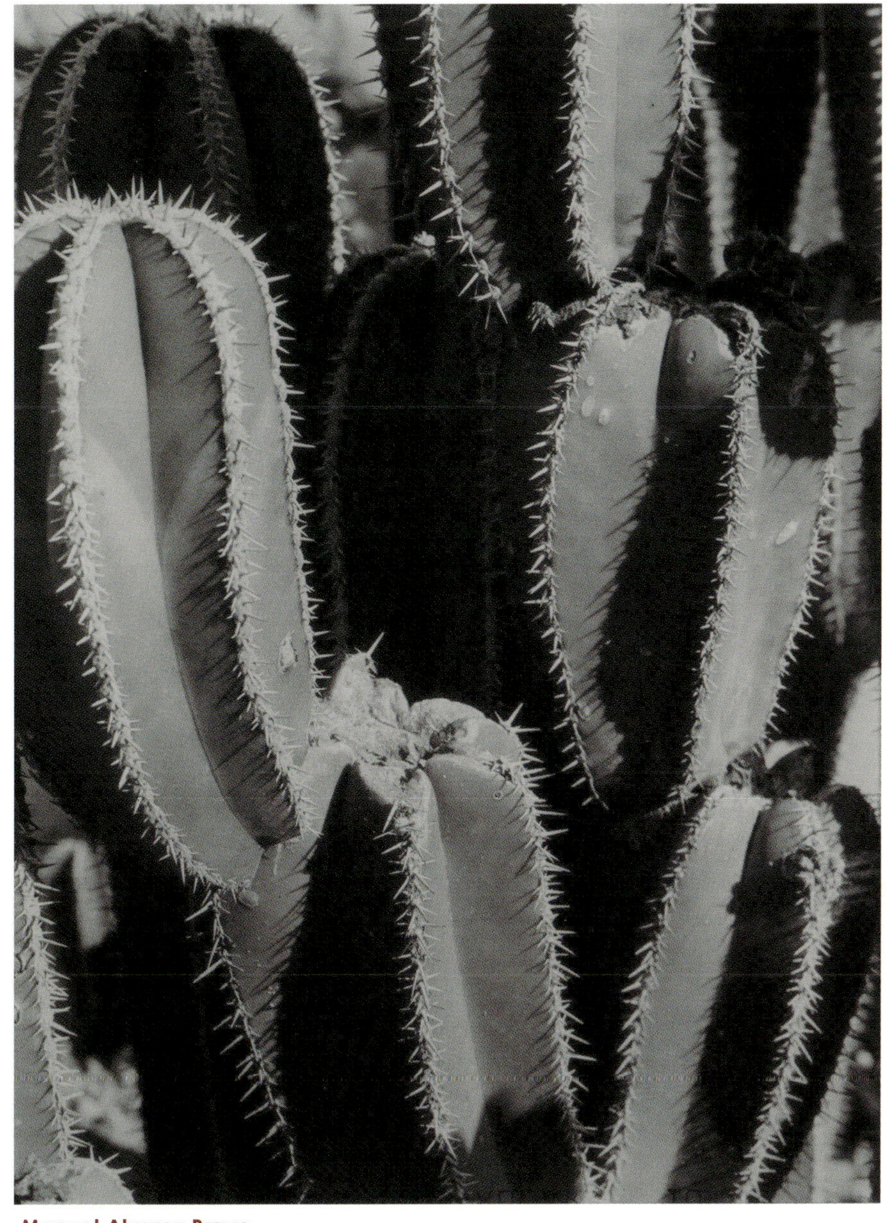

Manuel Alvarez Bravo
Organ Pipe Cacti / *Cactus*, 1929, Platinum print / *Platino*, 25.4 x 20.32 cm, 10" x 8"

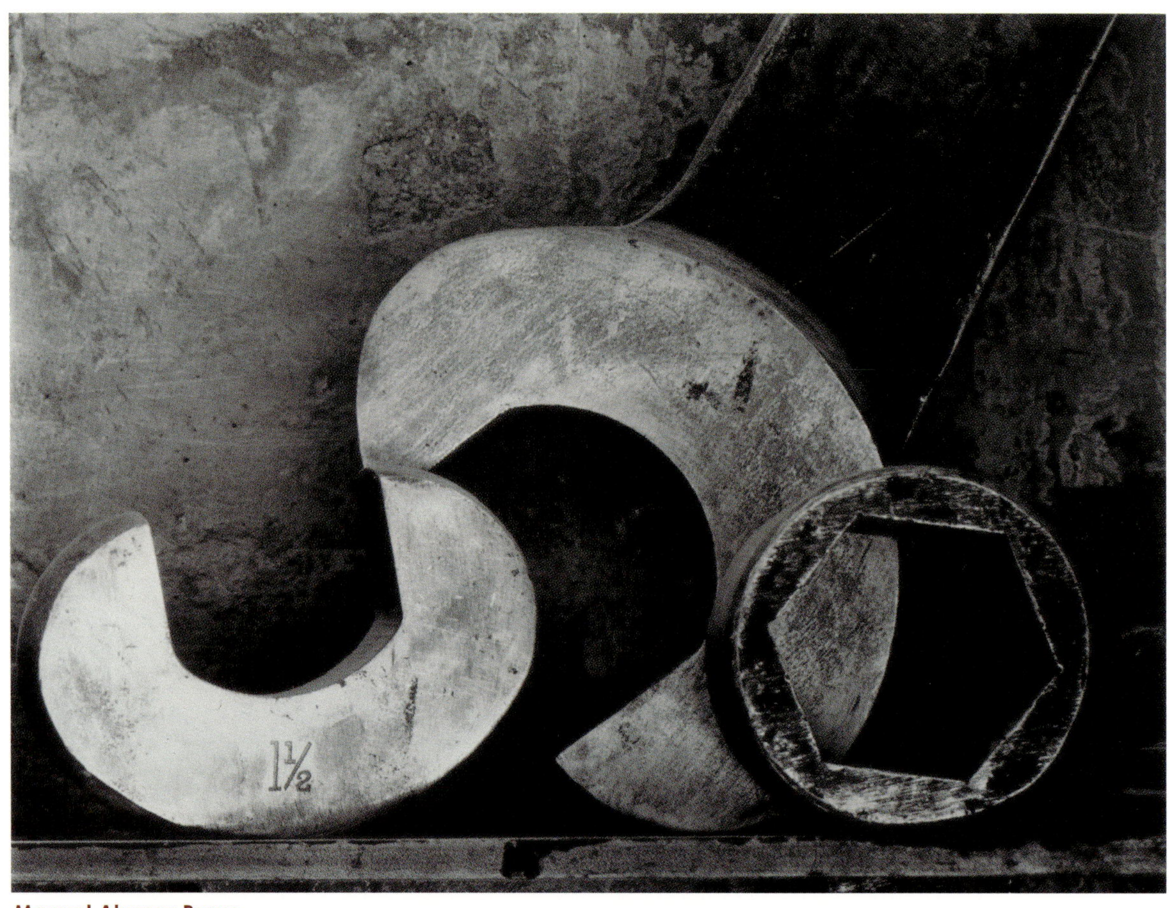

Manuel Alvarez Bravo
The Instruments / *El instrumental,* 1931, Silver gelatin print / *Plata gelatina*, 20.32 x 25.4 cm, 8" x 10"

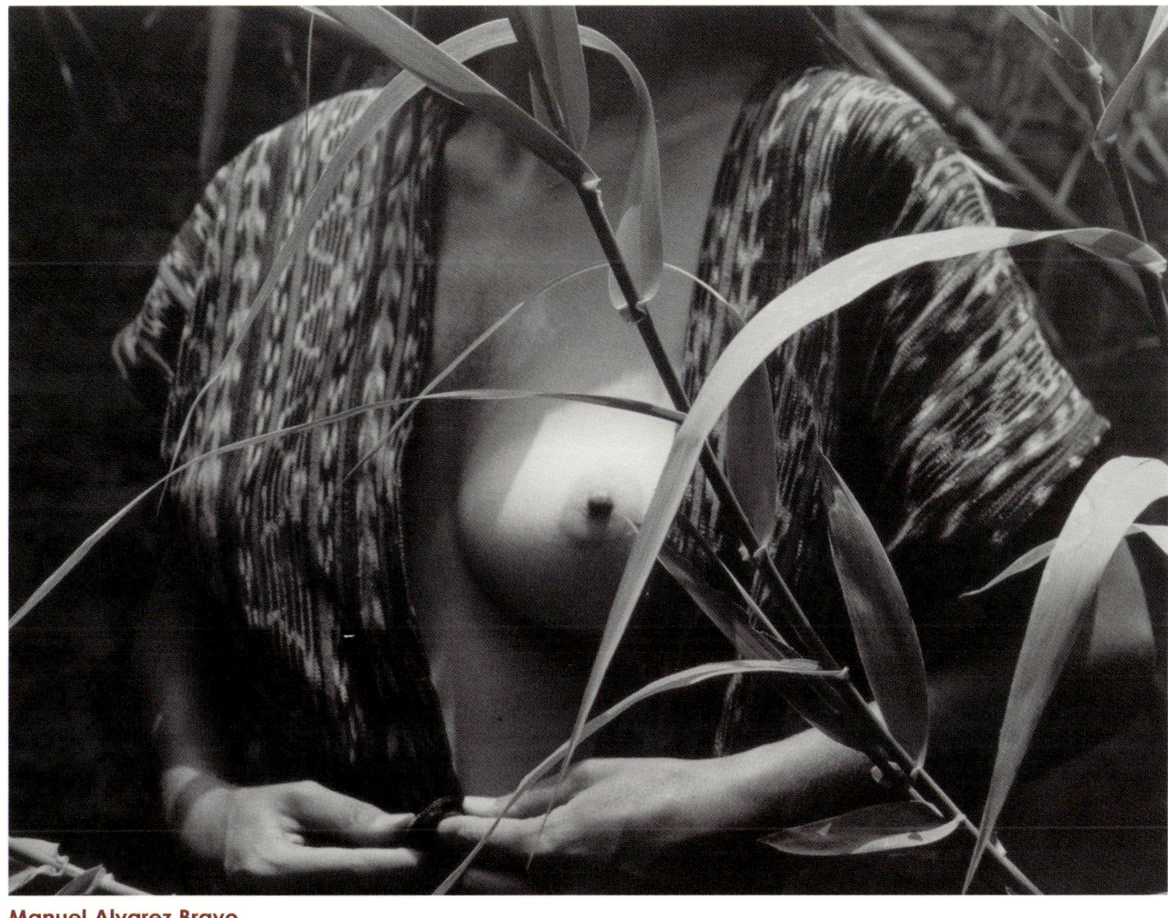

Manuel Alvarez Bravo
Forbidden Fruit / *Fruta prohibida*, 1976, Platinum print / *Platino*, 20.32 x 25.4 cm, 8" x 10"

Leonora Carrington

(1917-)

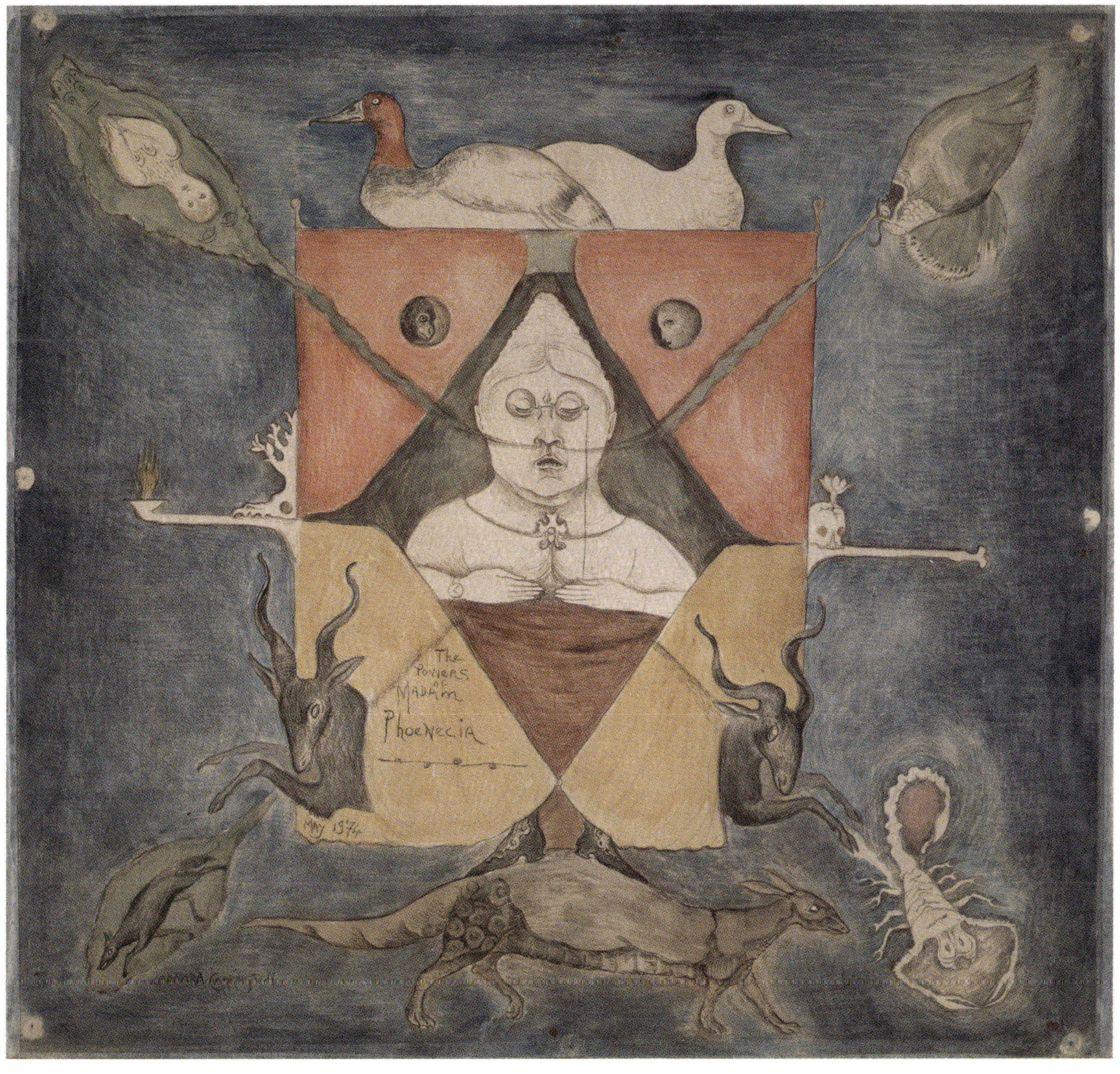

Leonora Carrington
The Powers of Madame Phoenicia / *Los poderes de Madame Phoenicia*, 1974, Mixed media on silk /
Técnica mixta sobre tela de seda, 42.5 x 44.5 cm, 16 3/4" x 17 1/2"

Elena Climent

(1955-)

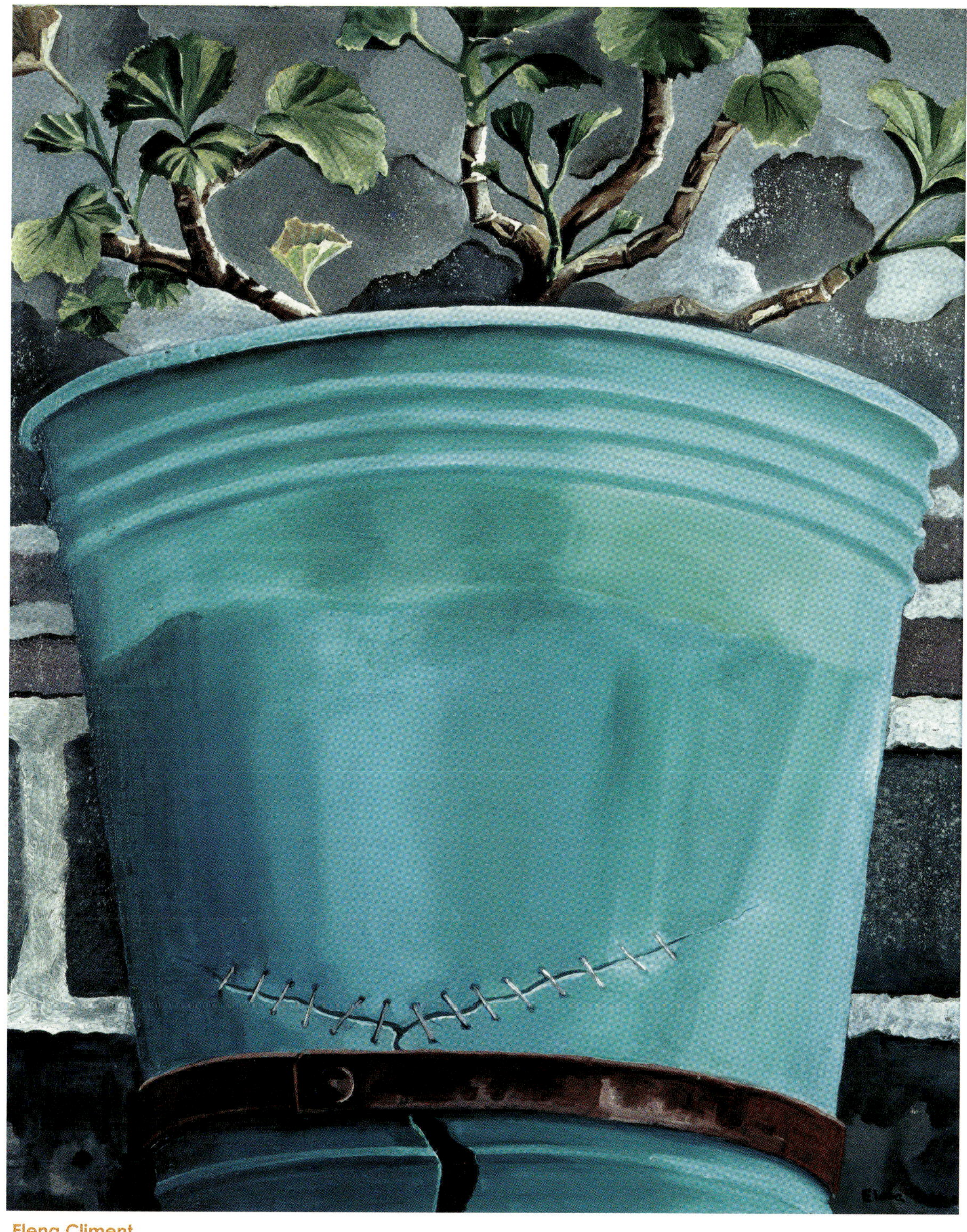

Elena Climent
Blue Pail / *Cubeta azul*, 1990, Oil on canvas / *Óleo sobre tela*, 28.5 x 23 cm, 11 1/4" x 9"

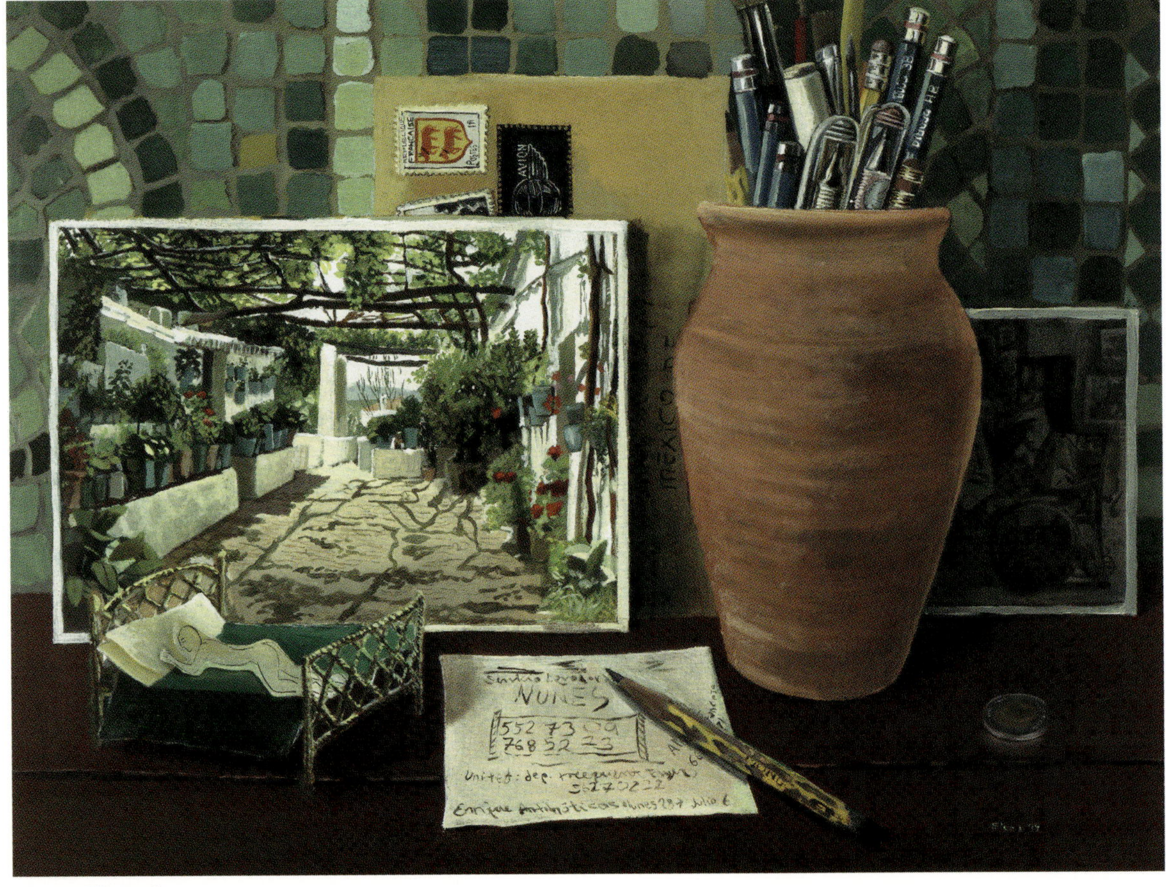

Elena Climent

Objects with Photo of Spanish Porch / *Objetos con foto en un pórtico español*, 1999, Oil on canvas on board / *Óleo sobre tela sobre madera*, 21.6 x 27.9 cm, $8^{1/4}$" x $10^{3/4}$"

Miguel Covarrubias
(1904-1957)

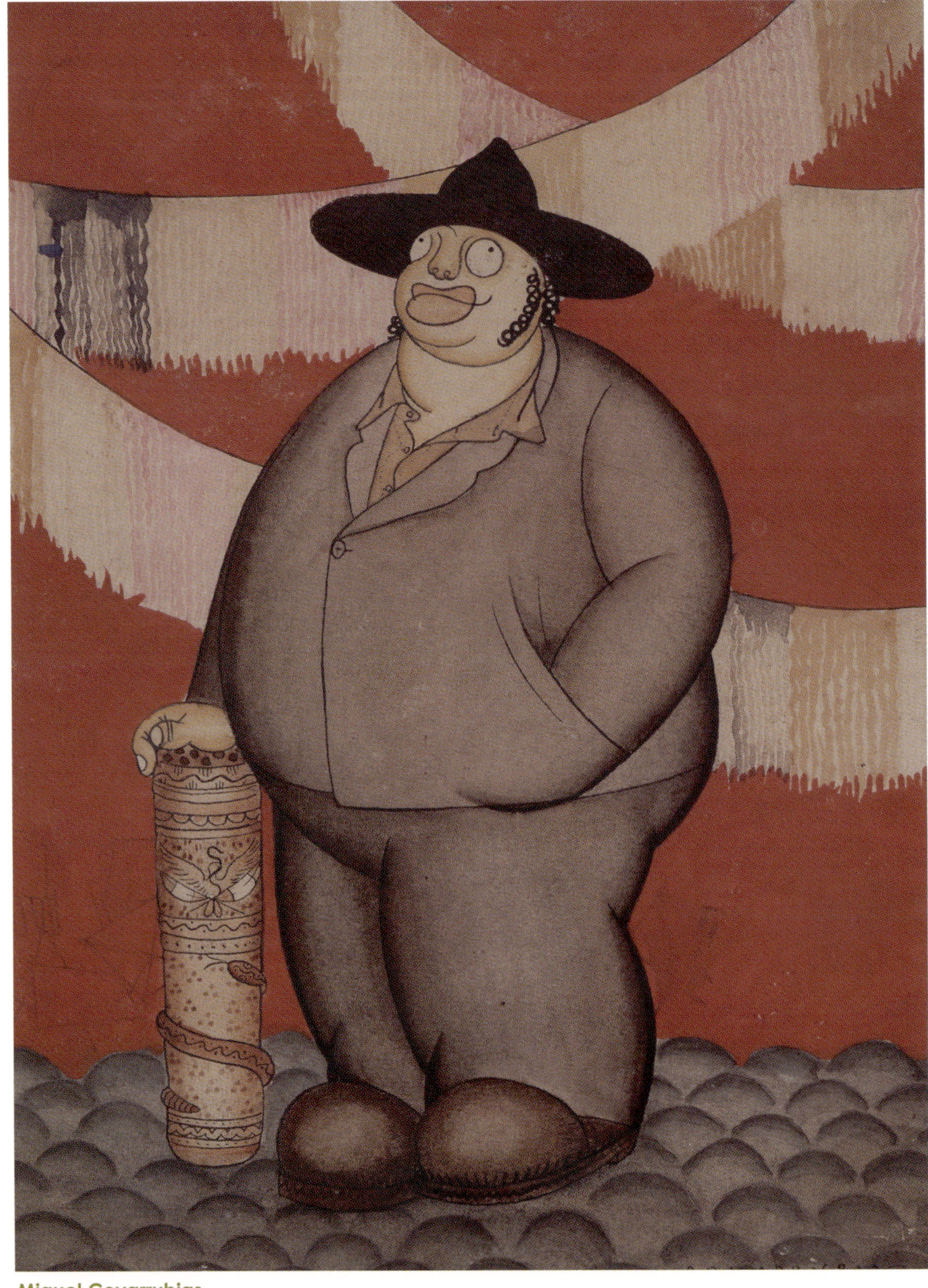

Miguel Covarrubias
Portrait of Diego Rivera / *Retrato de Diego Rivera*, 1920s, Ink and watercolor on paper / *Tinta y acuarela sobre papel*, 29 x 21 cm cm, 11 7/16" x 8 1/4"

Gabriel Figueroa
(1907-1997)

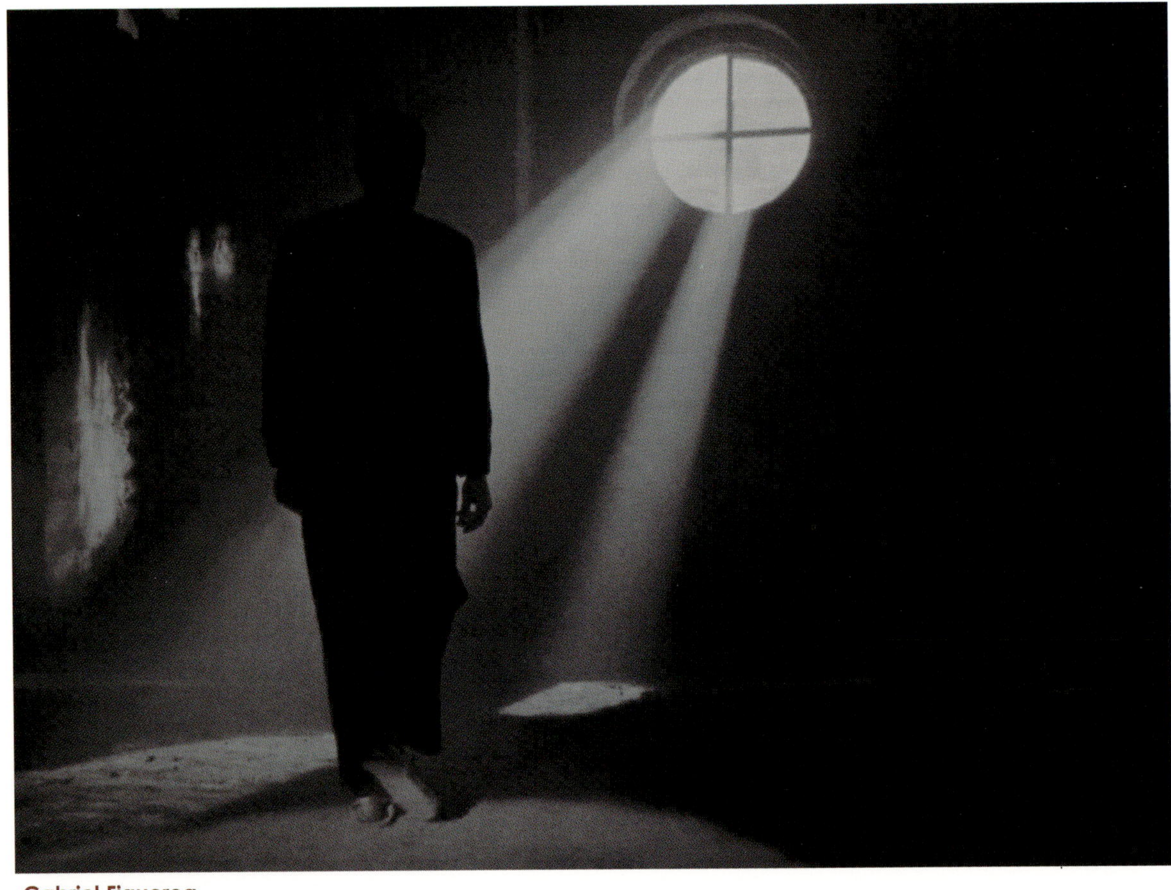

Gabriel Figueroa
Figure, from the movie "The Fugitive" / *Silueta, de la película "El fugitivo"*, 1947, Palladium Platinum print / *Platino*, 20 x 25 cm, 8" x 10"

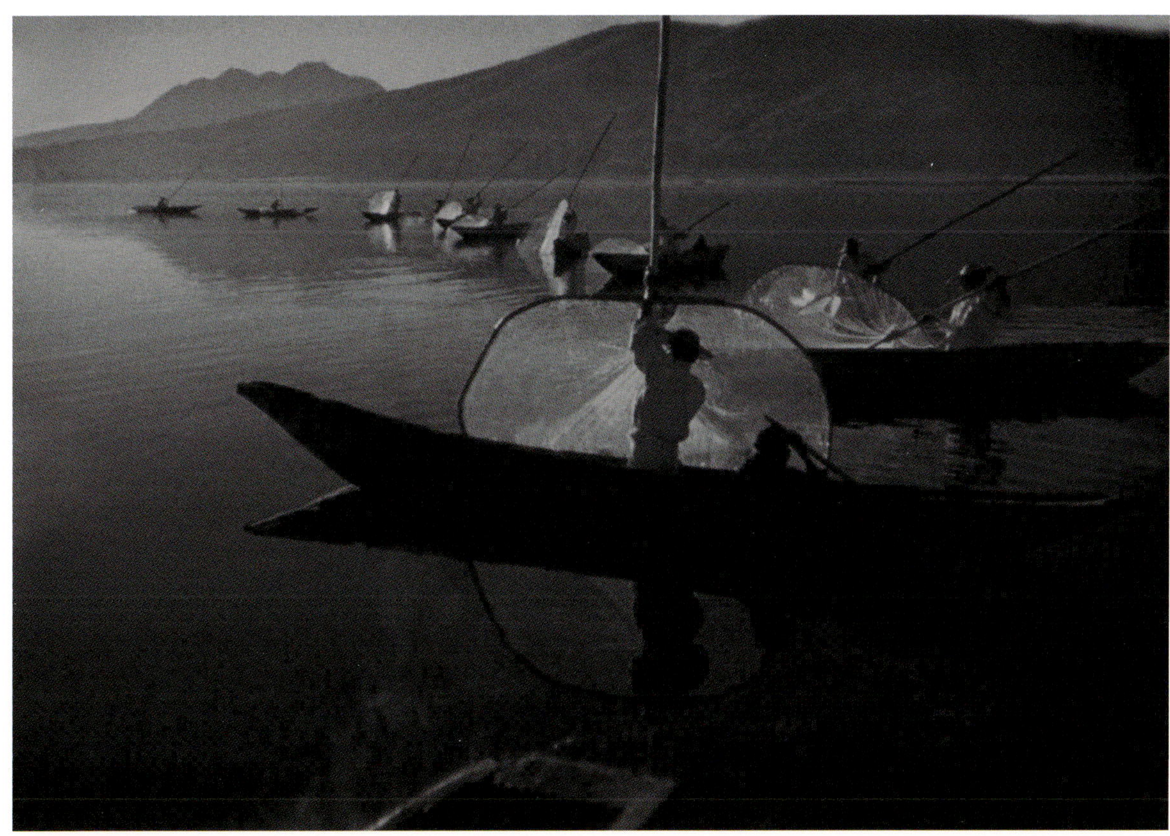

Gabriel Figueroa
Fishermen, from the movie "Maclovia" / *Pescadores, de la película "Maclovia"*, 1948, Palladium Platinum print / *Platino*, 20 x 25 cm, 8" x 10"

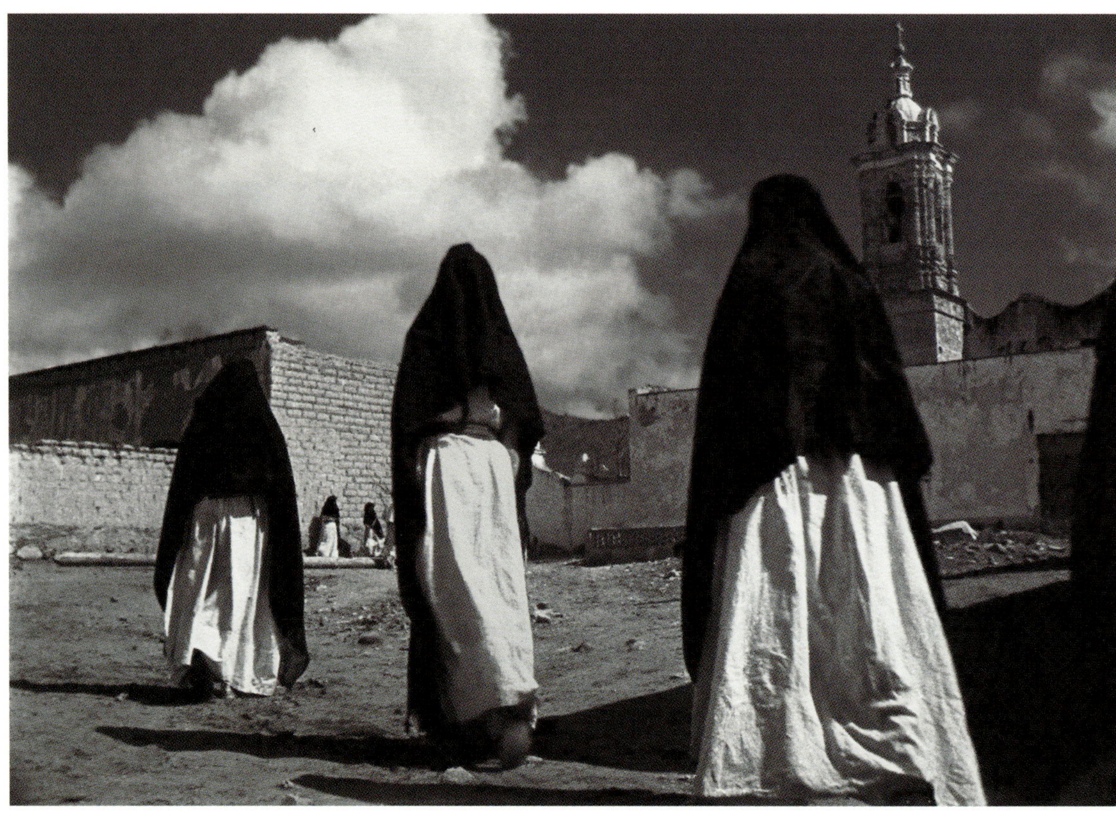

Gabriel Figueroa
Procession, from the movie "Hidden River" / *Procesión, de la película "Rio Escondido"*, 1947,
Palladium Platinum print / *Platino*, 20 x 27.5 cm, 8" x 10"

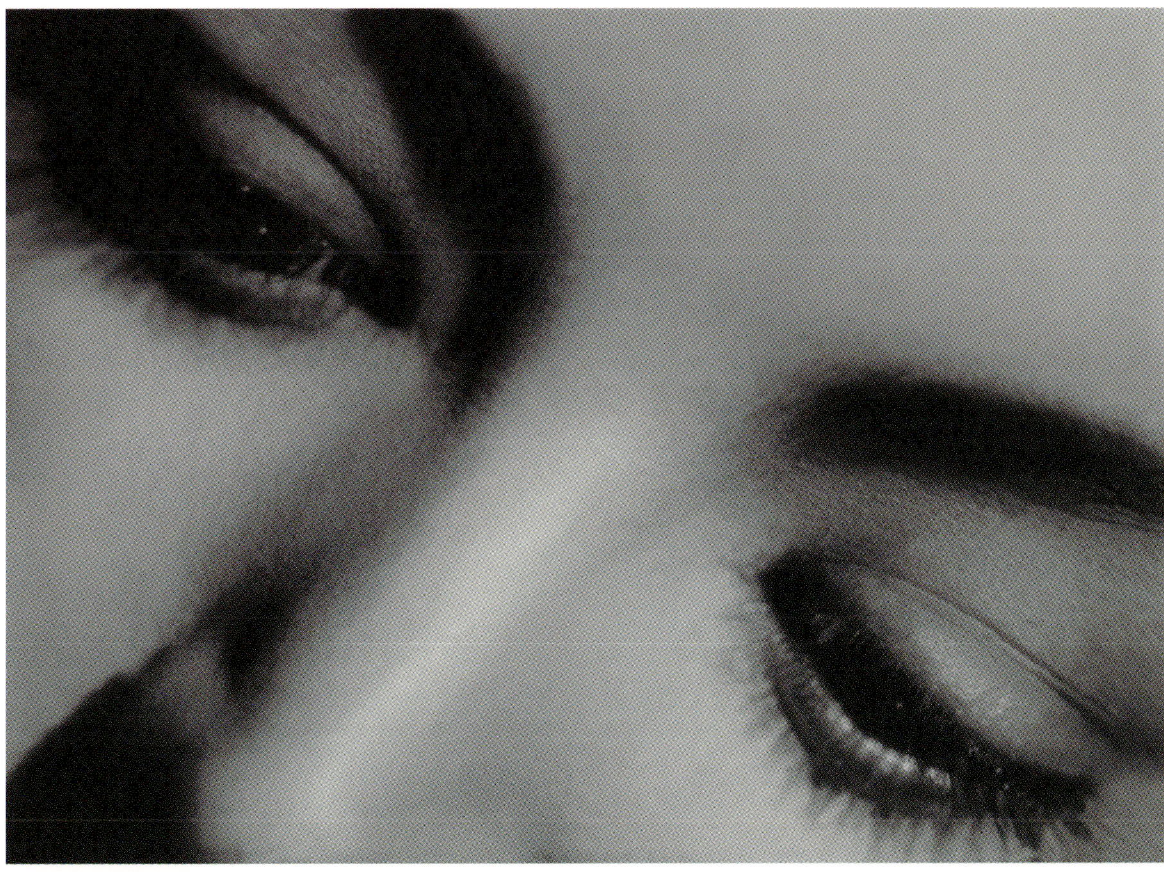

Gabriel Figueroa
The Eyes of Maria, from the movie "Woman in Love" / *Los ojos de María, de la película " Enamorada"*, 1948,
Palladium platinum print / *Platino*, 20 x 25 cm, 8" x 10"

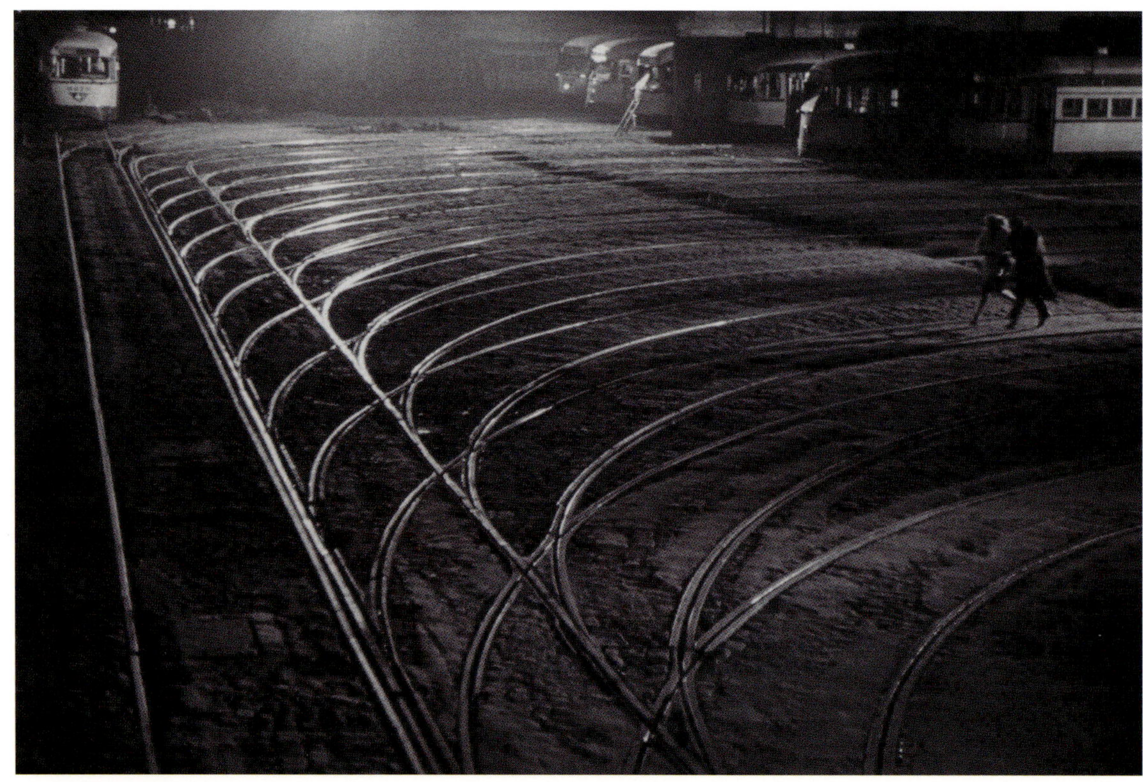

Gabriel Figueroa
Rails, from the movie "Victims of Sin" / *Rieles, de la película "Victimas del pecado"*, 1950, Palladium Platinum print / *Platino*, 20 x 25 cm, 8" x 10"

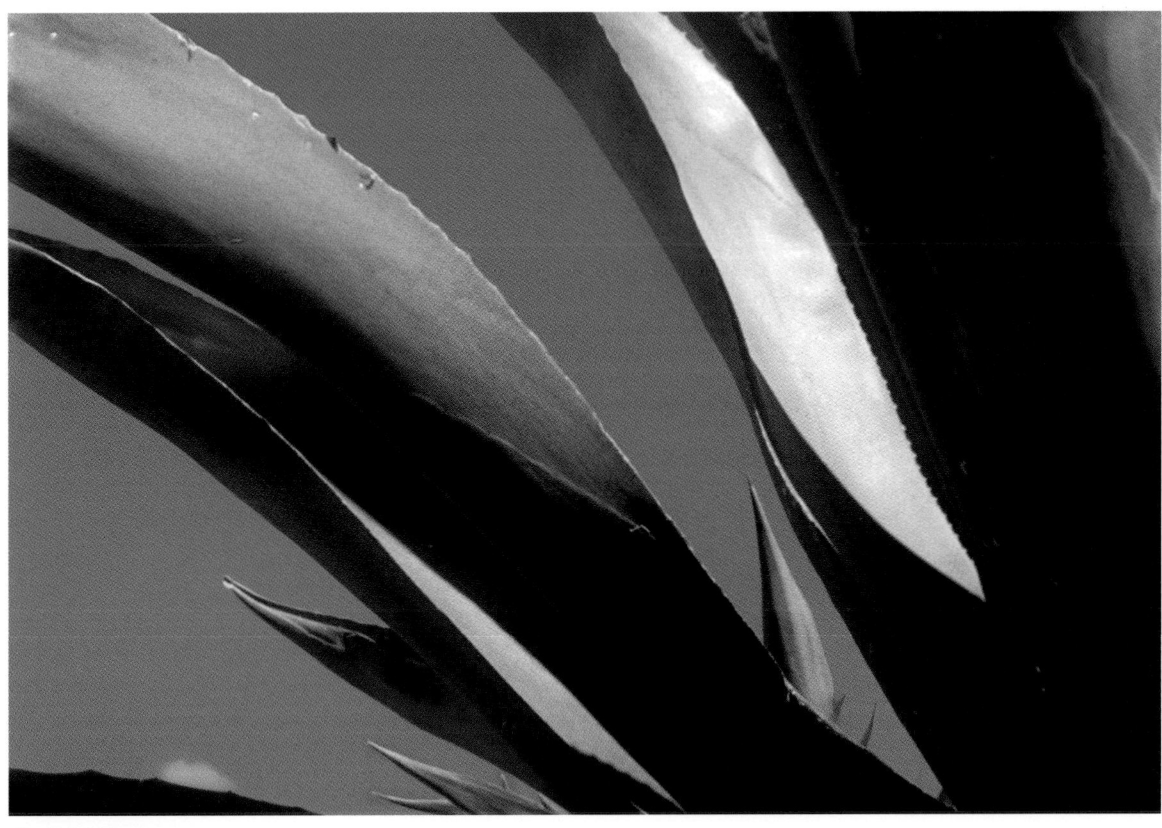

Gabriel Figueroa
Maguey, from the movie "A Love Date" / *Maguey, de la película "Una cita de amor"*, 1956, Palladium Platinum print / *Platino*, 20 x 25 cm, 8" x 10"

Gunther Gerzso

(1915-2000)

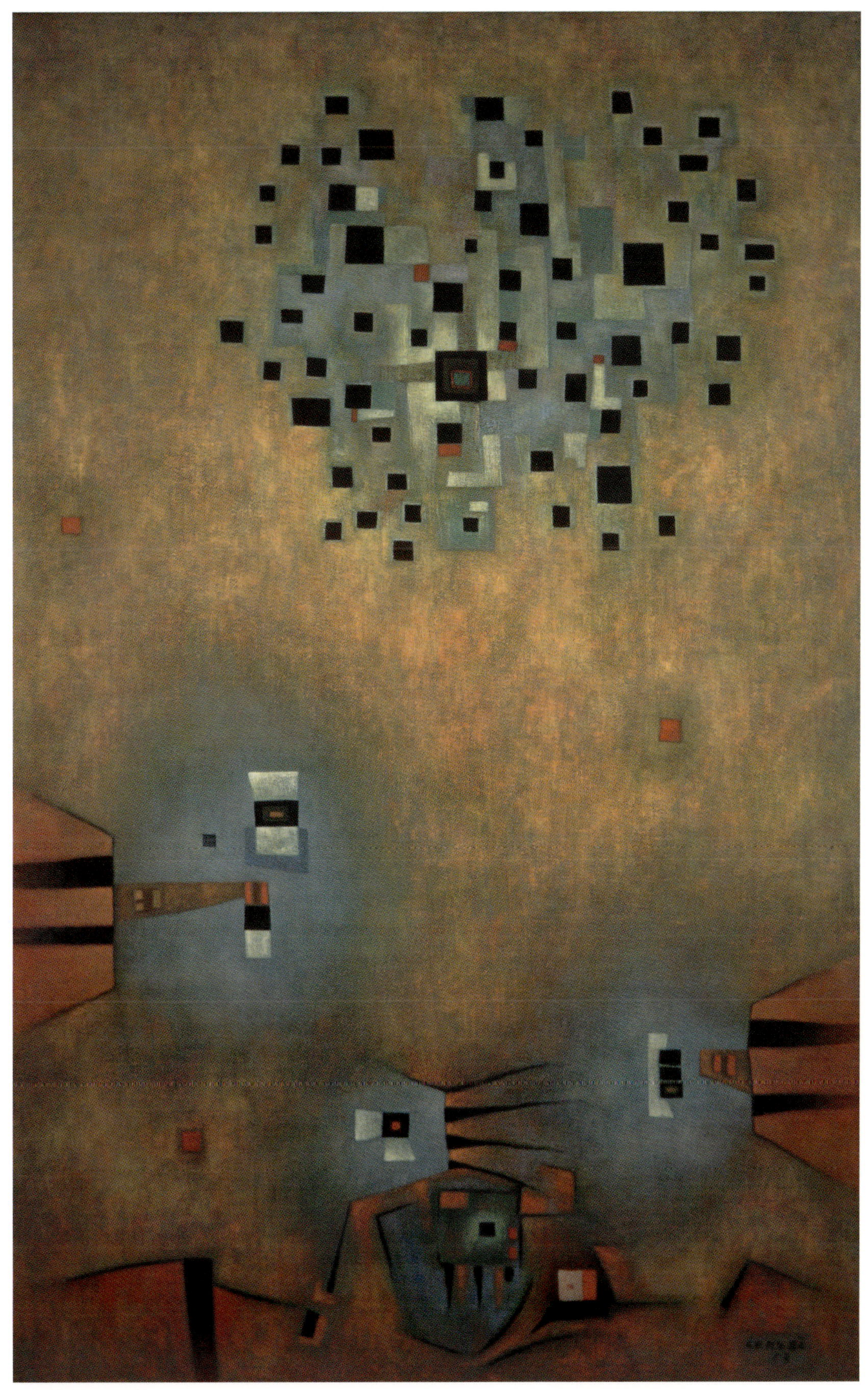

Gunther Gerzso
The Four Elements / *Los cuatro elementos*, 1953, Oil on canvas / *Óleo sobe tela*,
100 x 65 cm, 39 3/8" x 25 5/8"

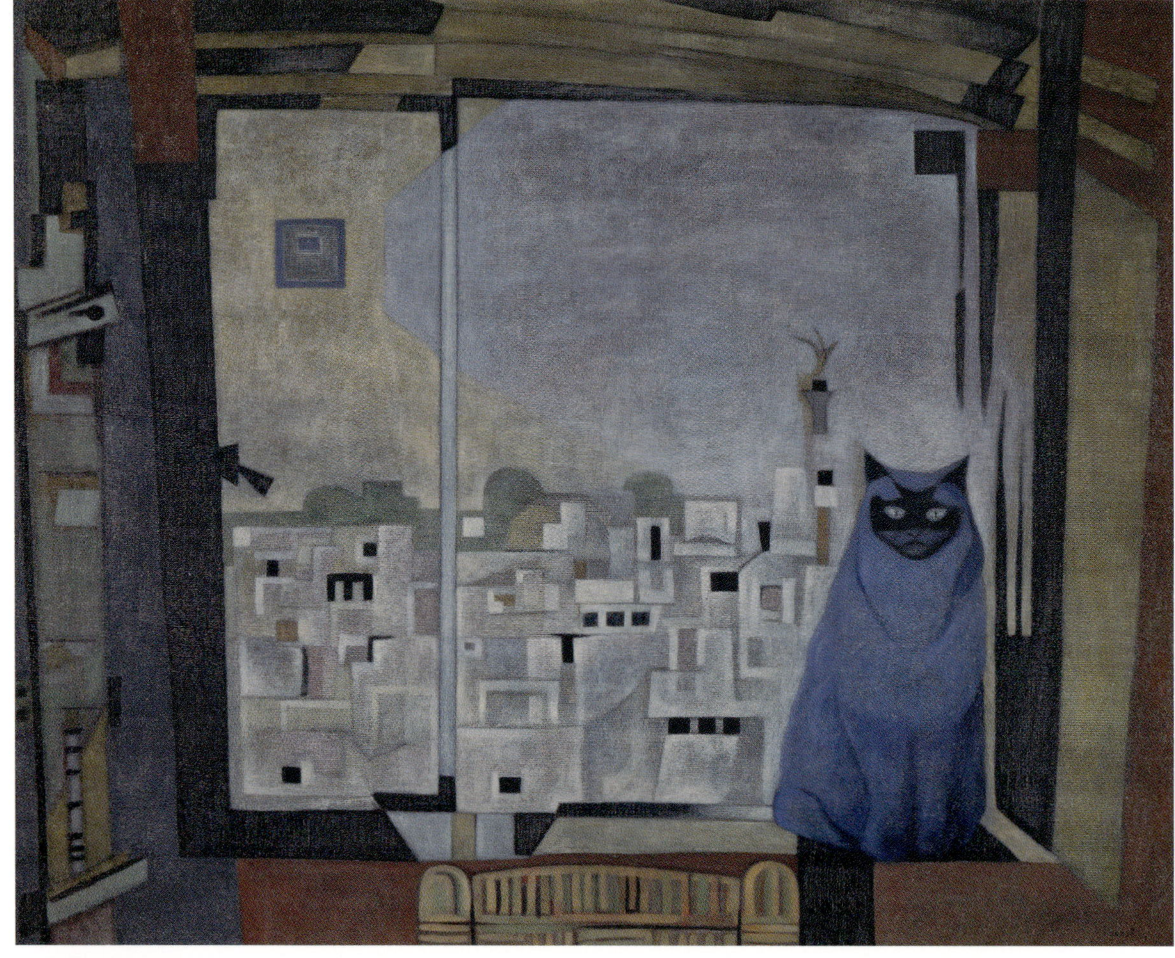

Gunther Gerzso
The Cat from London Street / *El gato de la calle Londres*, 1954, Oil on canvas / *Óleo sobre tela*, 64 x 80 cm, 25$^{3/16}$" x 31$^{1/2}$"

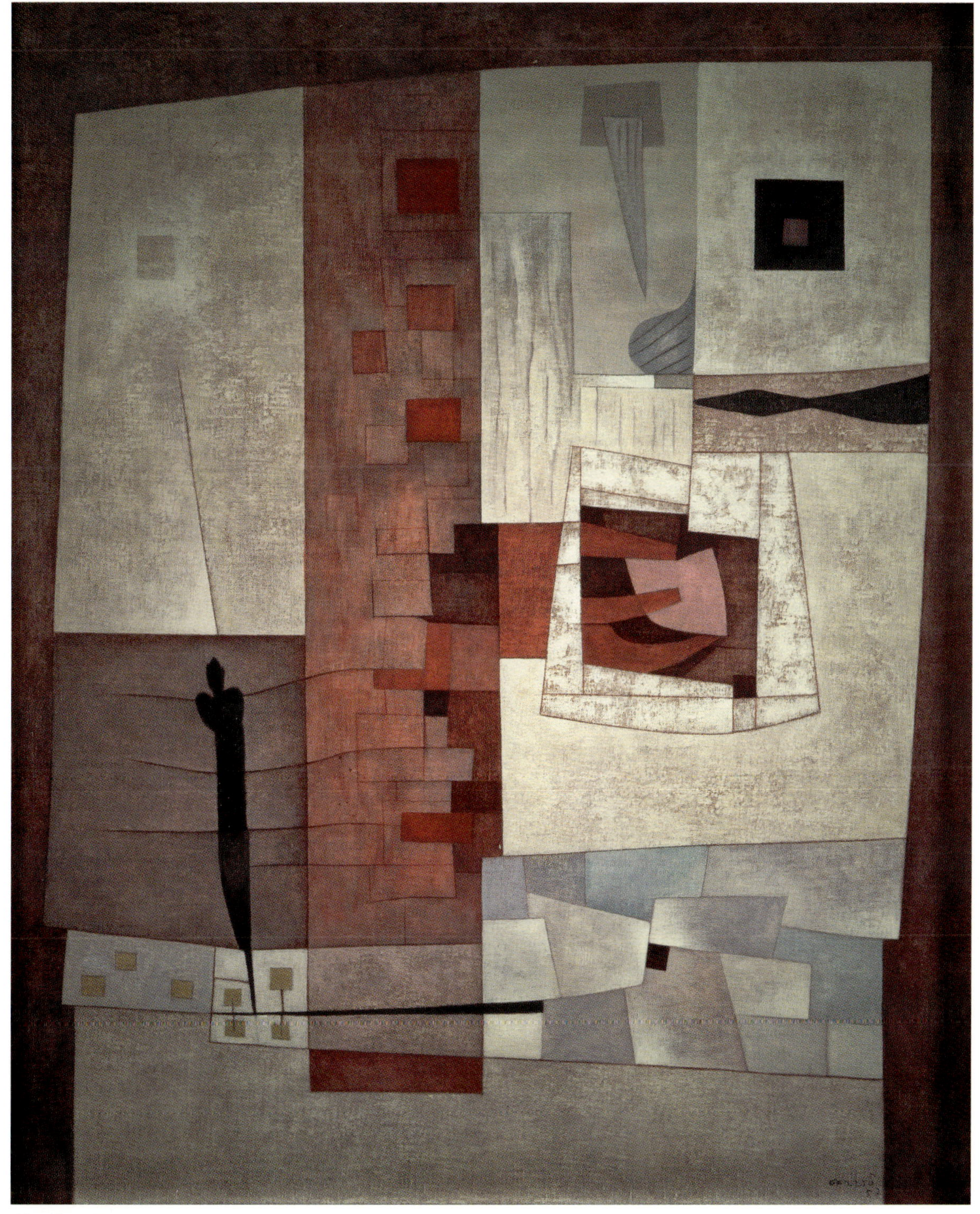

Gunther Gerzso
Archaic Landscape / *Paisaje arcaico*, 1956, Oil on Masonite / *Óleo sobre Masonite*, 80 x 53 cm , 31 1/2" x 20 7/8"

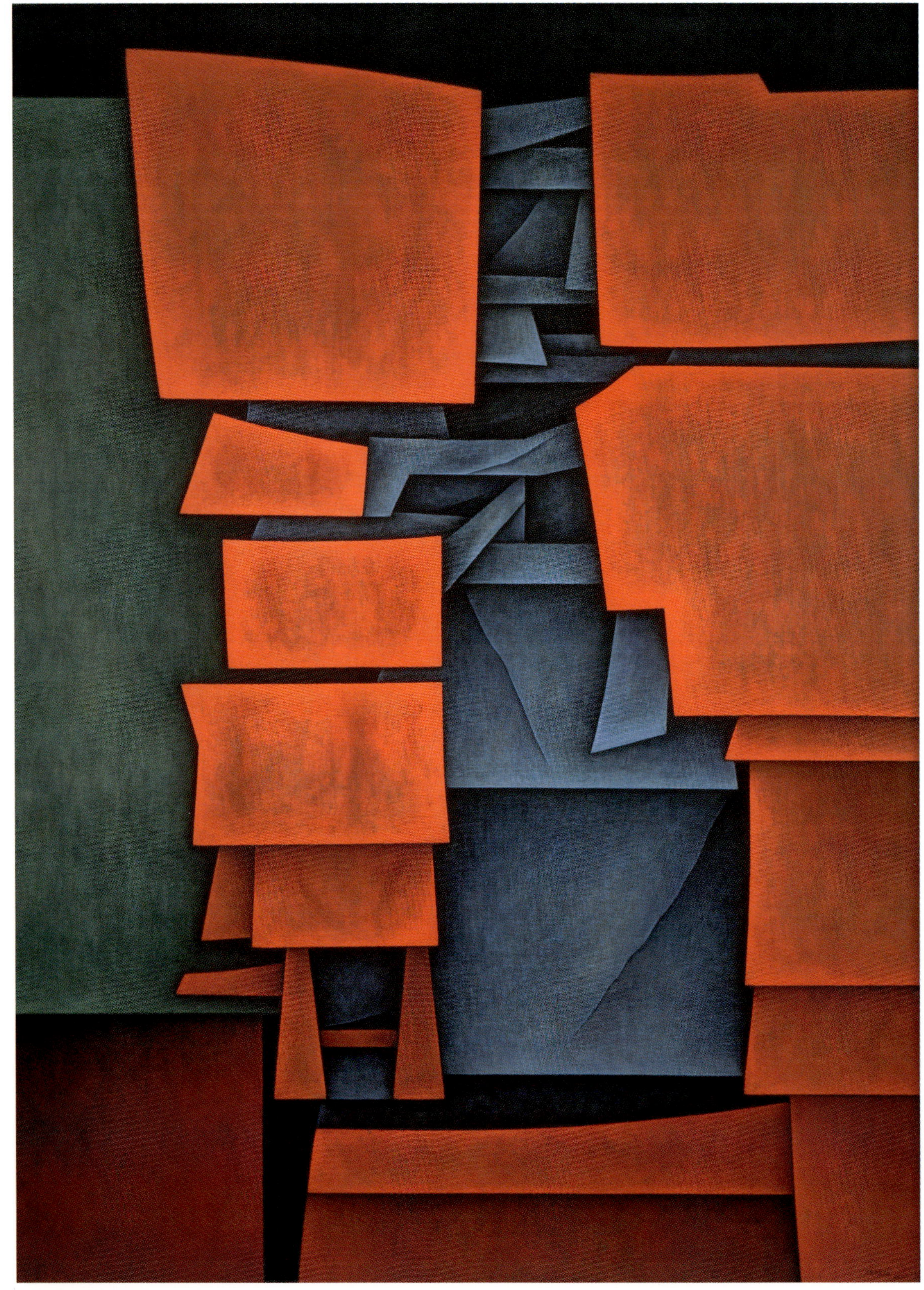

Gunther Gerzso
Figure in Red and Blue / *Personaje en rojo y azul,* 1964, Oil on canvas / *Óleo sobre tela,*
100 x 73 cm, $39^{3/8}$" x $28^{3/4}$"

María Izquierdo

(1902-1955)

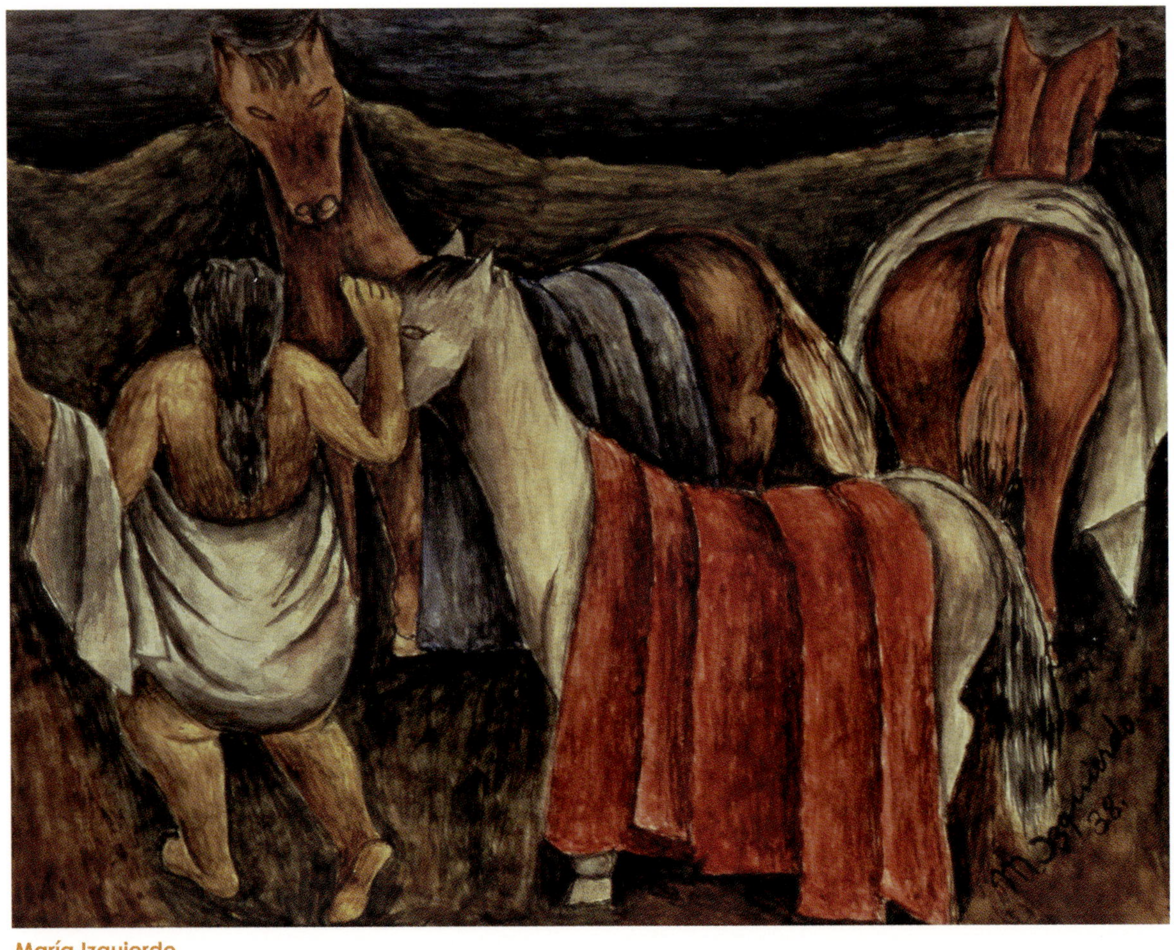

María Izquierdo
Horses / *Los caballos*, 1938, Watercolor on paper / *Acuarela sobre papel*, 21 x 28 cm, 8 1/4" x 11"

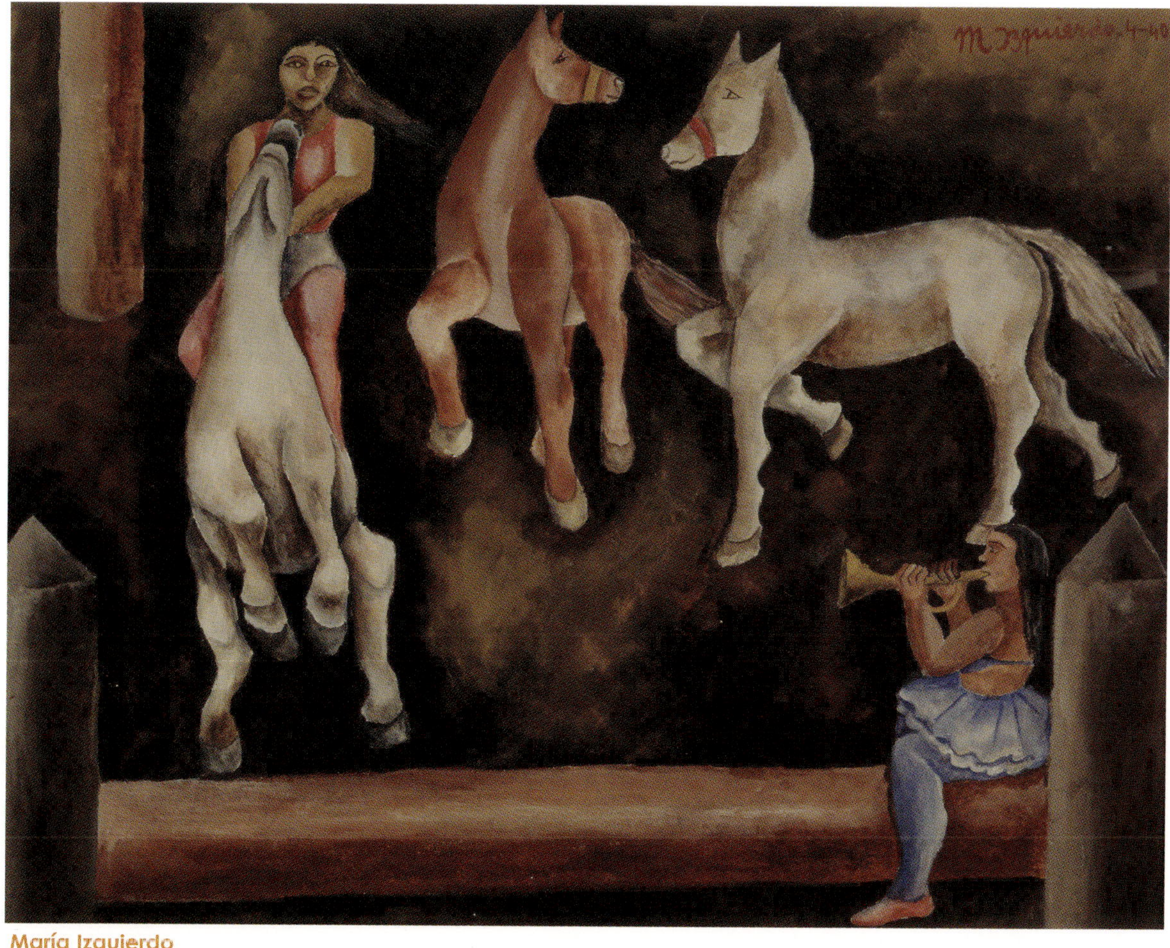

María Izquierdo
Circus Scene / *Escena de circo*, 1940, *Gouache* on paper / *Gouache sobre papel*, 42 x 54 cm, $16^{1/2}$" x $21^{1/4}$"

Frida Kahlo

(1907-1954)

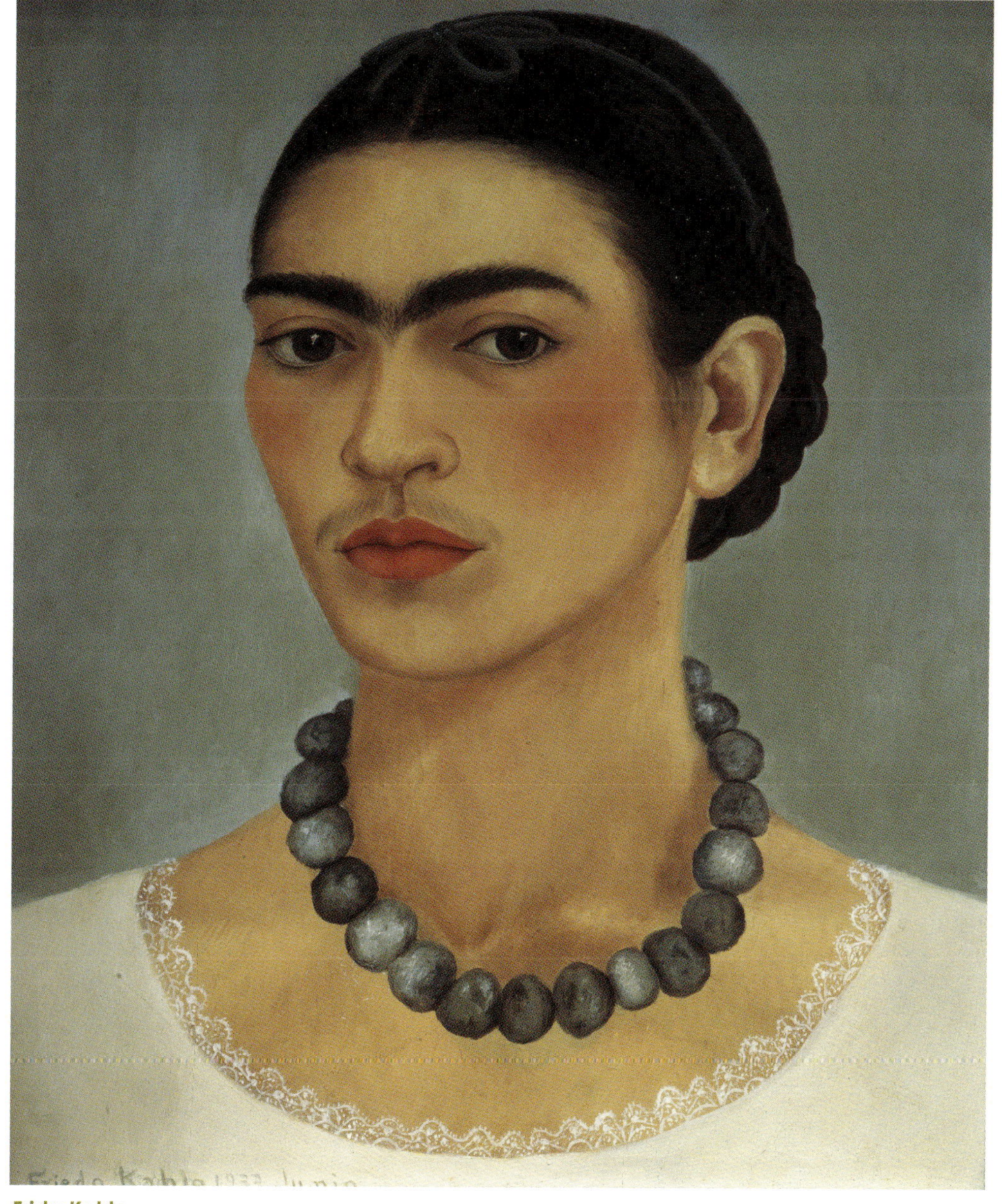

Frida Kahlo
Self-portrait with Necklace / *Autorretrato con collar*, 1933, Oil on metal / *Óleo sobre lámina*, 35 x 29 cm, $13^{3/4}$" x $11^{7/16}$"

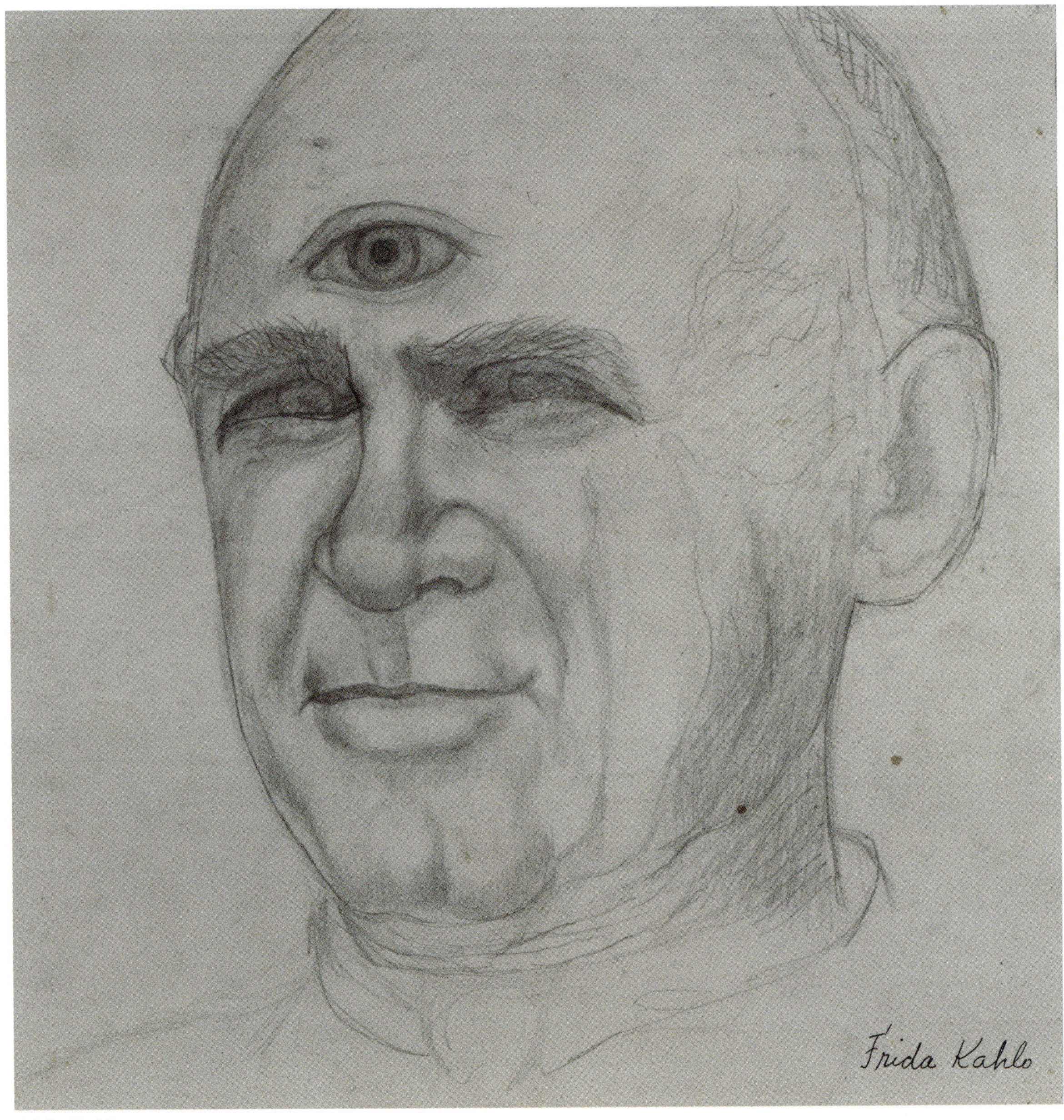

Frida Kahlo
Drawing of Nacho Aguirre / *Dibujo de Nacho Aguirre (anverso)*, 1935, Pencil on paper / *Lápiz sobre papel*, 22 x 22 cm, 8 3/4" x 8 3/4"

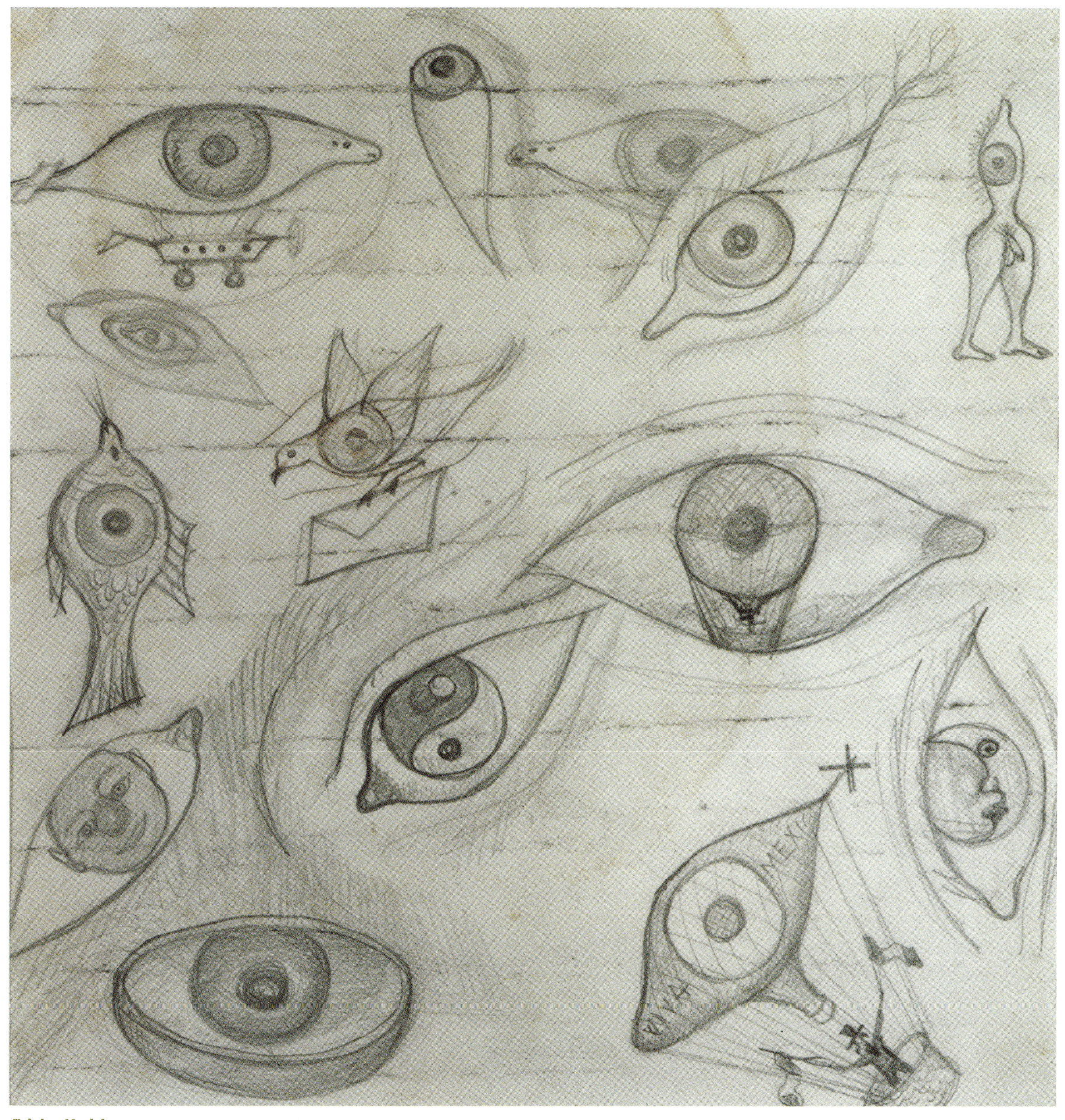

Frida Kahlo
Drawing of Eyes / *Dibujo de ojos (reverso)*, 1935, Pencil on Paper / Lápiz sobre papel , 22 x 22 cm, $8^{3/4}$" x $8^{3/4}$"

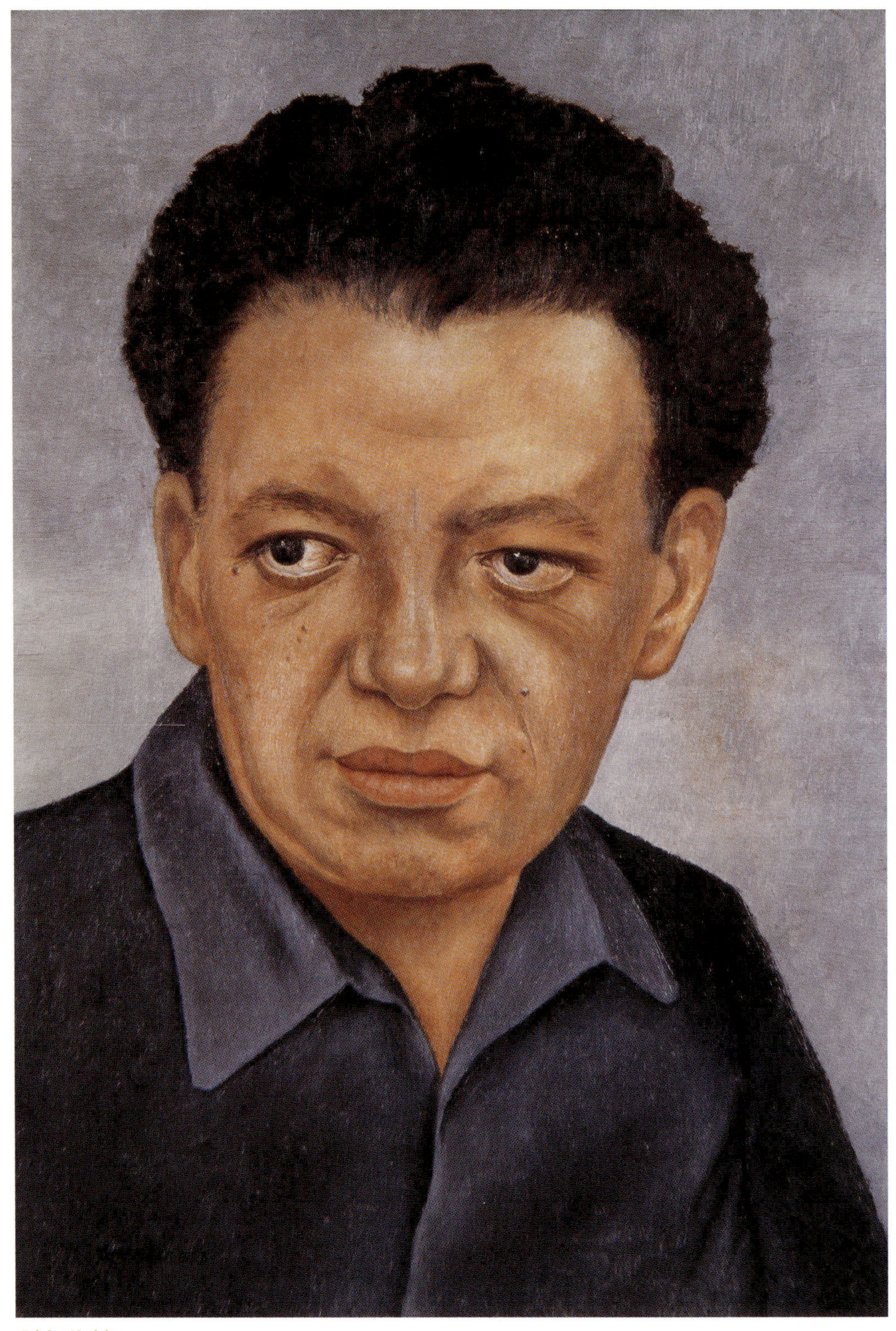

Frida Kahlo
Portrait of Diego Rivera / *Retrato de Diego Rivera*, 1937, Oil on Masonite / *Óleo sobre Masonite*, 53 x 39 cm, $20^{7/8}$" x $15^{3/8}$"

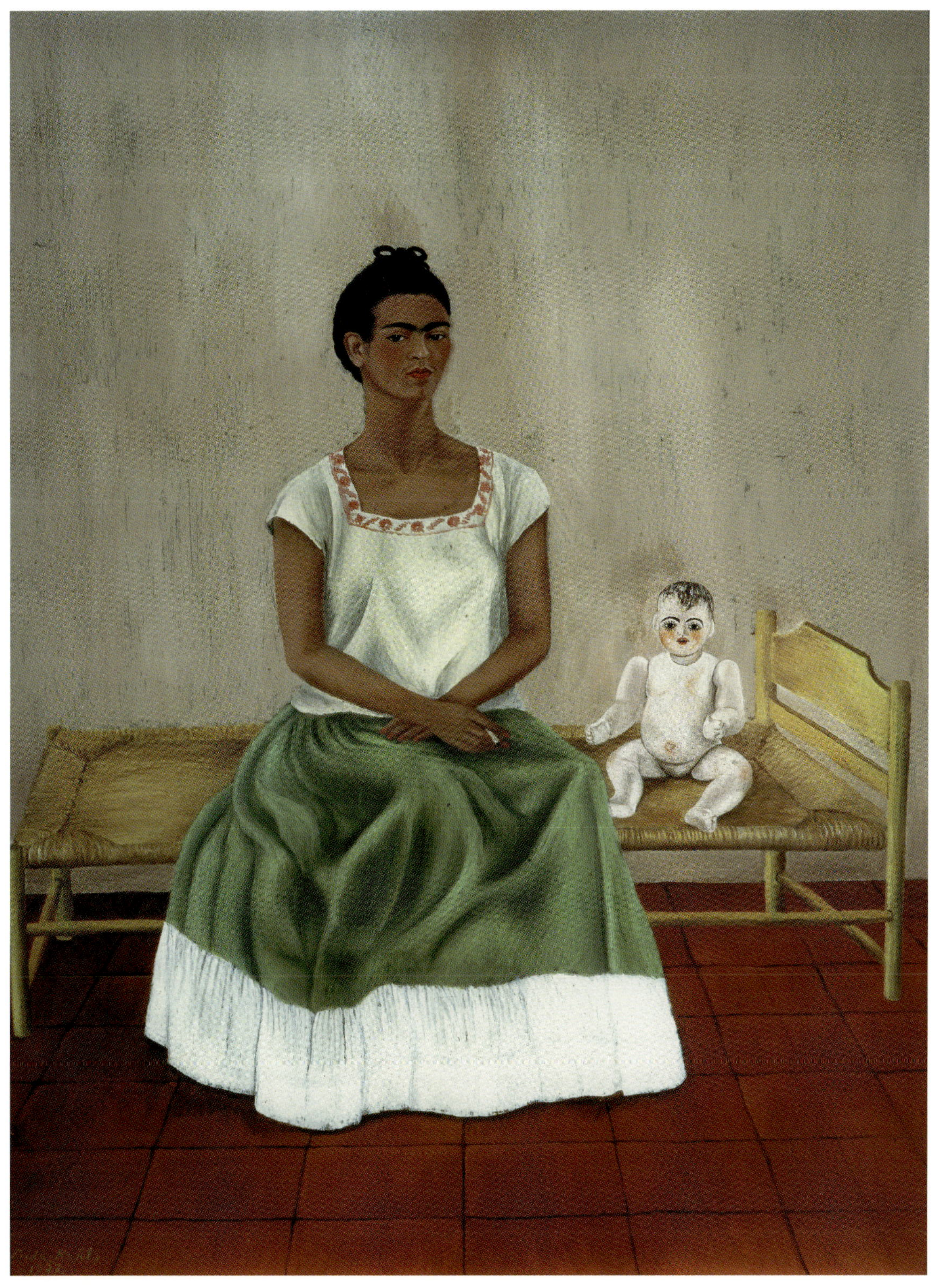

Frida Kahlo
Self-portrait with Bed / *Autorretrato con cama*, 1937, Oil on metal / *Óleo sobre lámina,*
40 x 30 cm, $15^{3/4}$" x $11^{3/4}$"

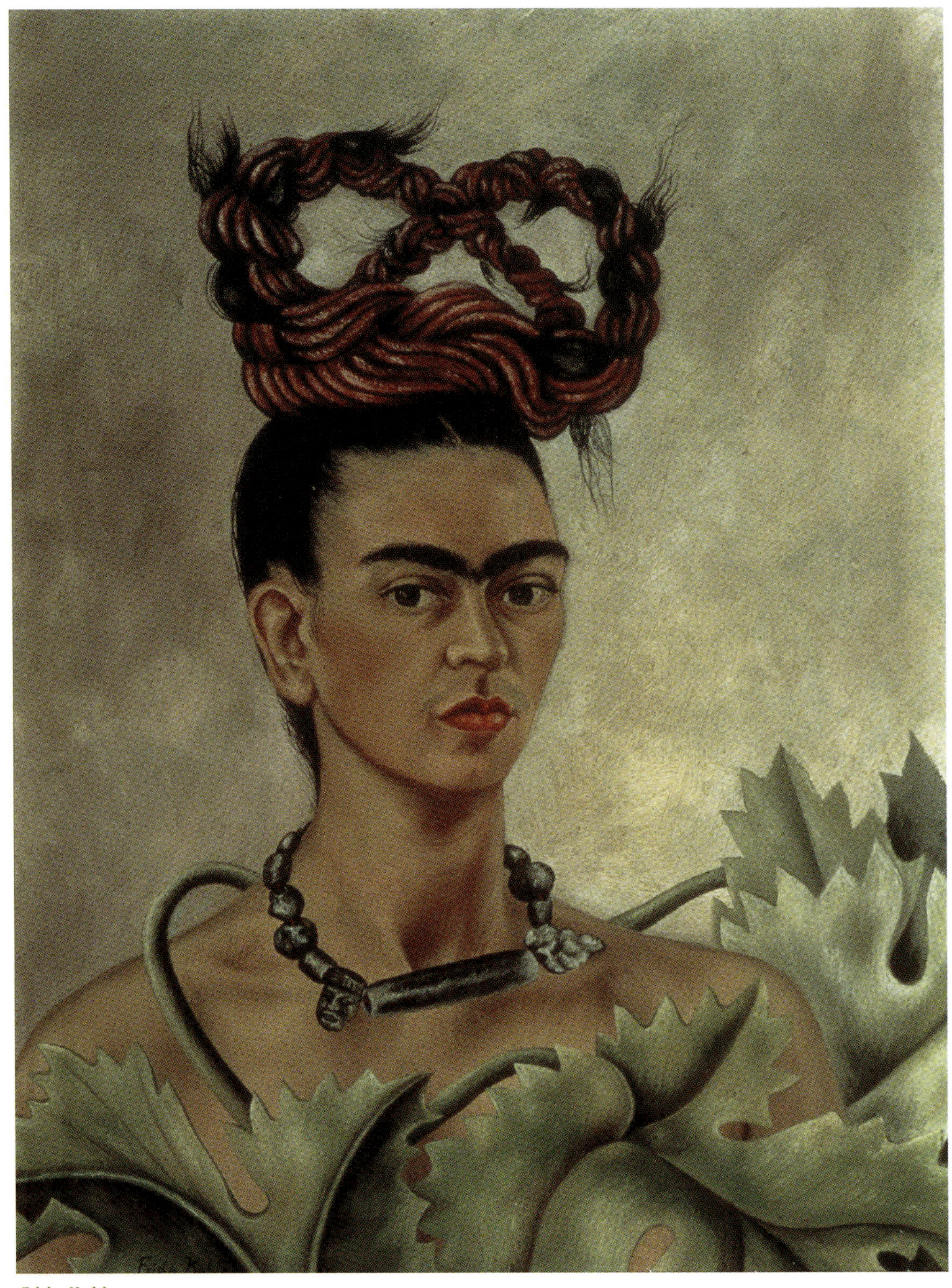

Frida Kahlo
Self-portrait with Braid / *Autorretrato con trenza*, 1941, Oil on canvas / *Óleo sobre tela*, 51 x 38.5 cm, 20" x 15$^{1/8}$"

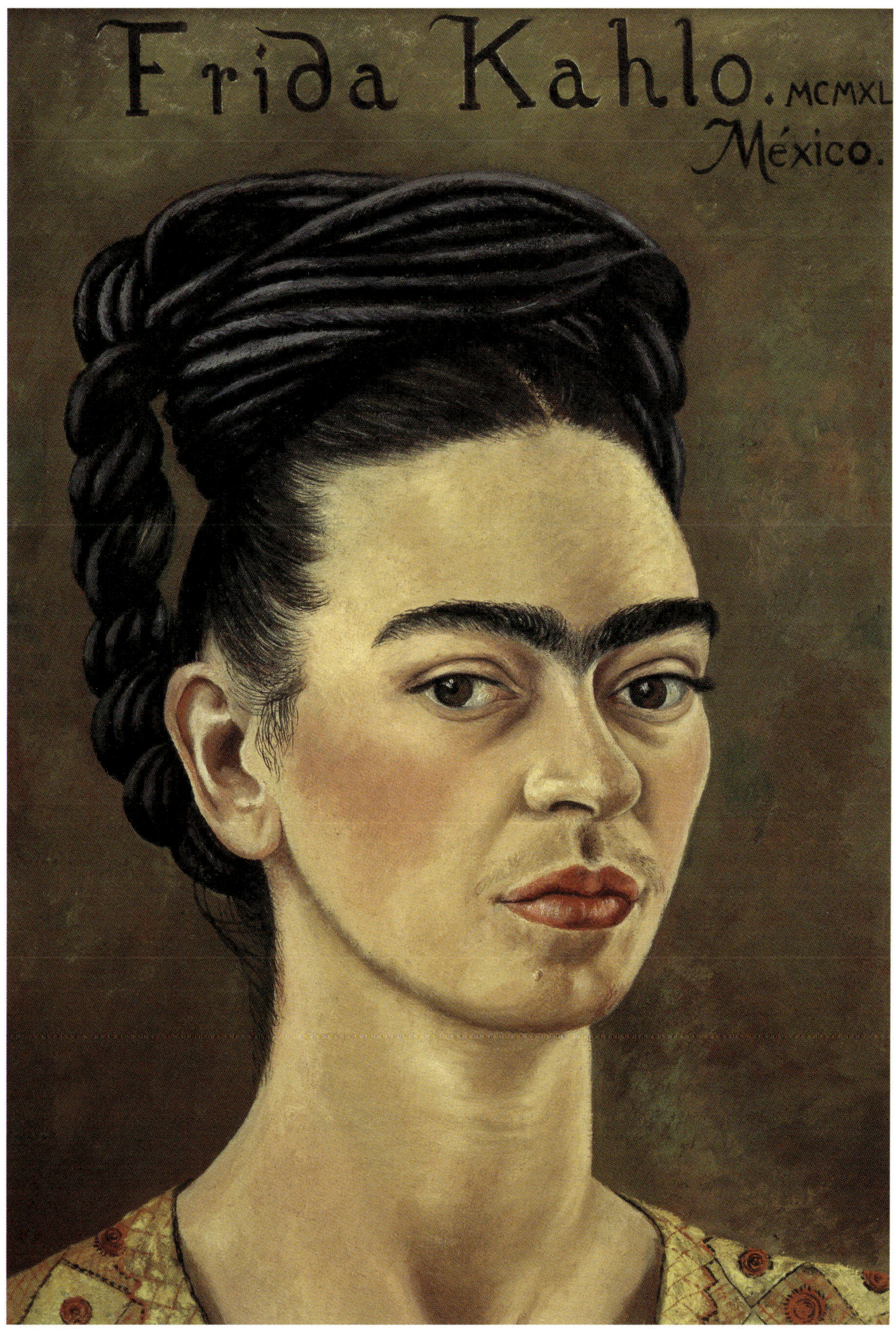

Frida Kahlo
Self-portrait with Red and Gold Dress / *Autorretrato con vestido rojo y dorado*, 1941, Oil on canvas / *Óleo sobre tela* , 39 x 27.5 cm, $15^{3/8}$" x $10^{7/8}$"

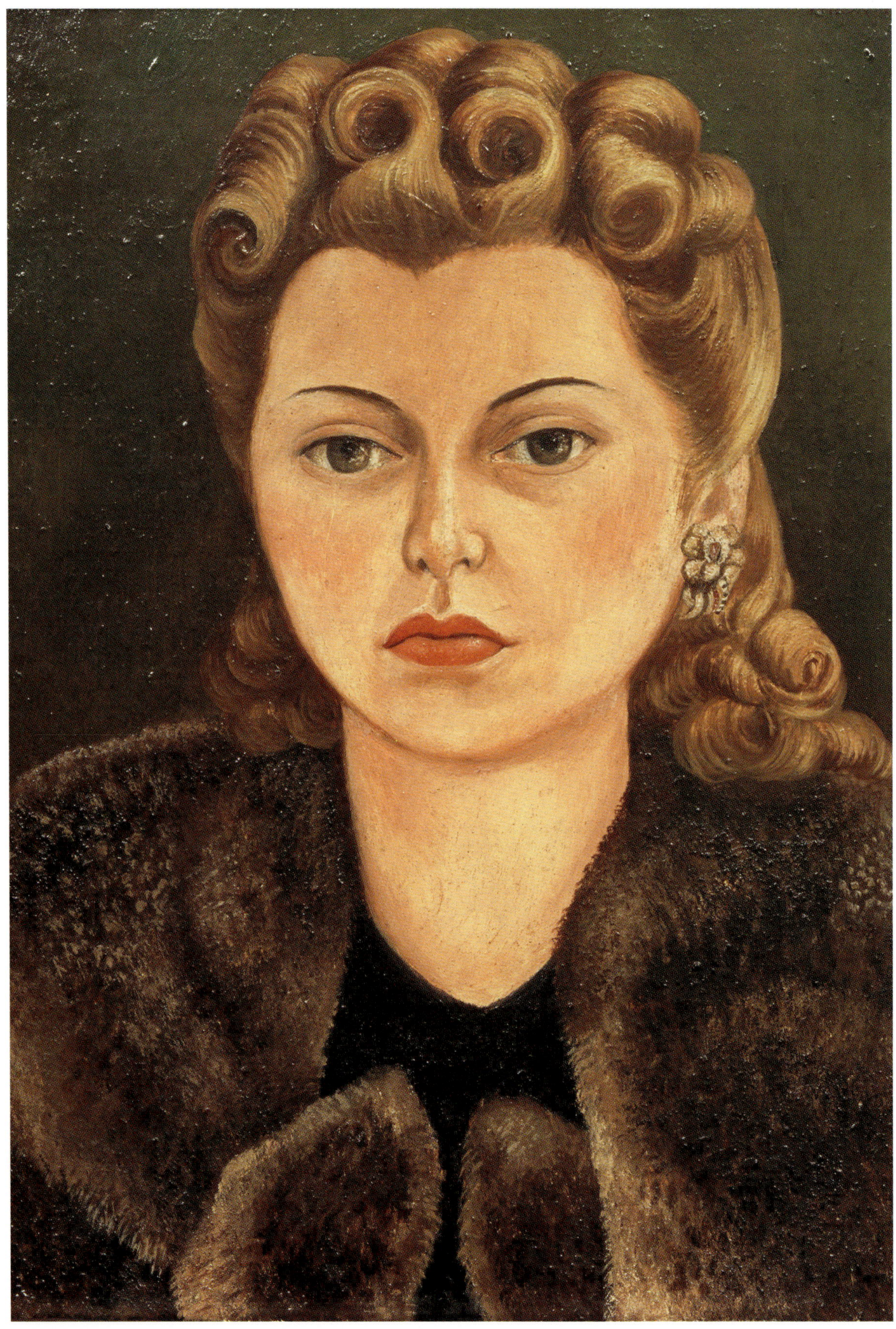

Frida Kahlo
Portrait of Mrs. Natasha Gelman / *Retrato de la Señora Natasha Gelman,* 1943, Oil on Masonite / *Óleo sobre Masonite*, 30 x 23 cm, 11 7/8" x 9"

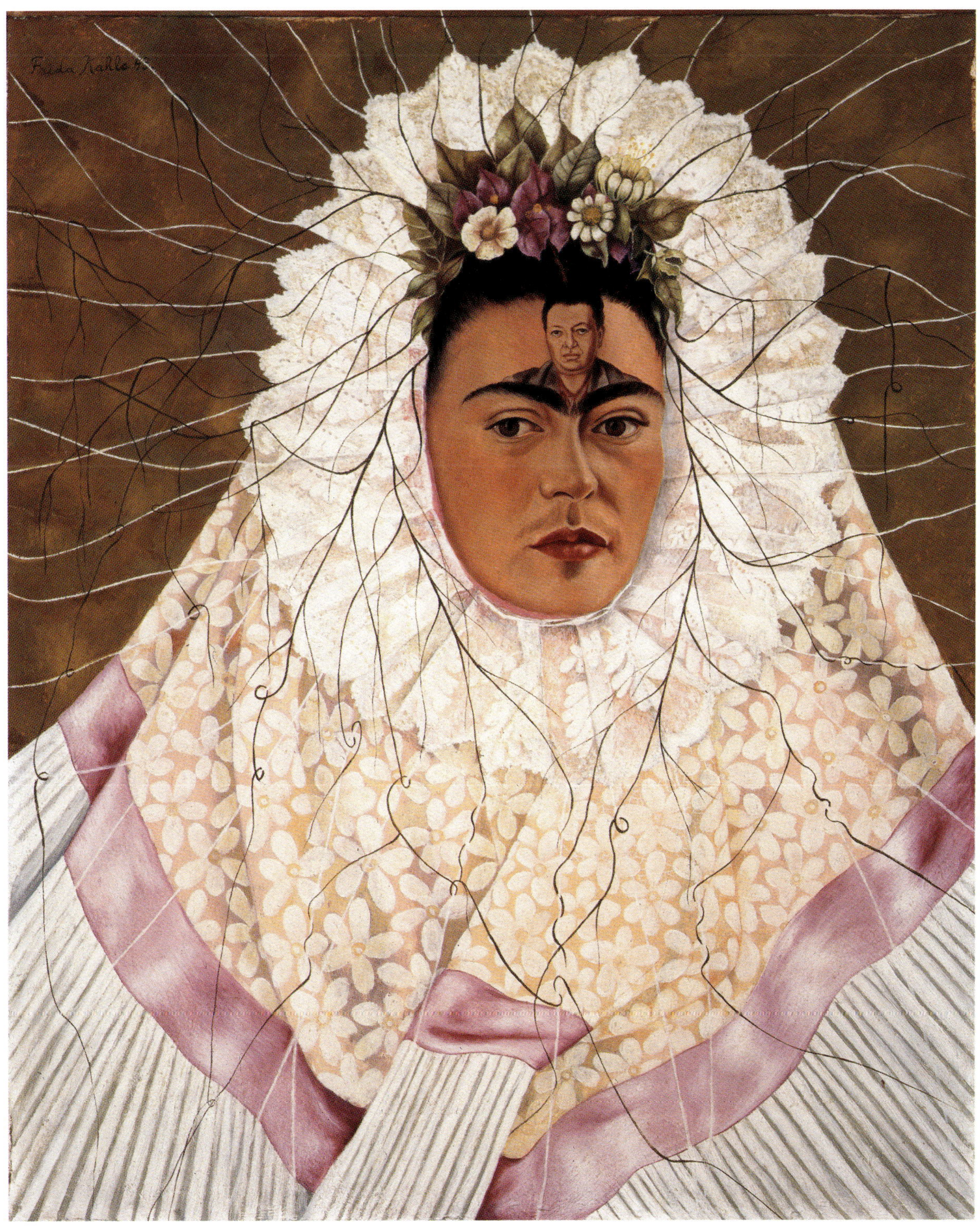

Frida Kahlo
Diego on My Mind / *Diego en mi pensamiento*, 1943, Oil on Masonite / *Óleo sobre Masonite*, 76 x 61 cm, $29^{7/8}$" x 24"

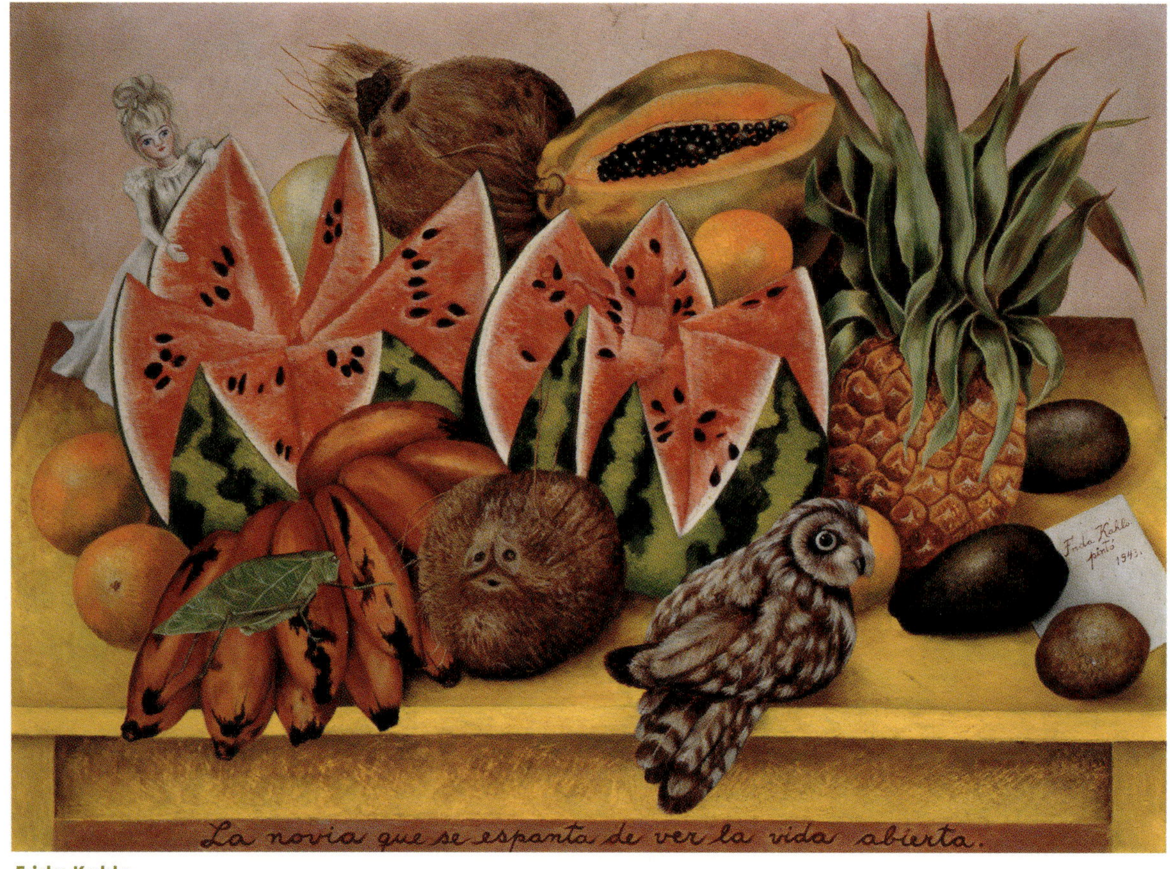

Frida Kahlo
The Bride Who Became Frightened When She Saw Life Opened / *La novia que se espanta de ver la vida abierta,* 1943, Oil on canvas / *Óleo sobre tela*, 63 x 81.5 cm, $24^{7/8}$" x 32"

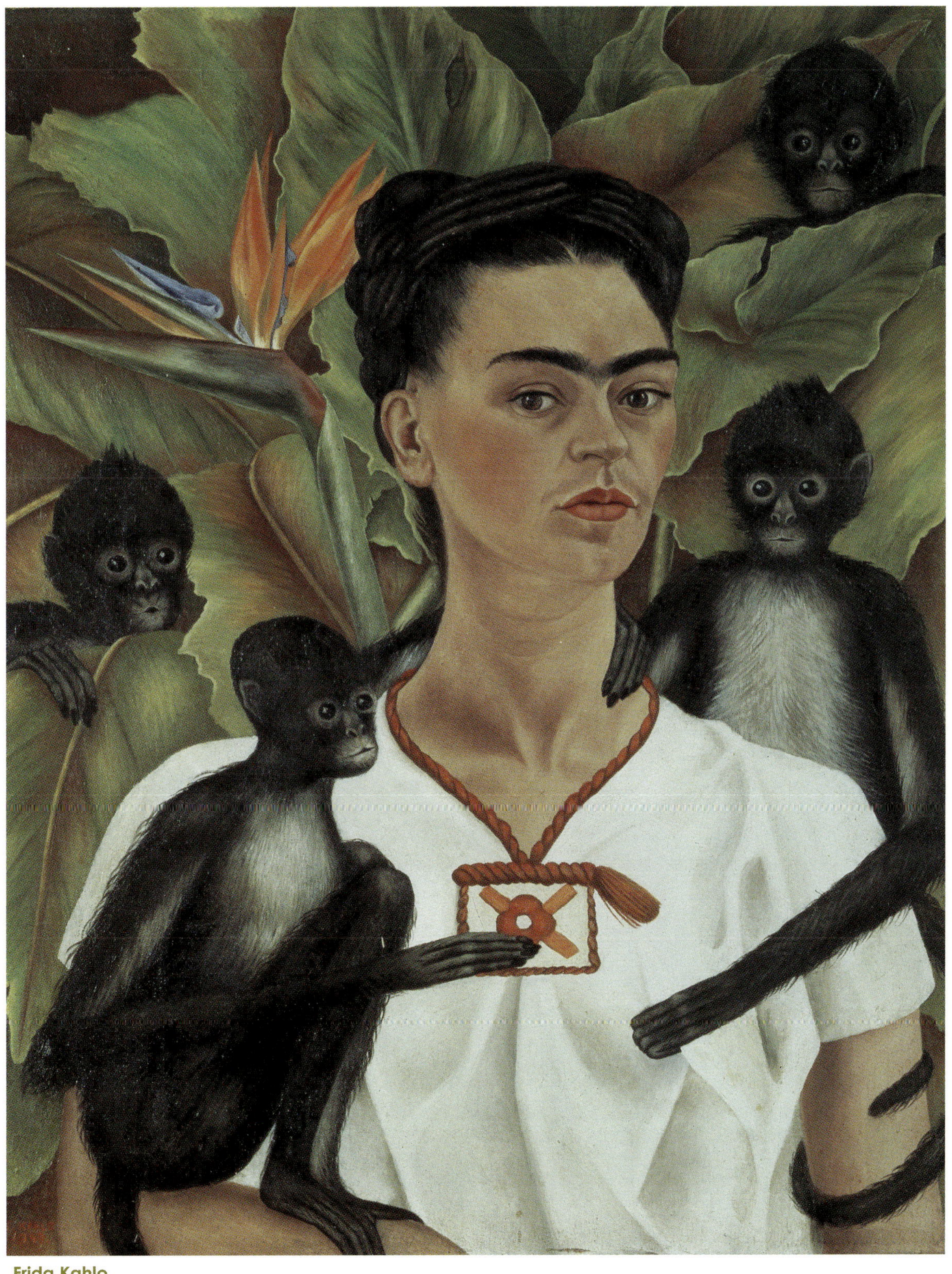

Frida Kahlo
Self-portrait with Monkeys / *Autorretrato con monos*, 1943, Oil on canvas / *Óleo sobre tela*, 81.5 x 63 cm, 32" x 24$^{7/8}$"

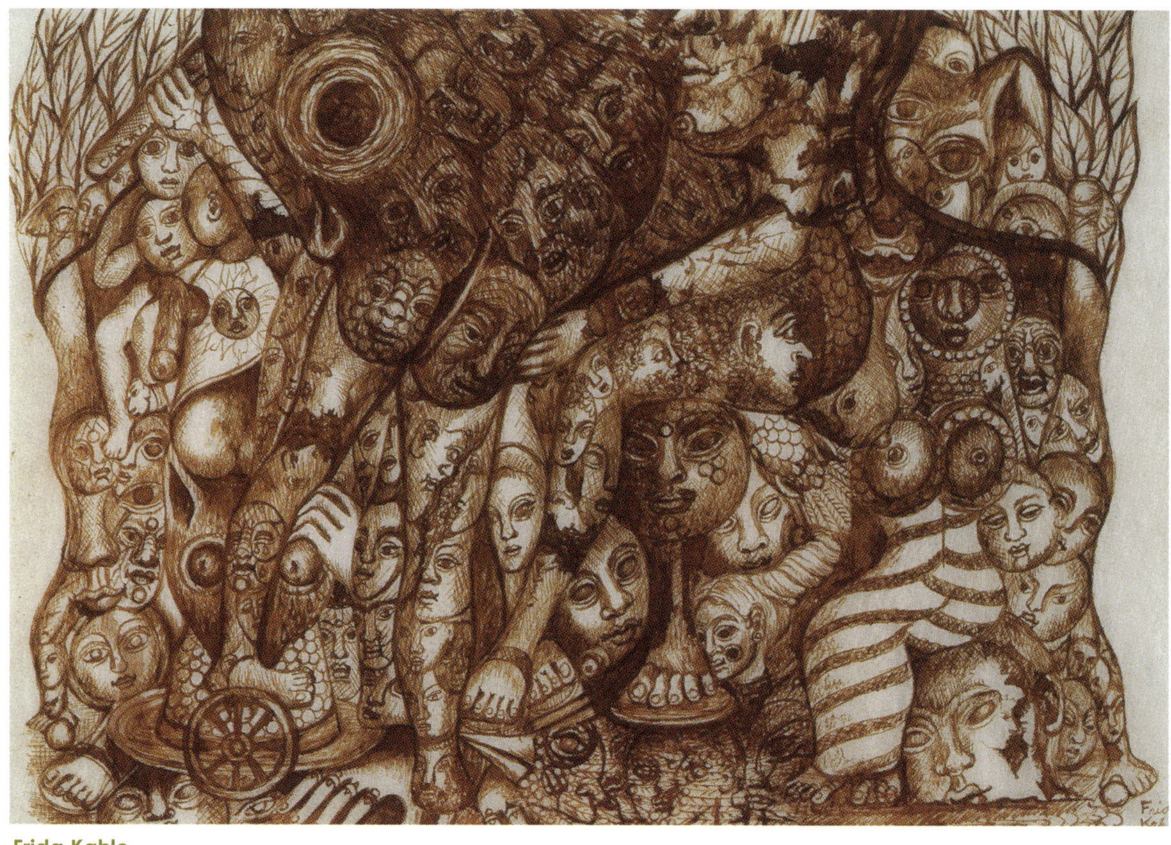

Frida Kahlo
Karma I , 1946, Sepia ink on paper / *Tinta sepia sobre papel*, 18 x 27 cm, $7^{1/4}$" x $10^{3/4}$"

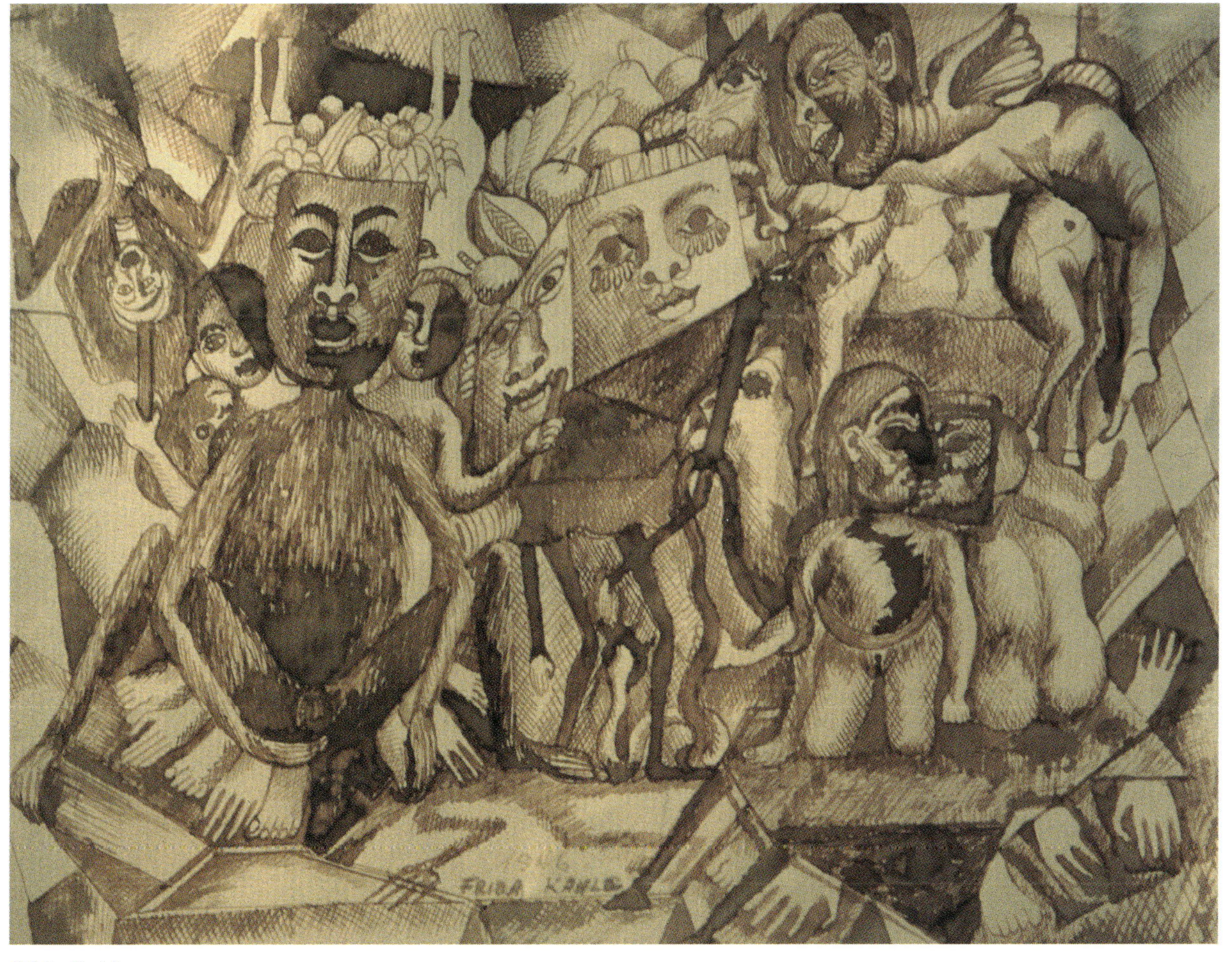

Frida Kahlo
Karma, 1946, Sepia ink on paper / *Tinta sepia sobre papel,* 21.3 x 27 cm, 8" x 10$^{3/4}$"

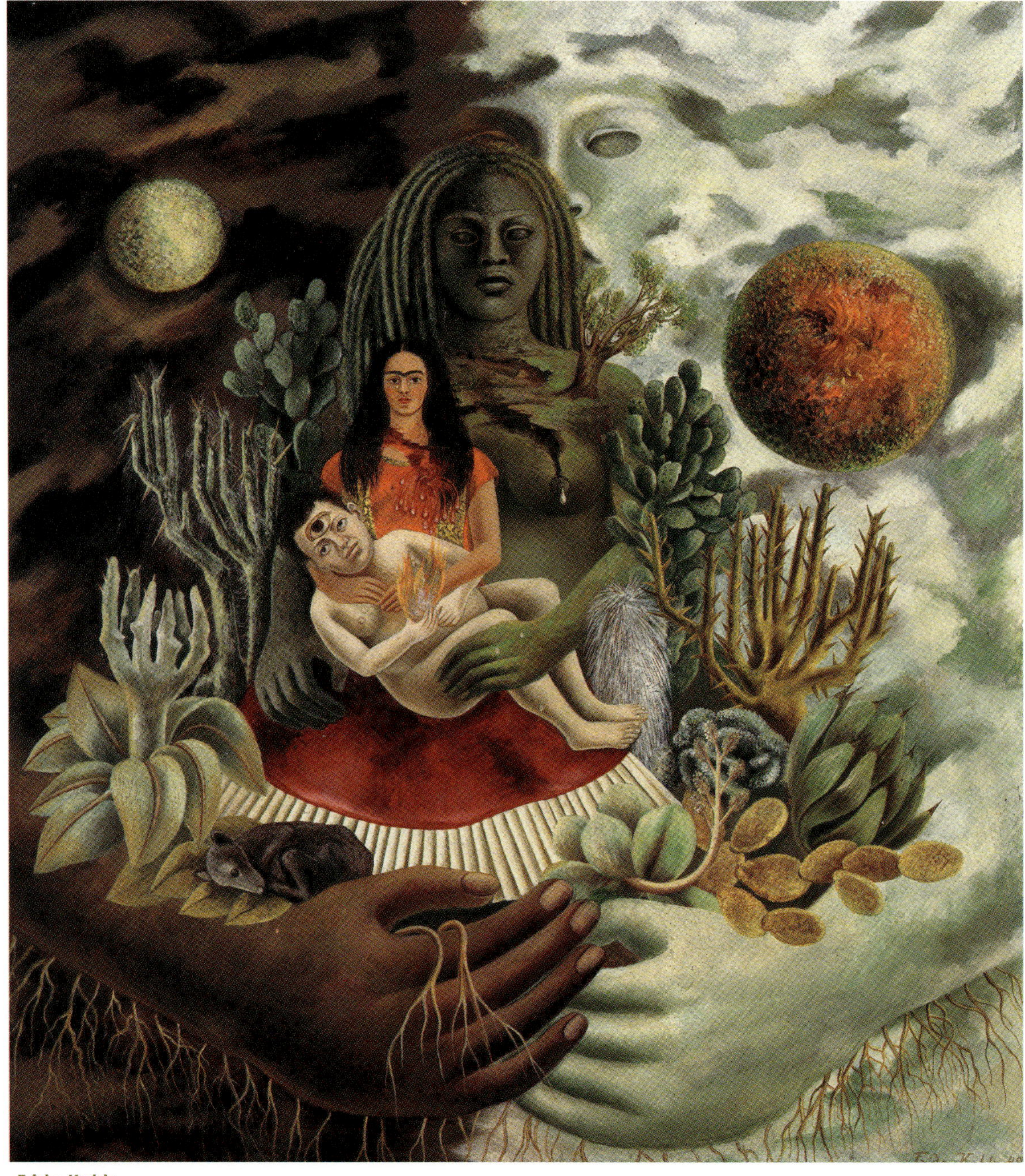

Frida Kahlo
The Love Embrace of the Universe, the Earth (Mexico) Diego, I and Señor Xolotl / *El Abrazo de Amor del Universo, la Tierra (México), Diego, yo y el Señor Xolotl,* 1949, Oil on Masonite / *Óleo sobre Masonite*, 70 x 60.5 cm, 27$^{1/2}$" x 23$^{7/8}$"

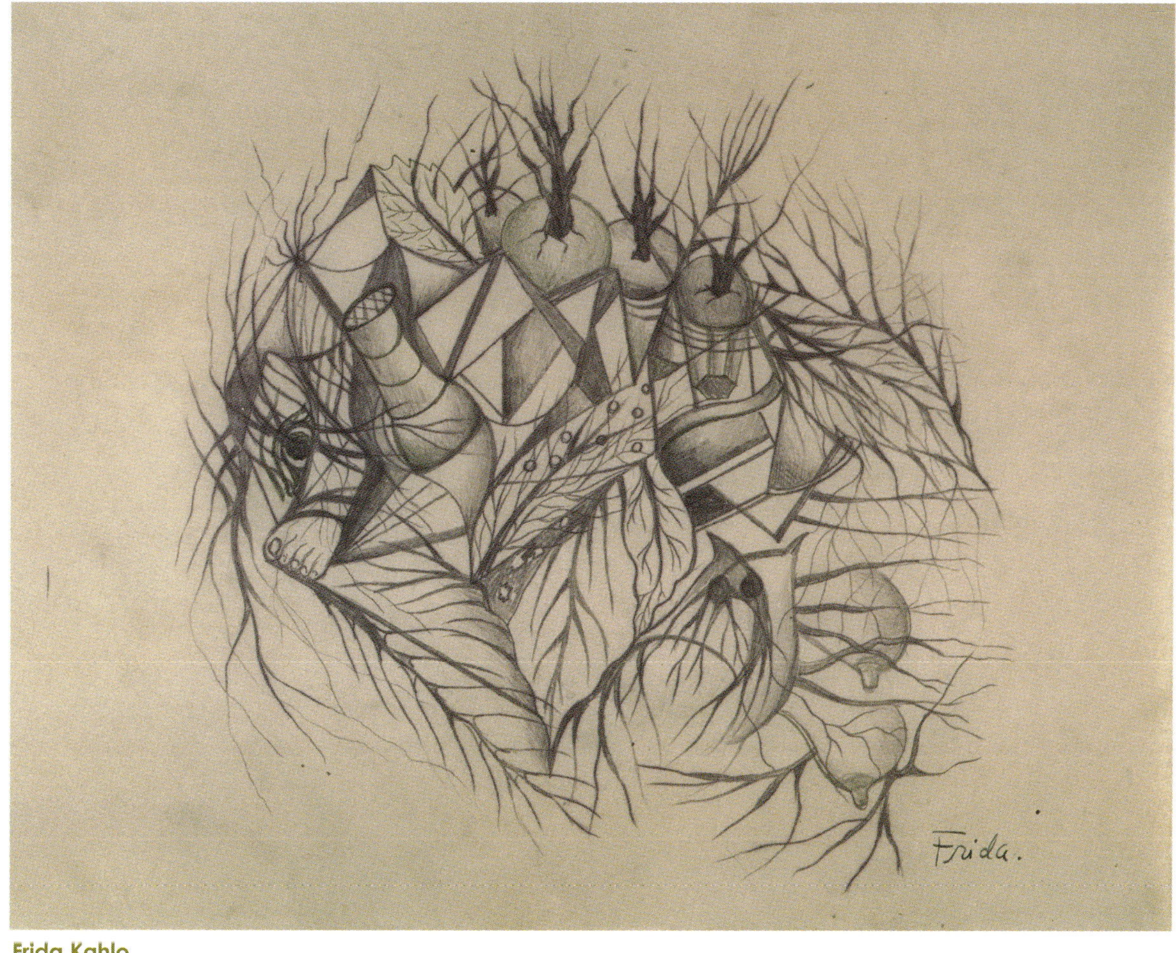

Frida Kahlo
Drawing with Foot / *Dibujo con pie*, Undated / *sin fecha*, Color pencil and graphite on paper / *Lápiz de color y grafito sobre papel*, 21.3 x 27 cm, 8" x 10$^{3/4}$"

Agustin Lazo

(1897-1971)

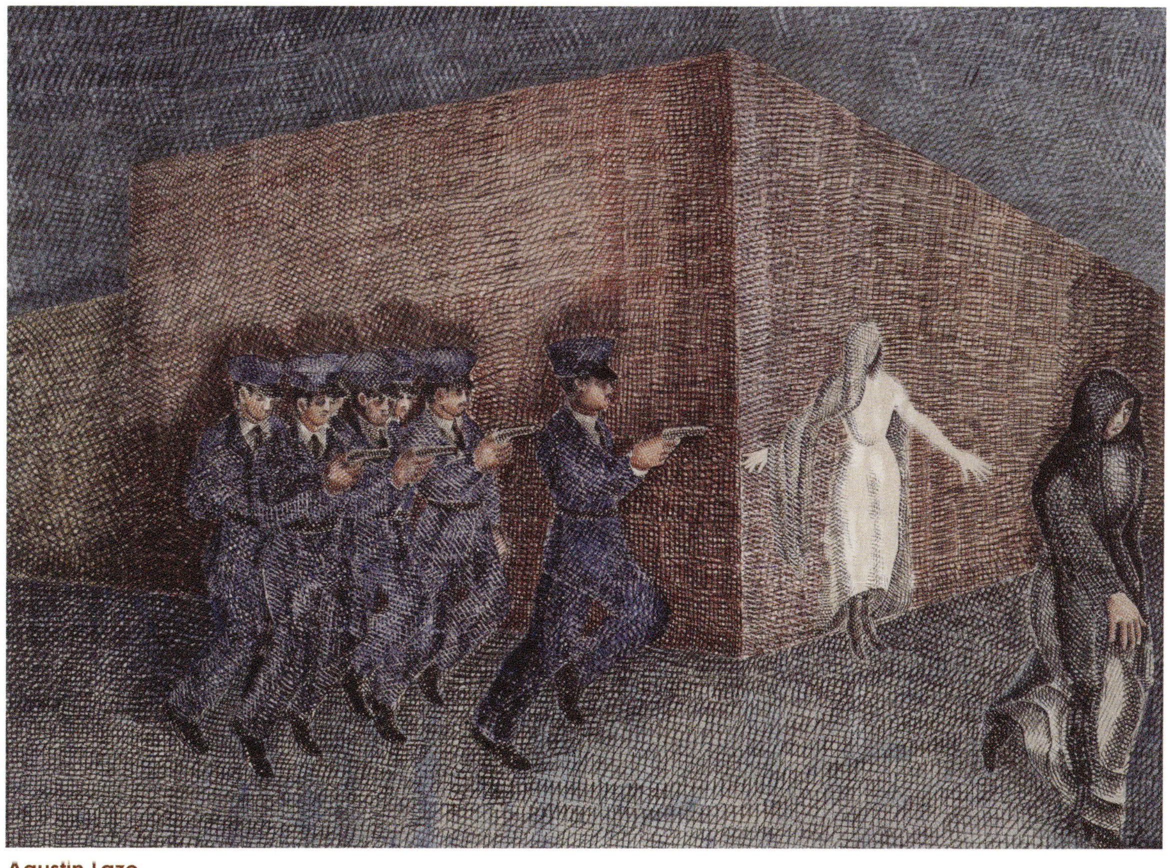

Agustin Lazo
Execution by Firing Squad / *Fusilamento*, ca. 1930 – 1932, Gouache and ink on paper / *Gouache y tinta sobre papel,* 24.6 x 33 cm, $9^{5/8}$" x 13"

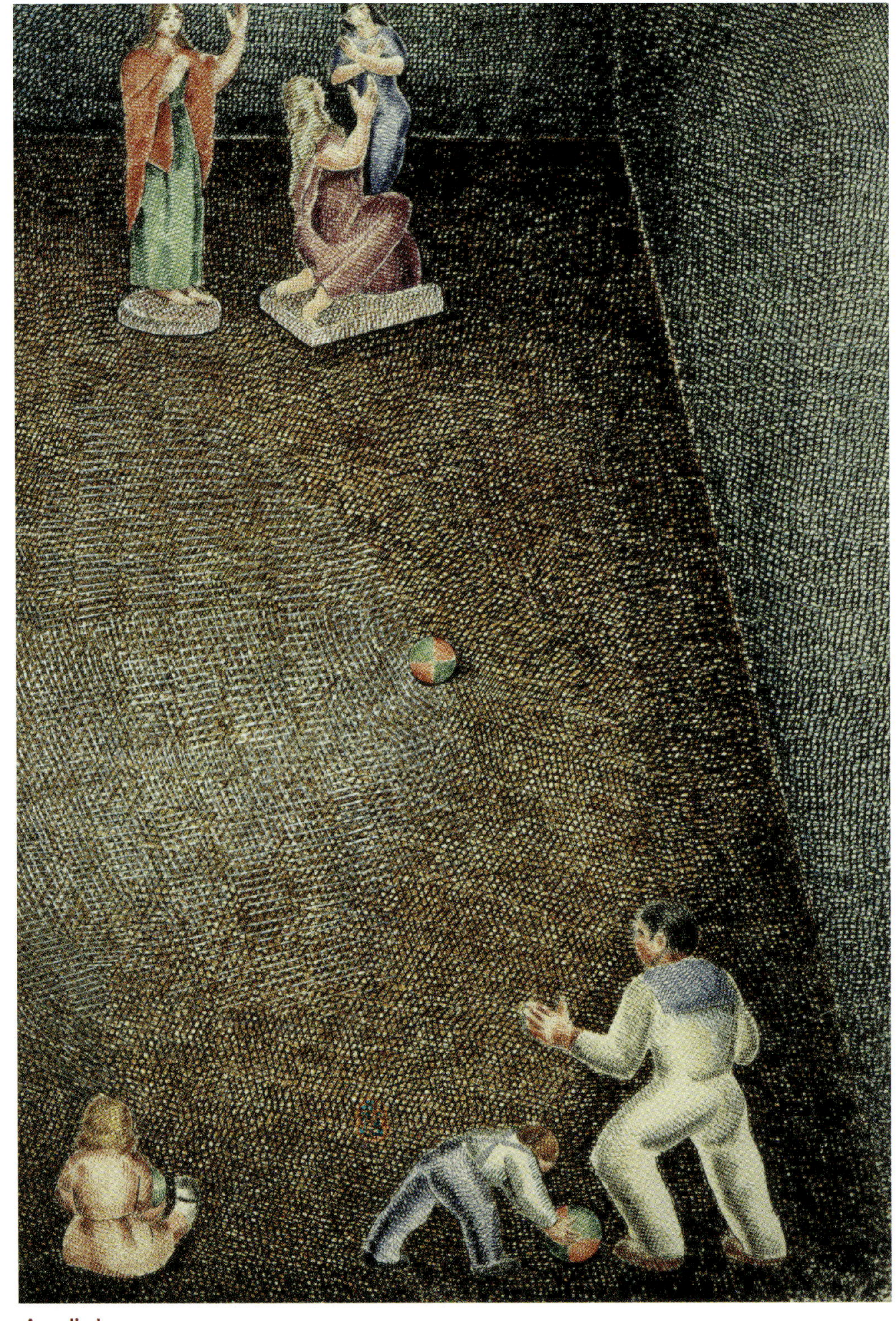

Agustin Lazo
Dangerous Games / *Juegos peligrosos*, ca. 1930 – 1932, Gouache and china ink on paper / *Gouache y tinta china sobre papel*, 35 x 23.5 cm, 13 3/4" x 9 1/4"

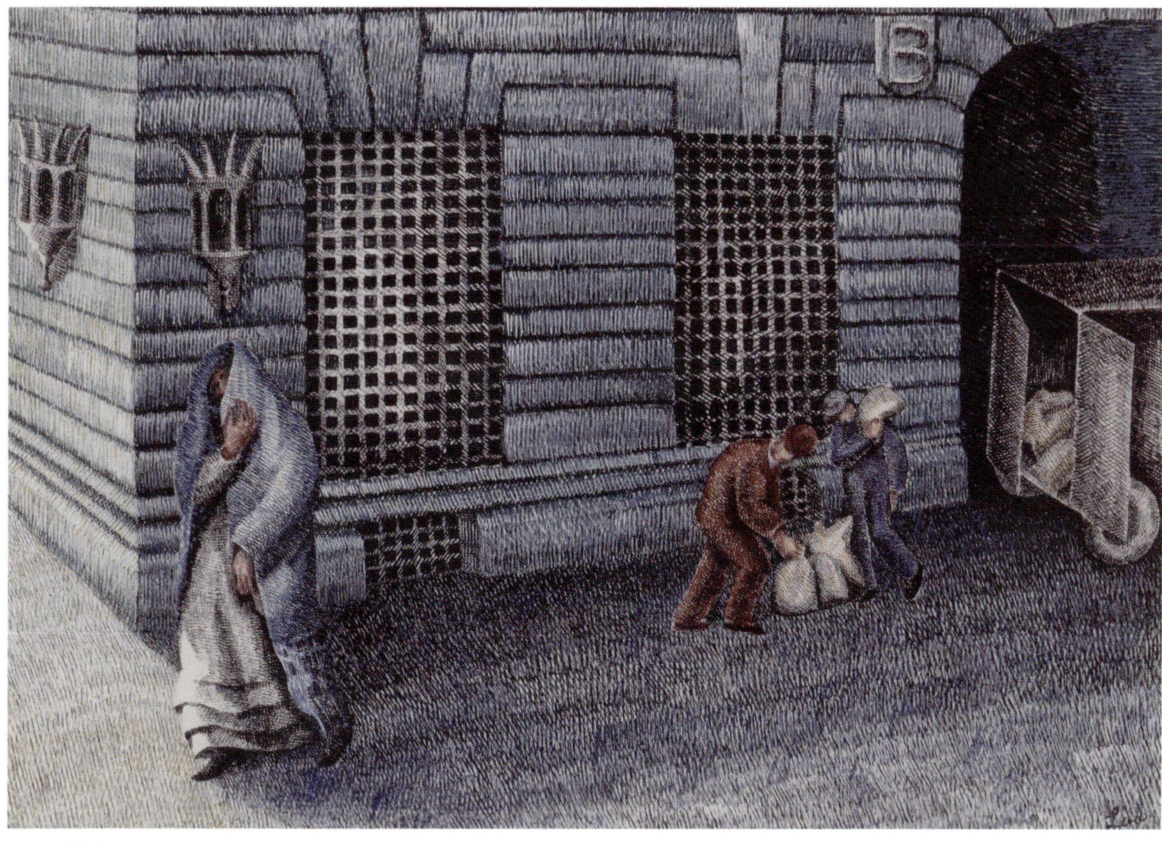

Agustin Lazo
Bank Robbery / *Robo al banco,* ca. 1930 – 1932, Gouache and ink on paper / *Gouache y tinta sobre papel,* 24.6 x 33 cm, 9 5/8" x 13"

Carlos Mérida
(1891-1984)

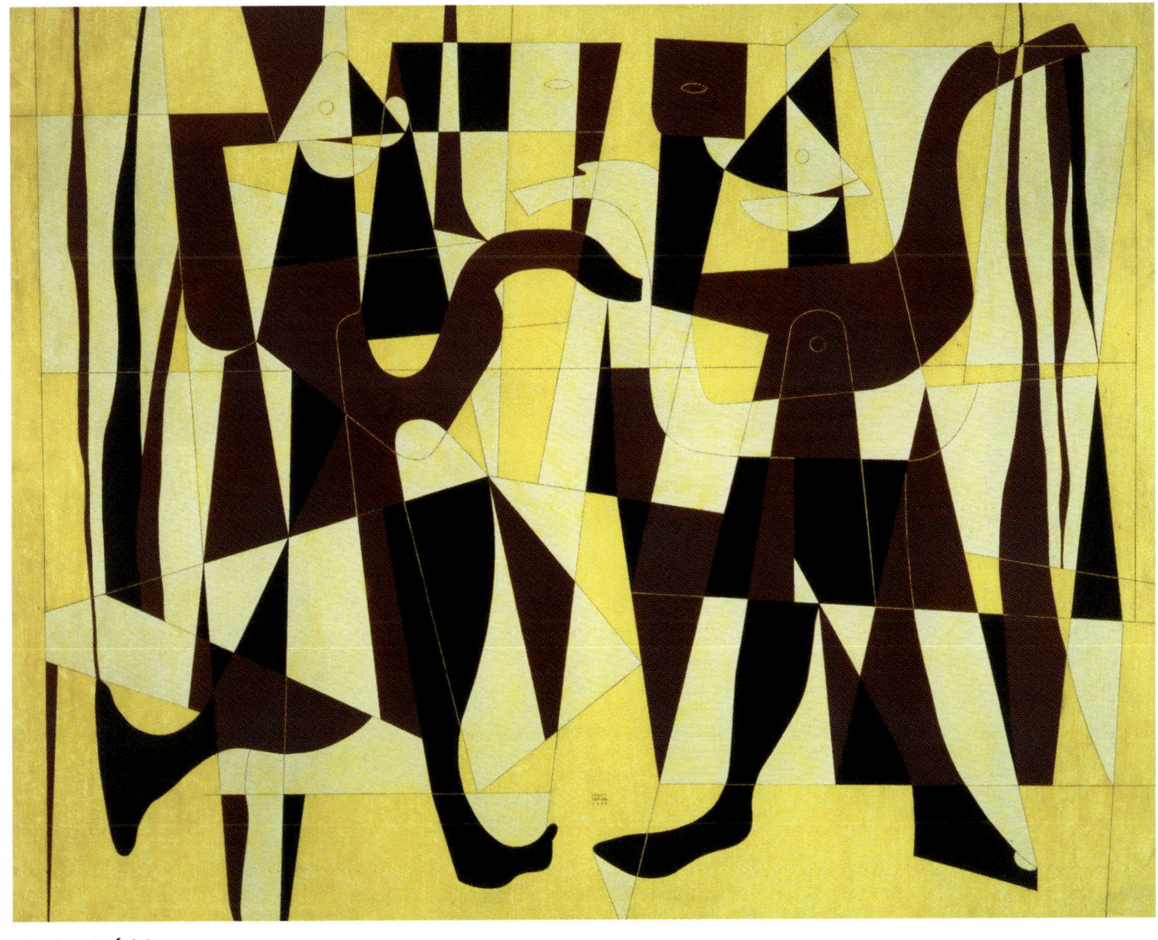

Carlos Mérida
Festival of the Birds / *Fiesta de pájaros*, 1959, Polished board / *Tablero pulido*, 50 x 40 cm, 19 3/4" x 15 3/4"

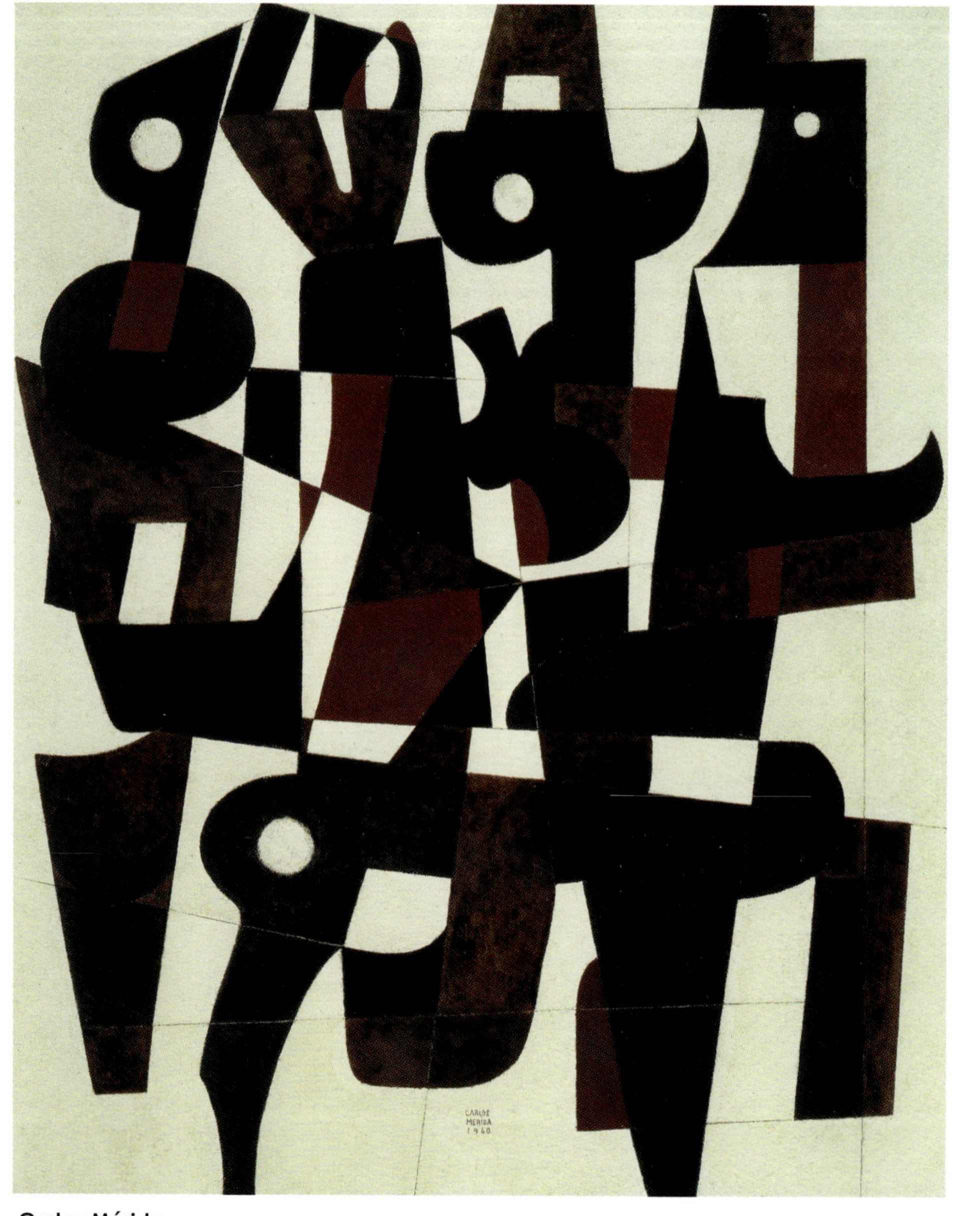

Carlos Mérida
The Message / *El mensaje*, 1960, Polished board / *Tablero pulido*, 71 x 88 cm, 28" x 34[5/8]"

José Clemente Orozco

(1883-1949)

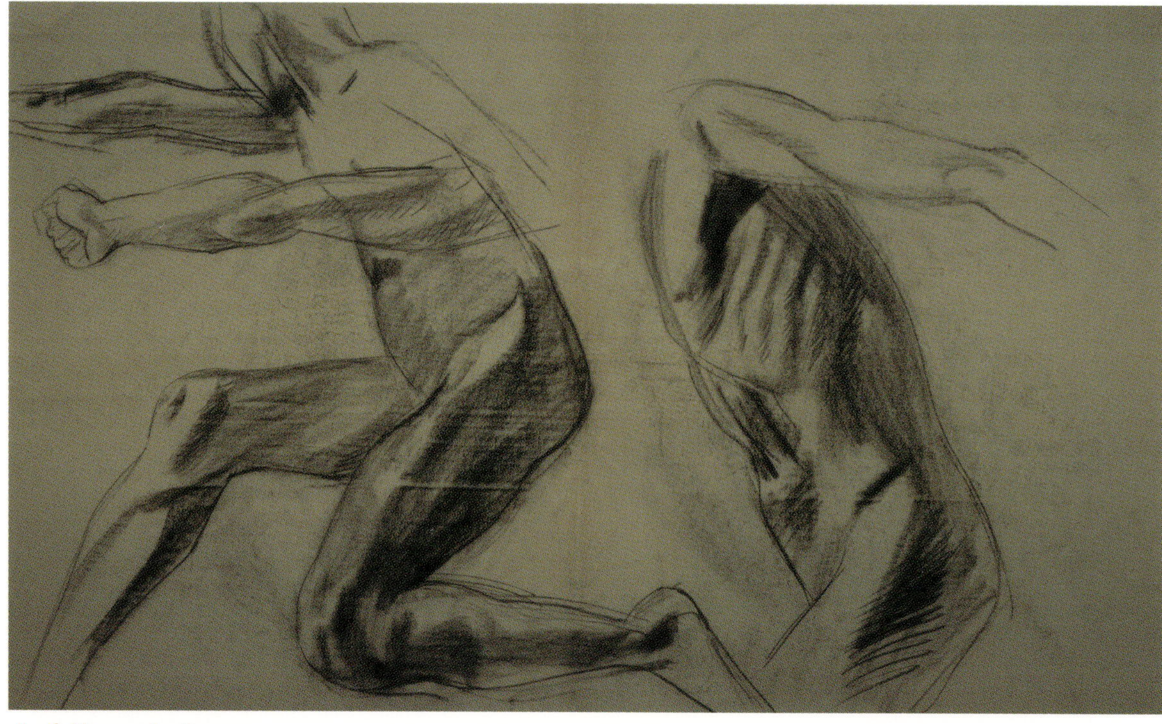

José Clemente Orozco
Torso Study (Studio drawing for the murals of the National Preparatory School) / *Estudios de figura (para los murales de la Escuela Nacional Preparatoria),* ca. 1926, Charcoal on *kraft* paper / *Carboncillo sobre papel kraft,* 61.5 x 96.5 cm, 24 1/2" x 38"

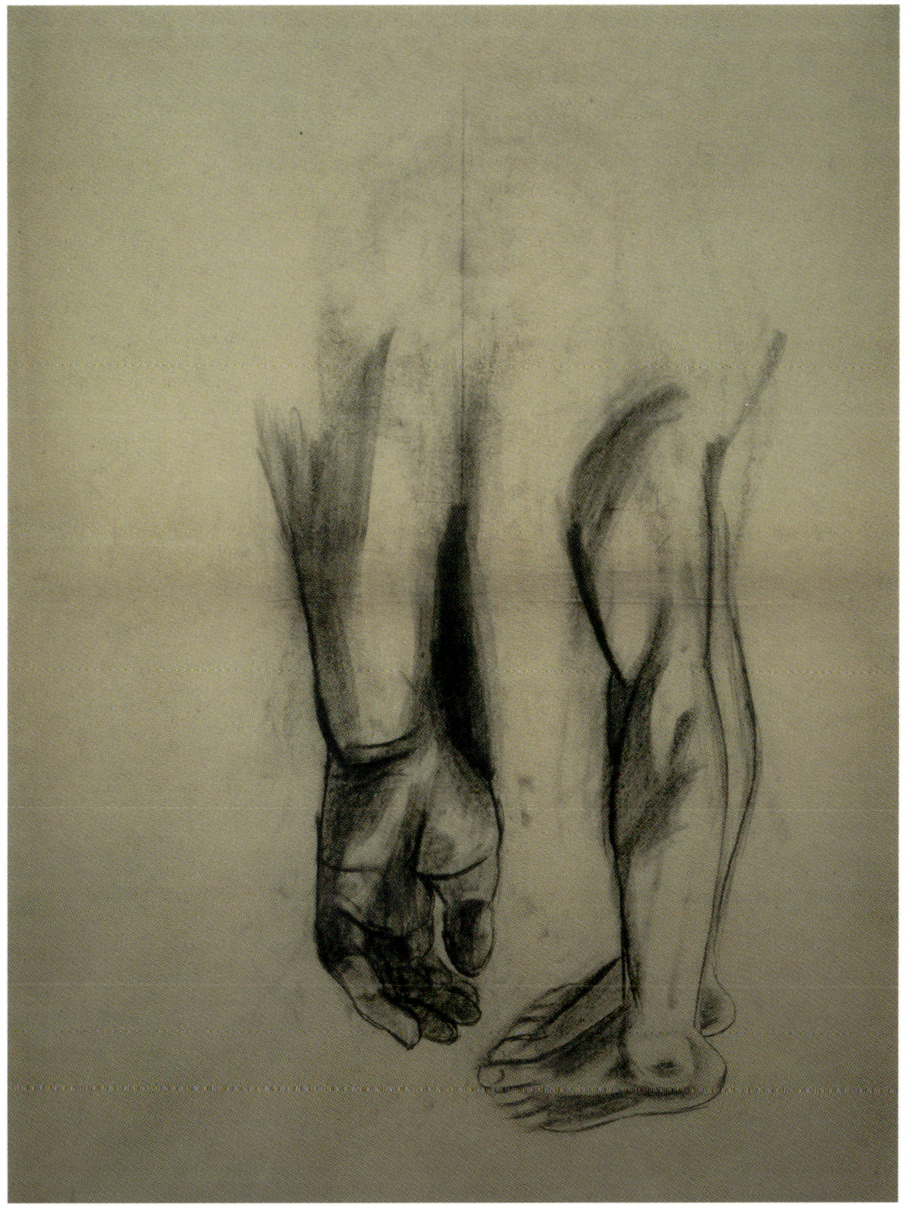

José Clemente Orozco
Figure Study (Studio drawing for the murals of the National Preparatory School) / *Estudios de figura (para los murales de la Escuela Nacional Preparatoria)*, ca. 1926, Charcoal on *kraft* paper / *Carboncillo sobre papel kraft*, 95 x 71 cm, 37$^{3/8}$" x 28"

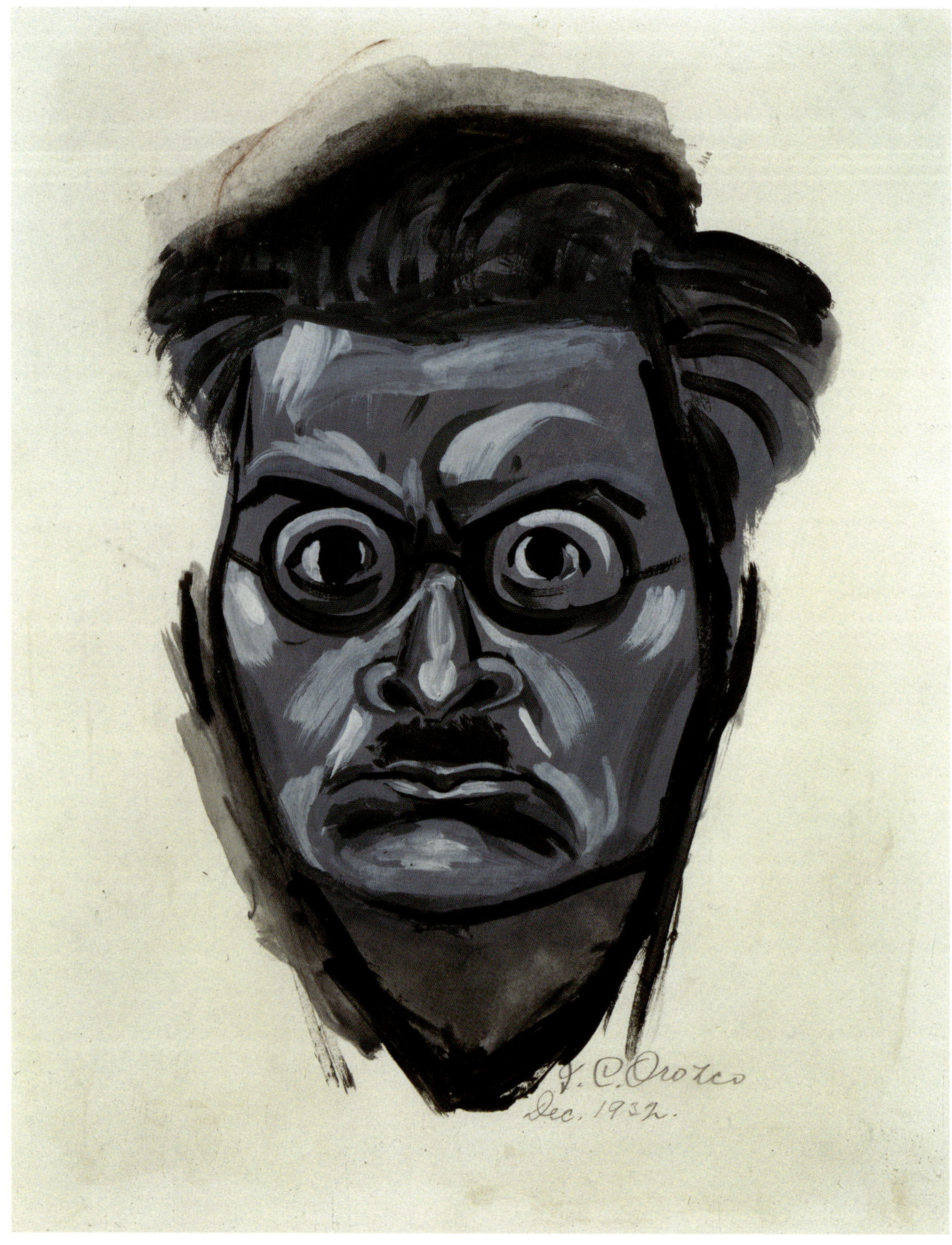

José Clemente Orozco
Self-portrait / *Autorretrato,* 1932, Watercolor and gouache on paper / *Acuarela y gouache sobre papel,*
37 x 30 cm, $14^{1/2}$" x $11^{7/8}$"

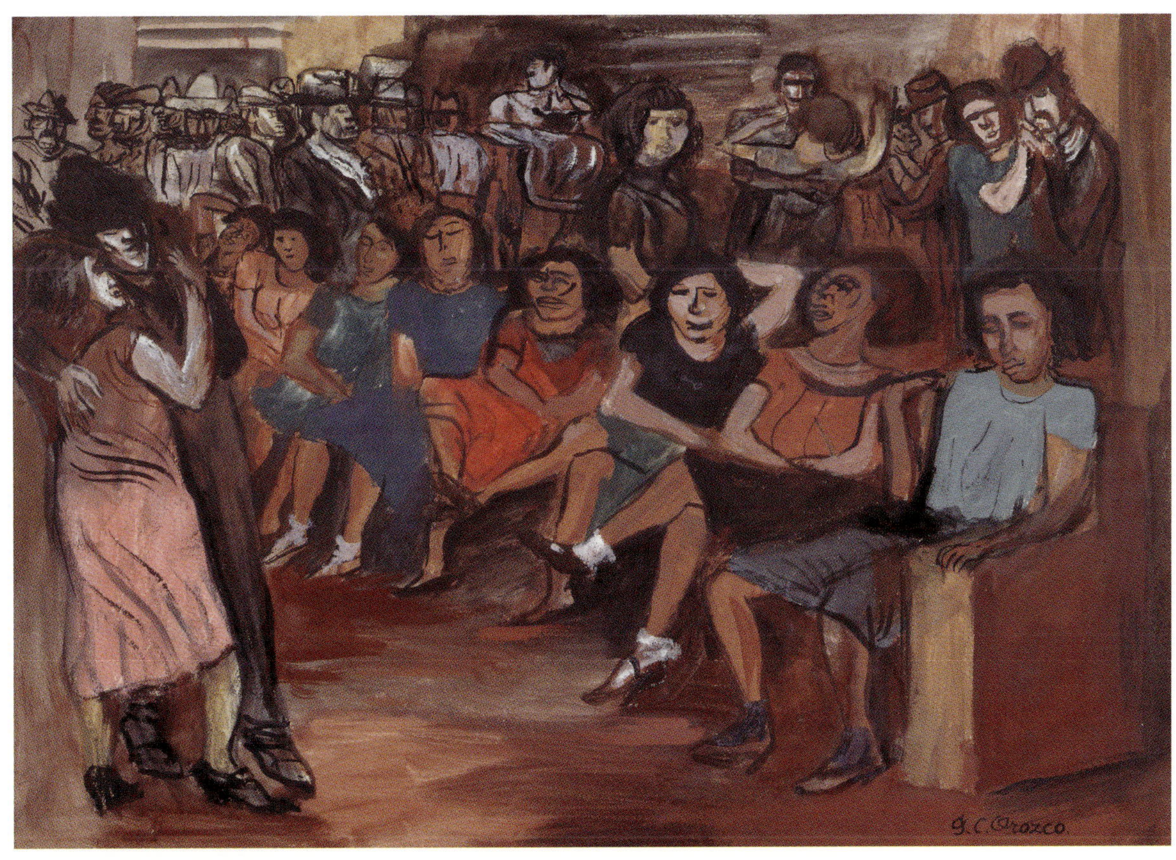

José Clemente Orozco
Untitled (Salon Mexico) / *Sin título (Salón México)*, 1940, Gouache on paper / *Gouache sobre papel,*
49 x 67 cm, $19^{1/4}$" x $26^{3/8}$"

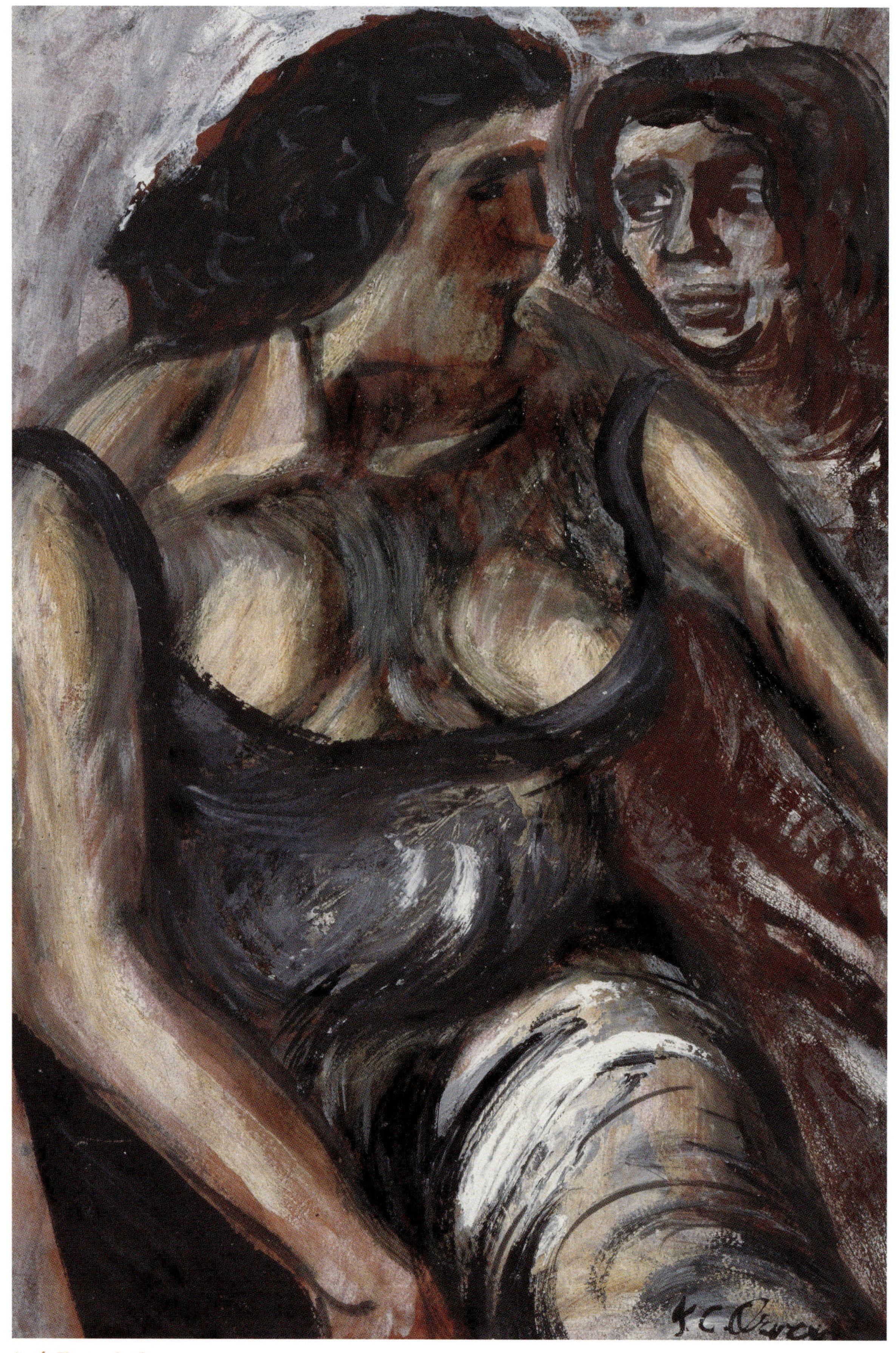

José Clemente Orozco
Painting / *Pintura*, 1942, Oil on paper / *Óleo sobre papel*, 37 x 25 cm, 14 1/2" x 9 7/8"

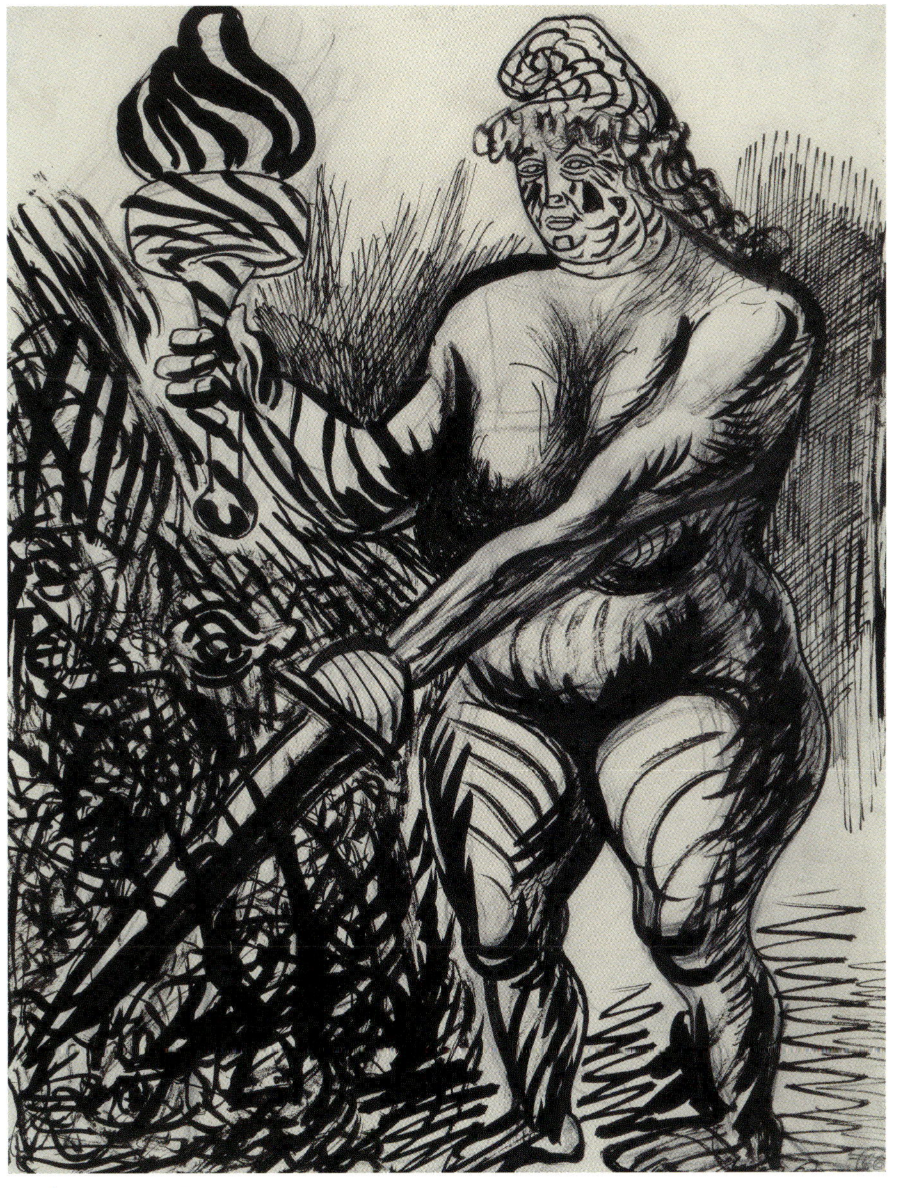

José Clemente Orozco
Liberty / *Libertad*, 1945, Pencil and ink on paper / *Lápiz y tinta sobre papel*, 37.5 x 28 cm , 15$^{3/4}$" x 11"

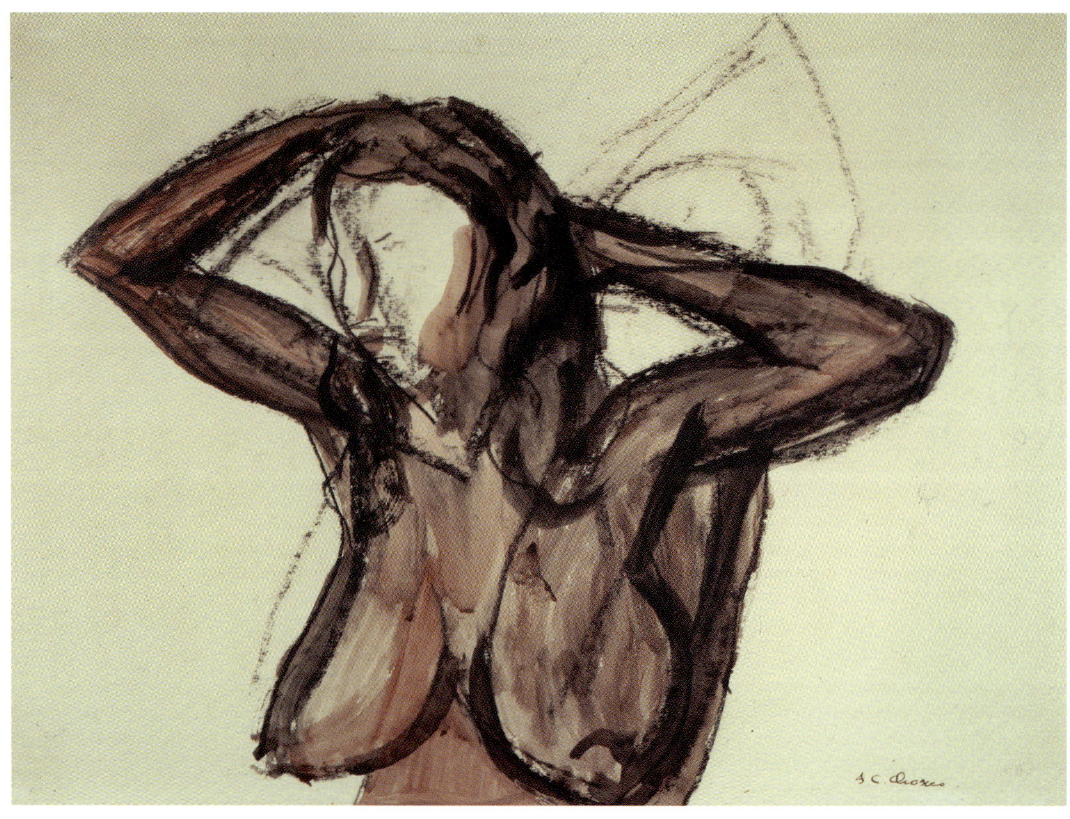

José Clemente Orozco
Female Nude / *Desnudo femenino*, Undated / *Sin fecha*, Ink and charcoal on paper / *Tinta y carboncillo sobre papel*, 48 x 64 cm, 18 7/8" x 25 1/4"

Carlos Orozco Romero

(1898-1984)

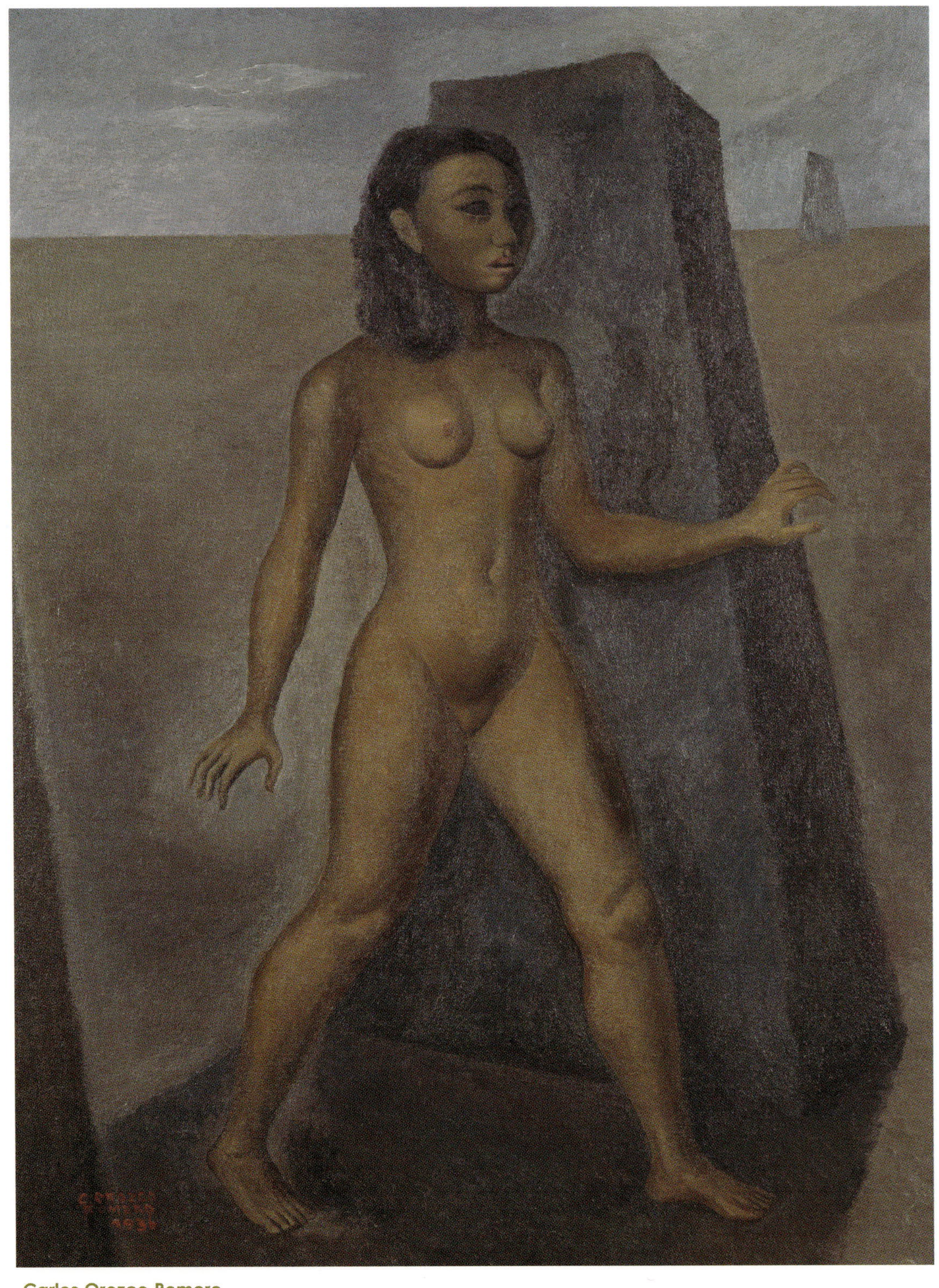

Carlos Orozco Romero
Entrance to Infinity / *Entrada al infinito*, 1936, Oil on canvas / *Óleo sobre tela*, 75 x 55 cm, 29$^{1/2}$" x 19$^{3/4}$"

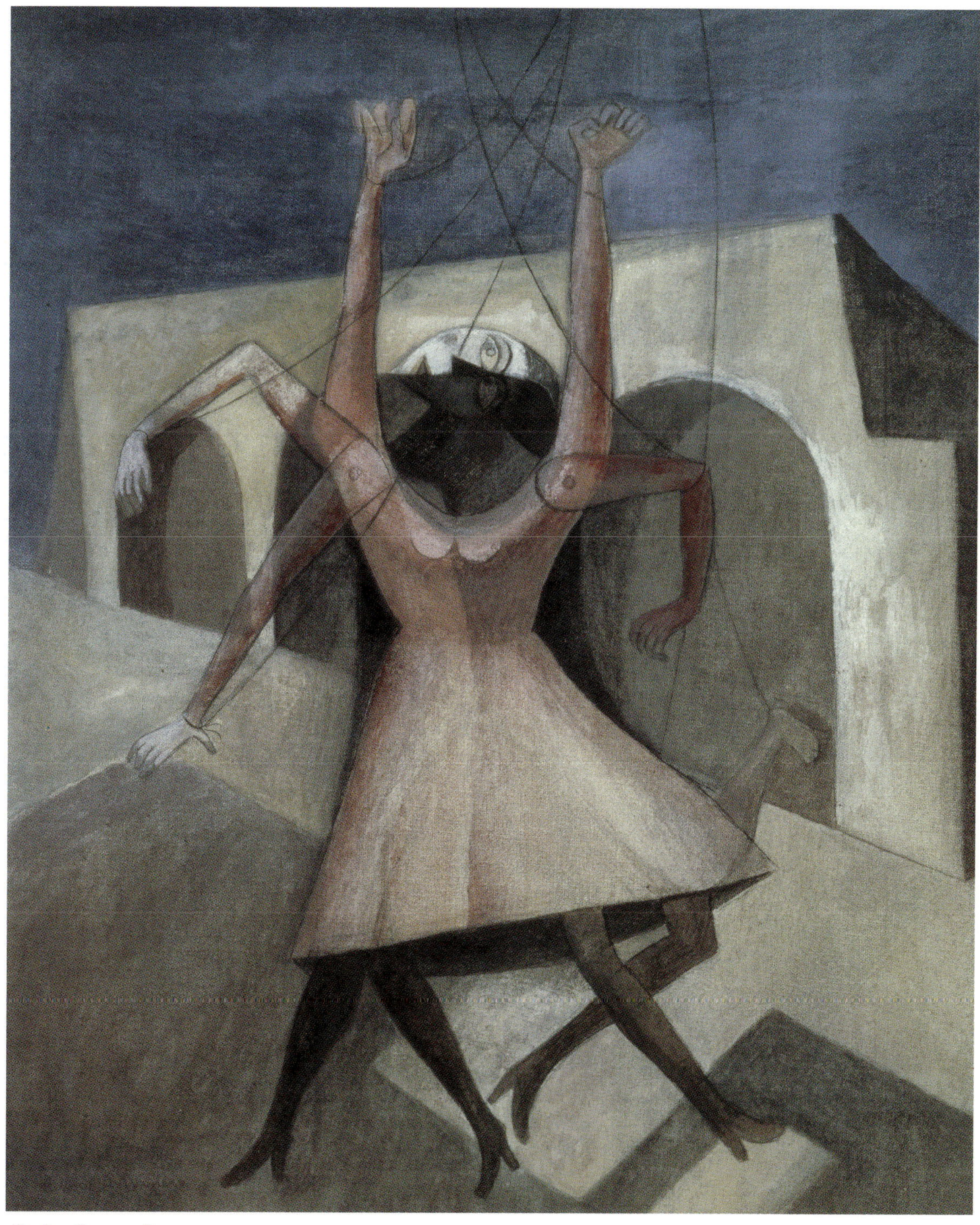

Carlos Orozco Romero
Protest / *Protesta*, 1939, Oil, gouache and pencil on canvas / *Aguada de óleo y lápiz sobre tela*,
39 x 32 cm, 15 3/8" x 12 5/8"

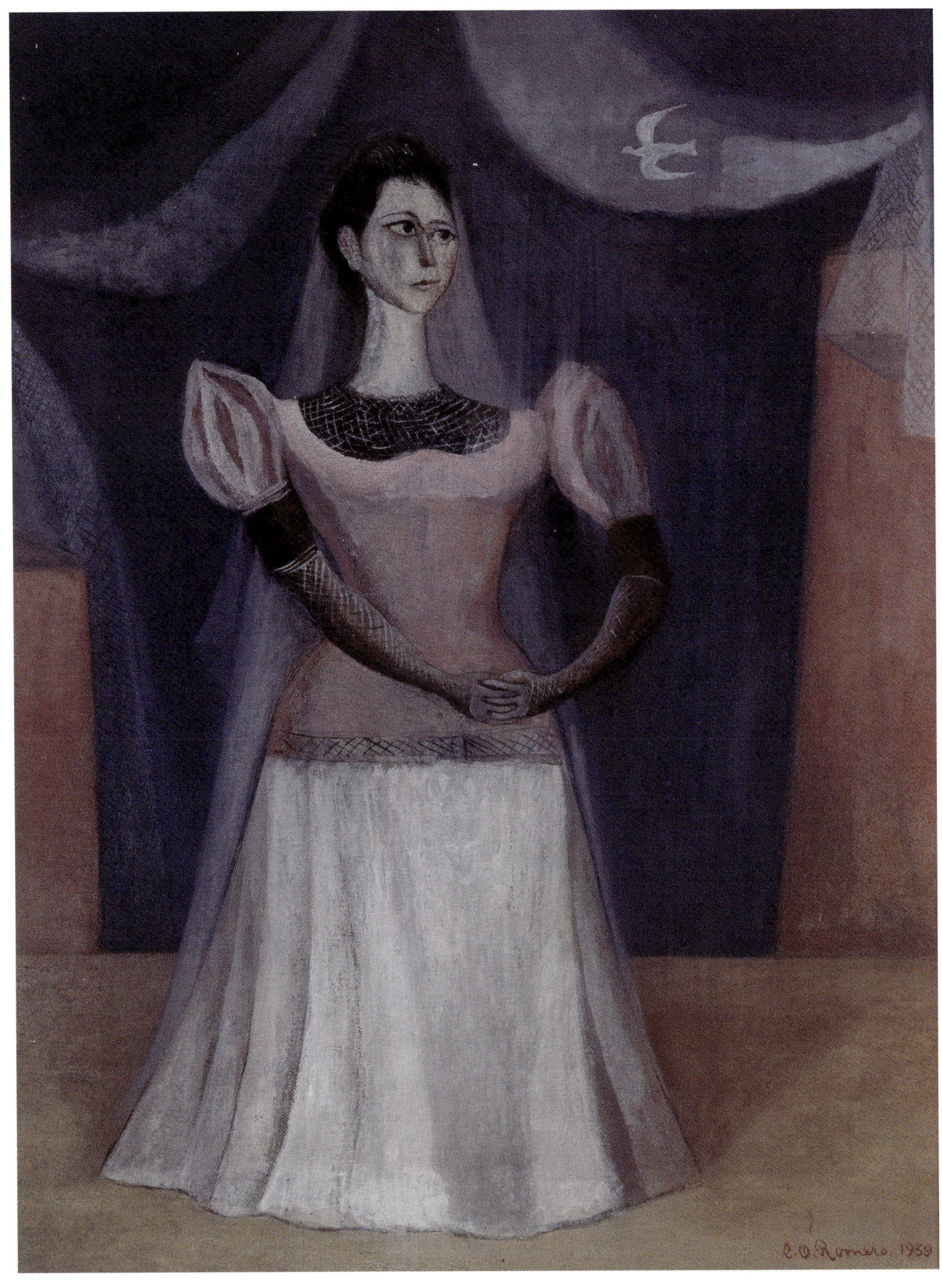

Carlos Orozco Romero
The Bride / *La novia*, 1939, Oil on canvas / *Óleo sobre tela* , 41 x 31 cm, $16^{1/8}$" x $12^{1/8}$"

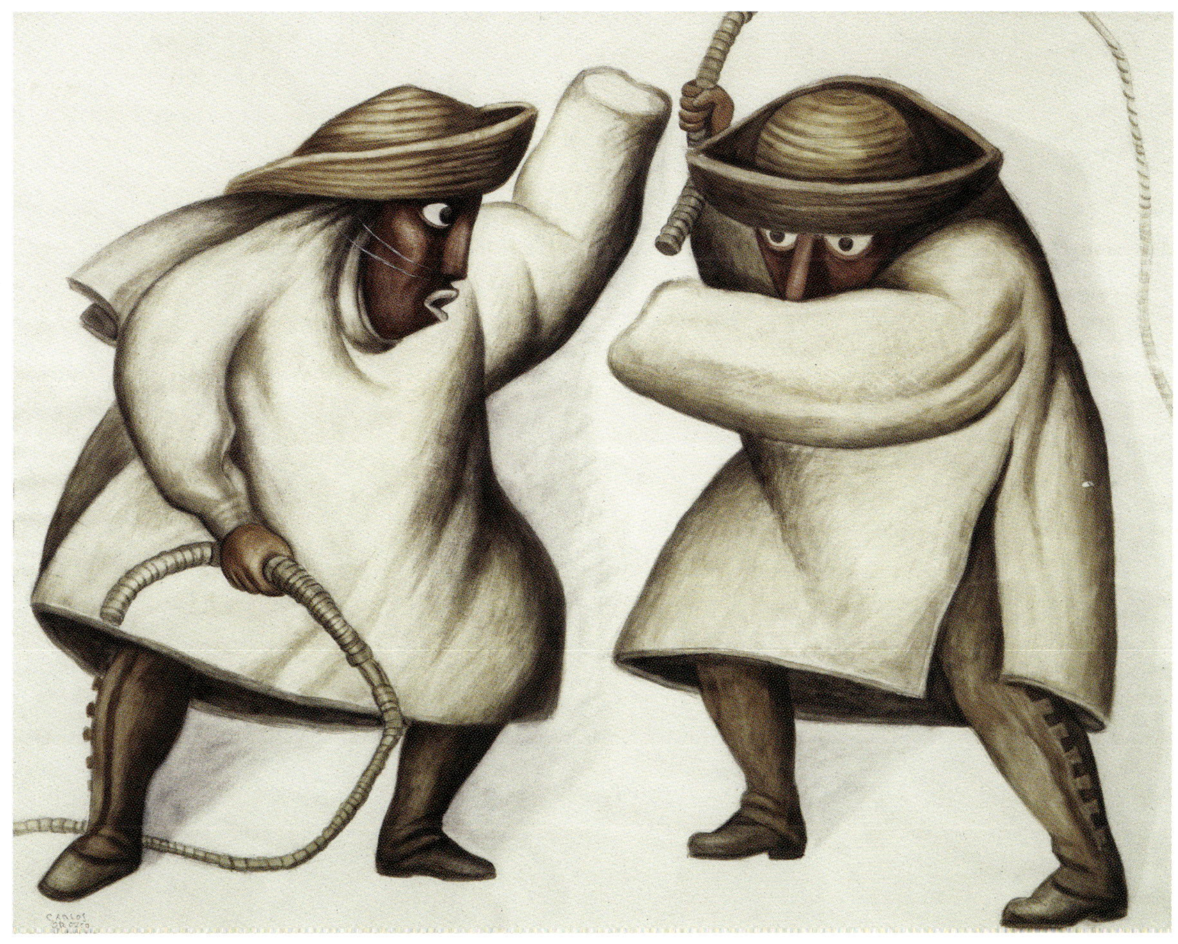

Carlos Orozco Romero
Dancers / *Danzantes*, Undated / *Sin fecha*, Pencil and watercolor on paper / *Lápiz y acuarela sobre papel*, 48 x 59 cm, 18$^{7/8}$" x 68$^{1/4}$"

Diego Rivera

(1886-1957)

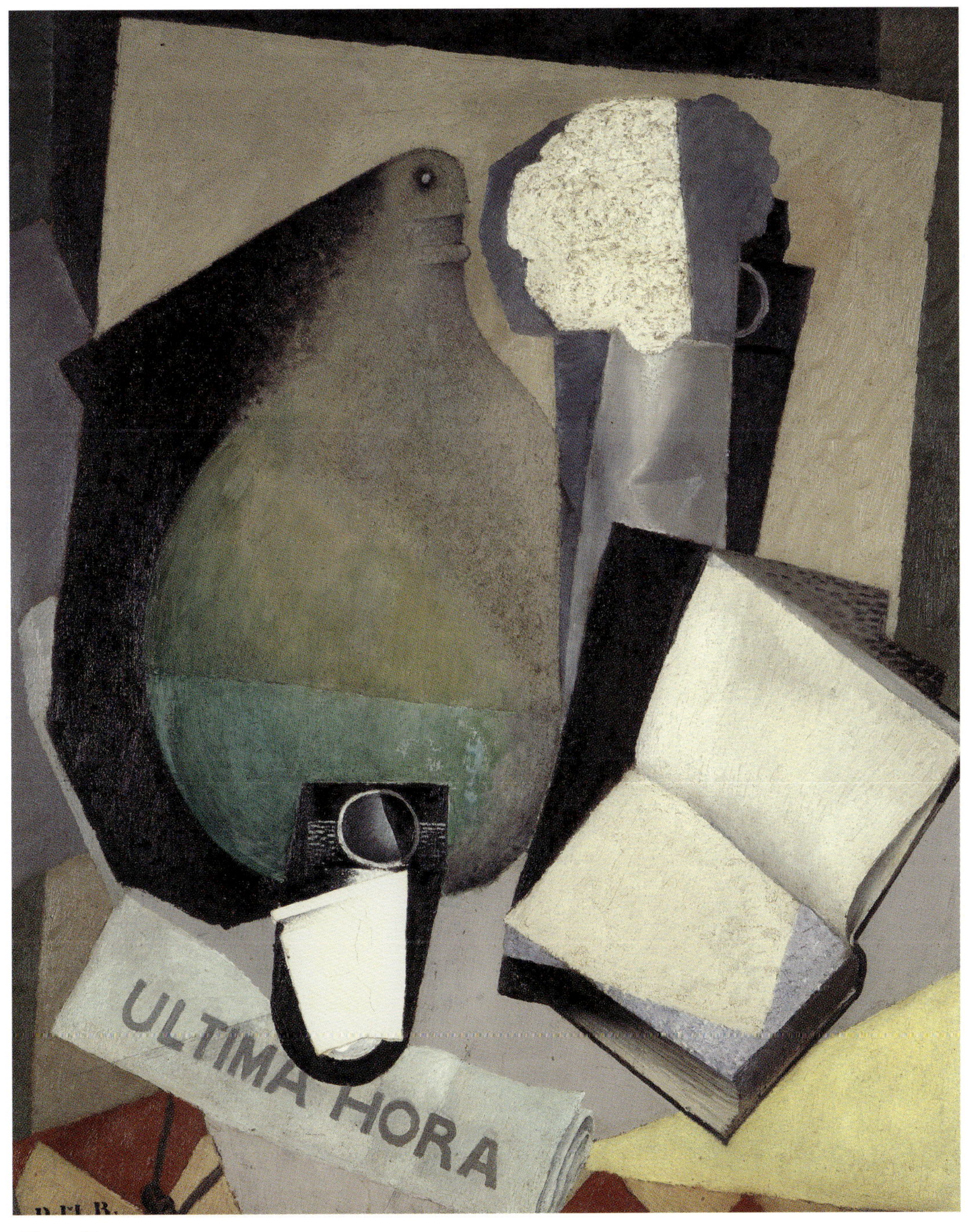

Diego Rivera
The Last Hour / *Última hora*, 1915, Oil on canvas / *Óleo sobre tela*, 92 x 73 cm, 36$^{1/4}$" x 28$^{3/4}$"

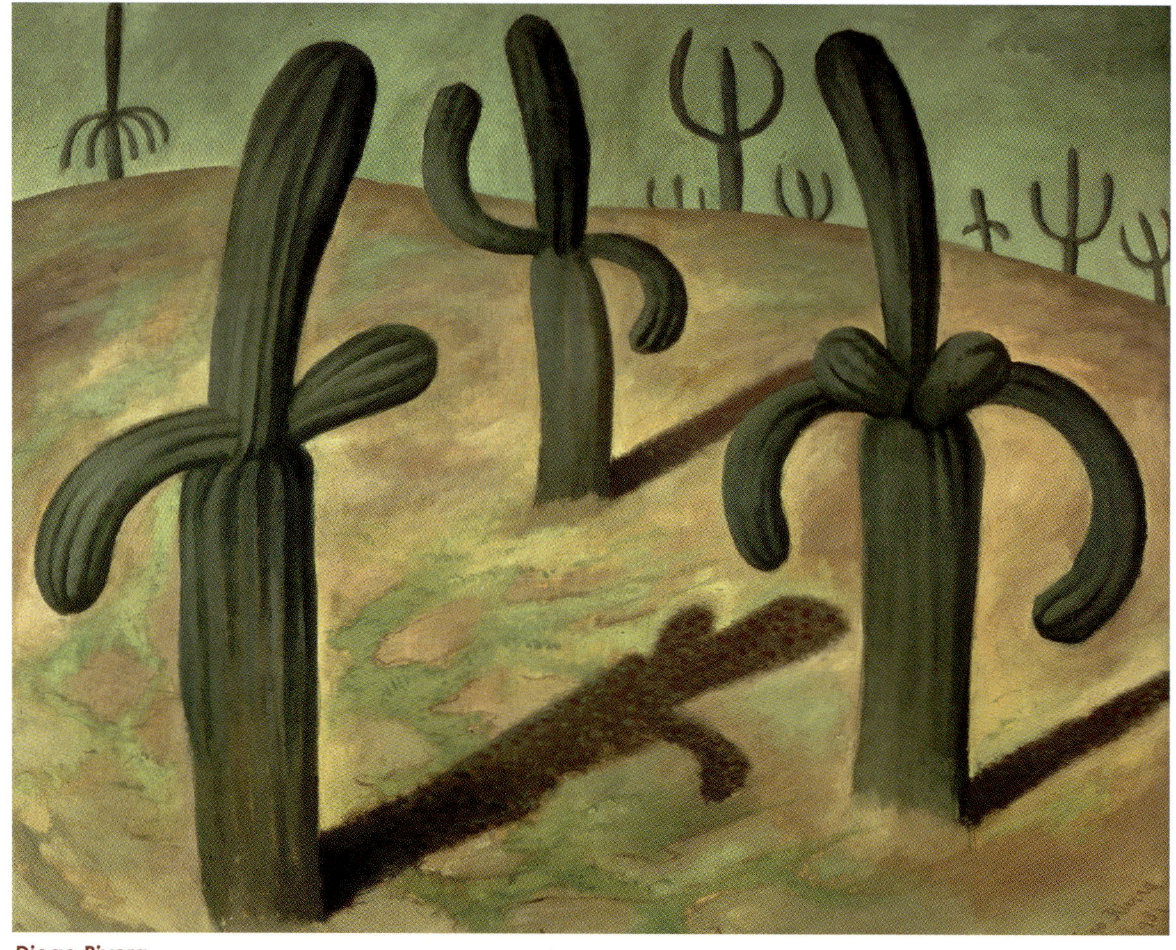

Diego Rivera
Landscape with Cactus / *Paisaje con cactus,* 1931, Oil on canvas / *Óleo sobre tela,* 125.5 x 150 cm, $49^{3/8}$" x 59"

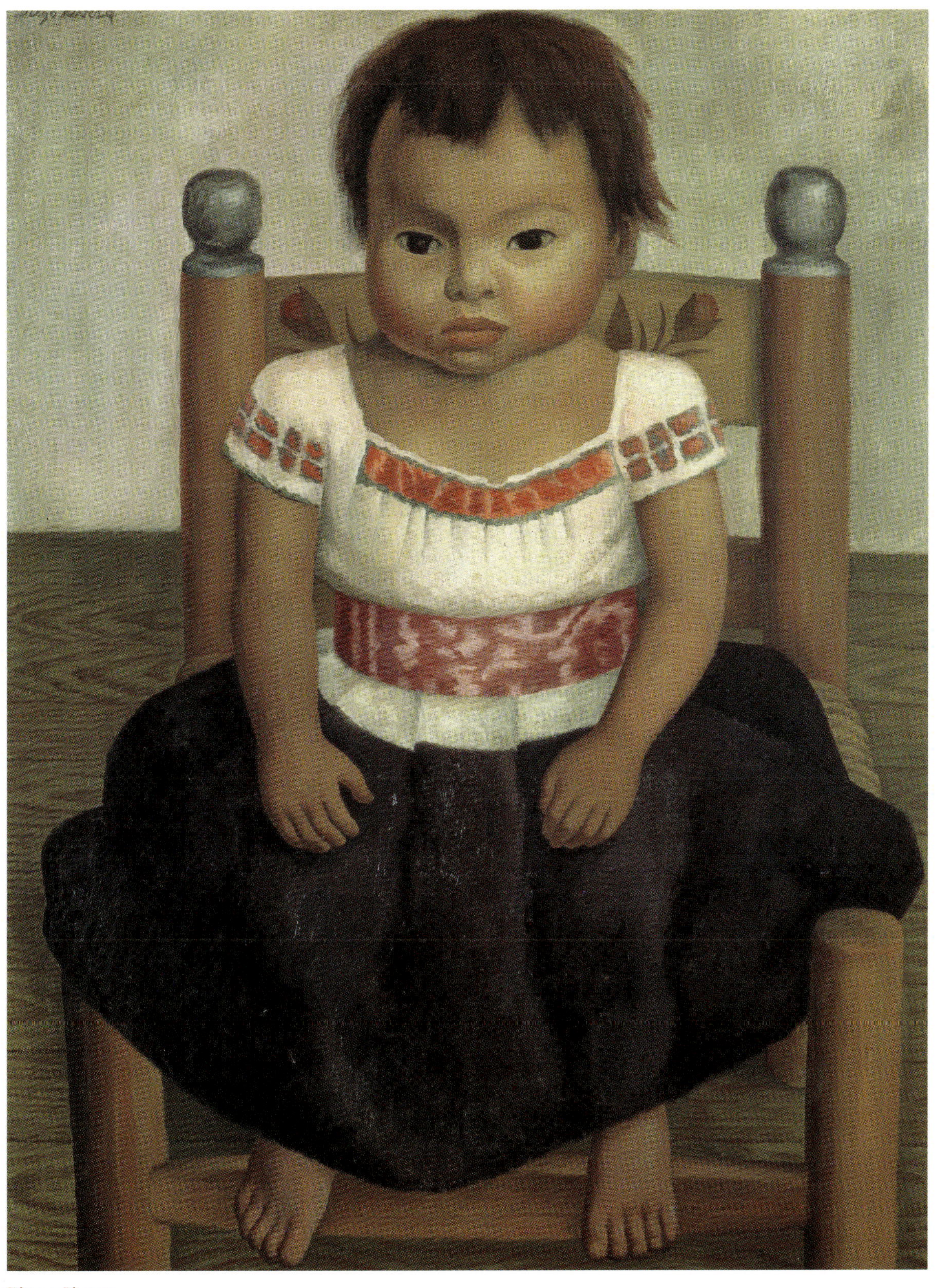

Diego Rivera
Modesta, 1937, Oil on canvas / *Óleo sobre tela*, 80 x 59 cm, $3^{11/2}$" x $23^{1/4}$"

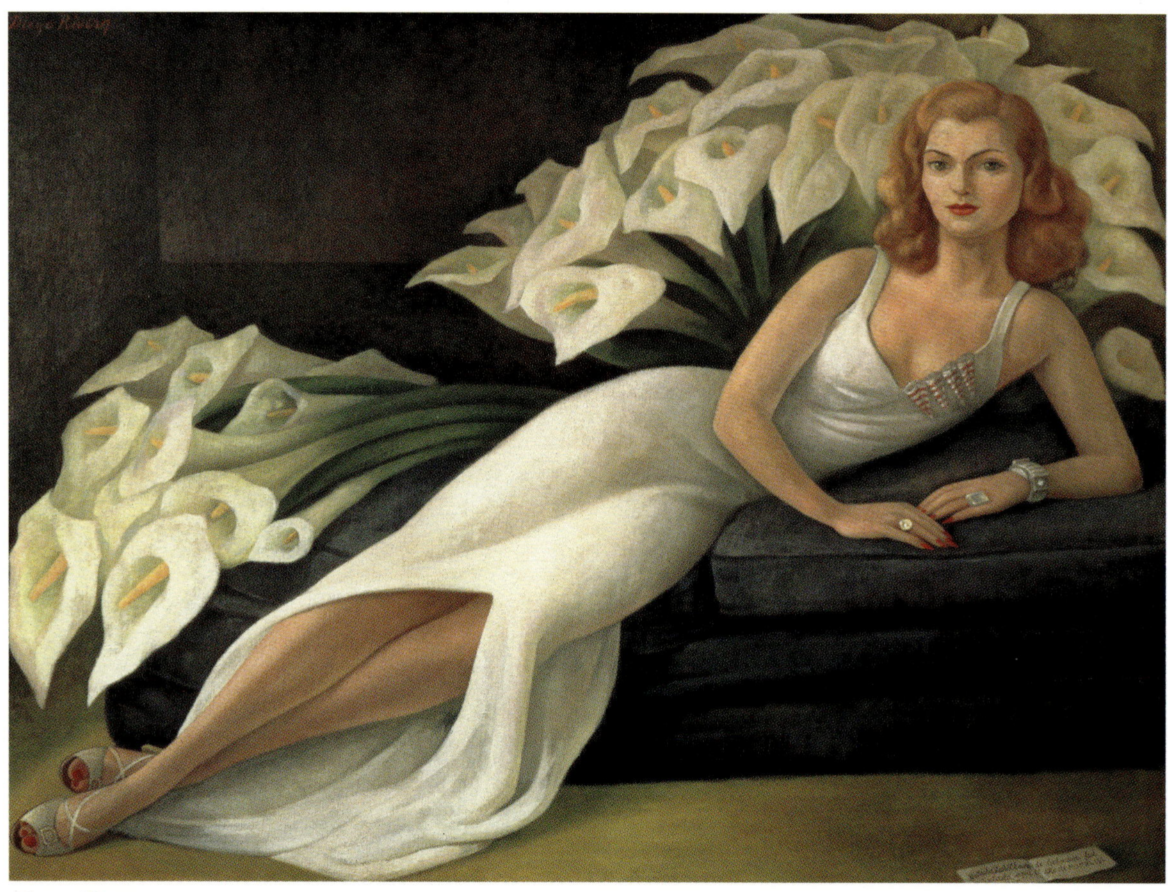

Diego Rivera
Portrait of Mrs. Natasha Gelman / *Retrato de la Señora Natasha Gelman*, 1943, Oil on canvas / *Óleo sobre tela*, 115 x 153 cm, $45^{1/4}$" x $60^{1/4}$"

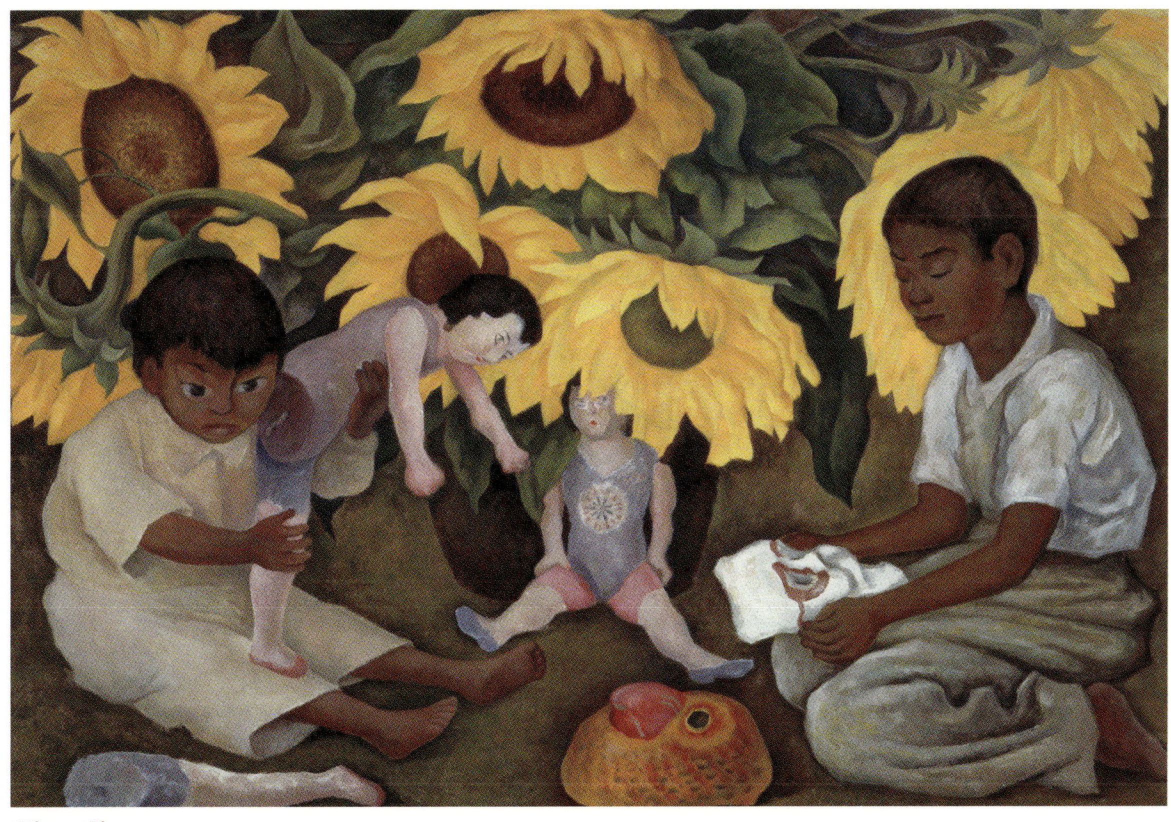

Diego Rivera
Sunflowers / *Girasoles,* 1943, Oil on wood / *Óleo sobre madera*, 90 x 130 cm, 35 1/2" x 51 1/8"

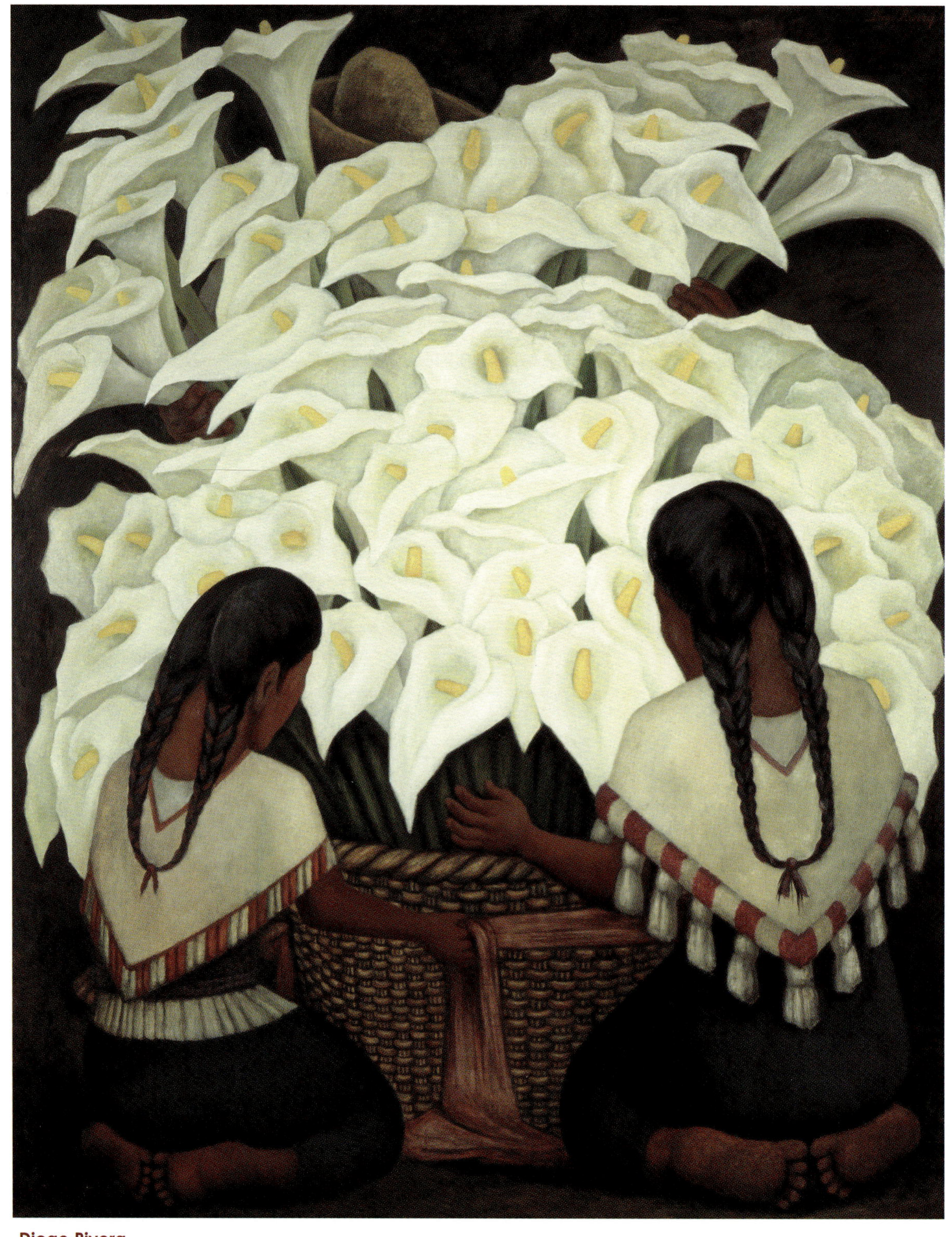

Diego Rivera
Calla Lily Vendor / *Vendedora de alcatraces*, 1943, Oil on Masonite / *Óleo sobre Masonite*, 150 x 120 cm, 59" x 47$^{1/4}$"

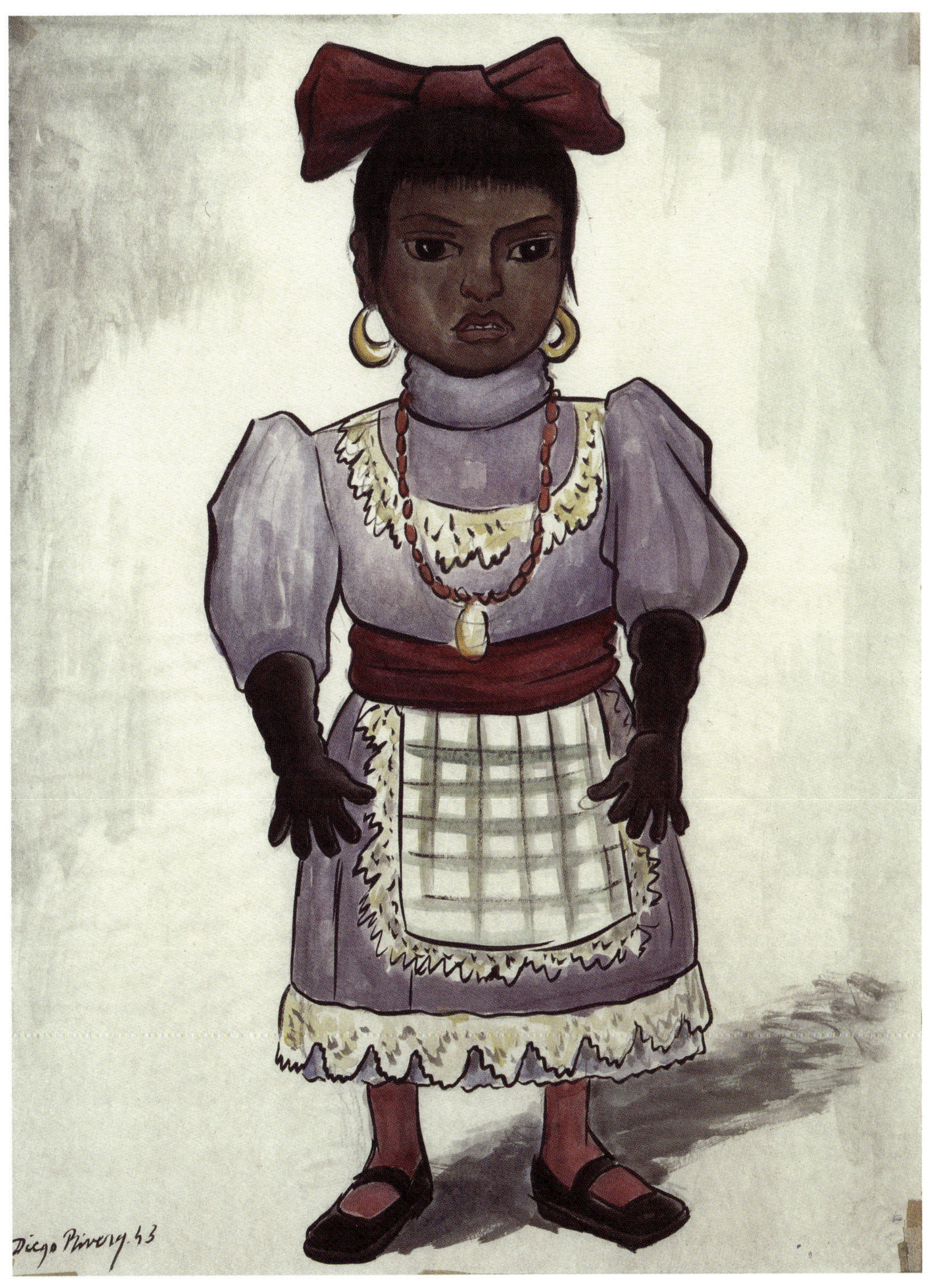

Diego Rivera
Girl with gloves / *Niña con guantes*, 1943, Watercolor on paper / *Acuarela sobre papel*, 73 x 53 cm, 28$^{3/4}$" x 20$^{7/8}$"

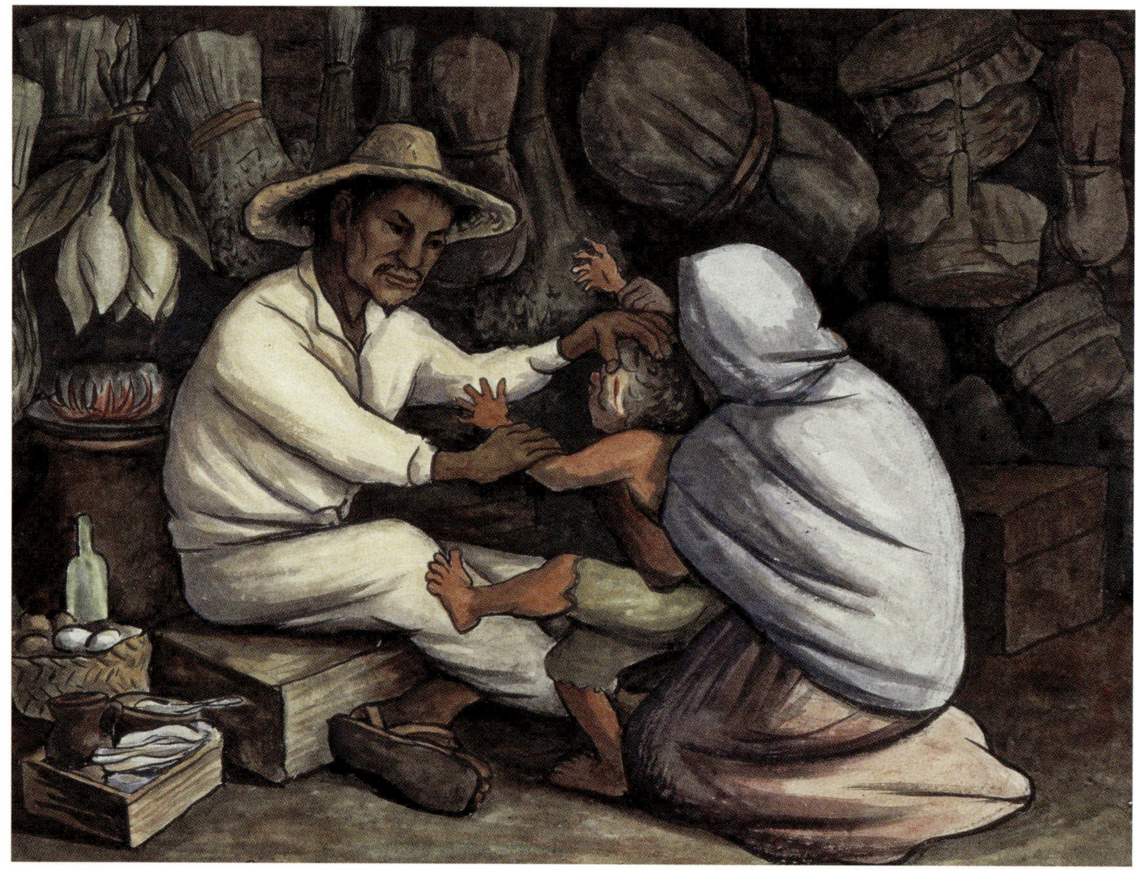

Diego Rivera
The Healer / *El curandero*, 1943, Gouache on paper / *Gouche sobre papel*, 47 x 61 cm, 18 1/2" x 24"

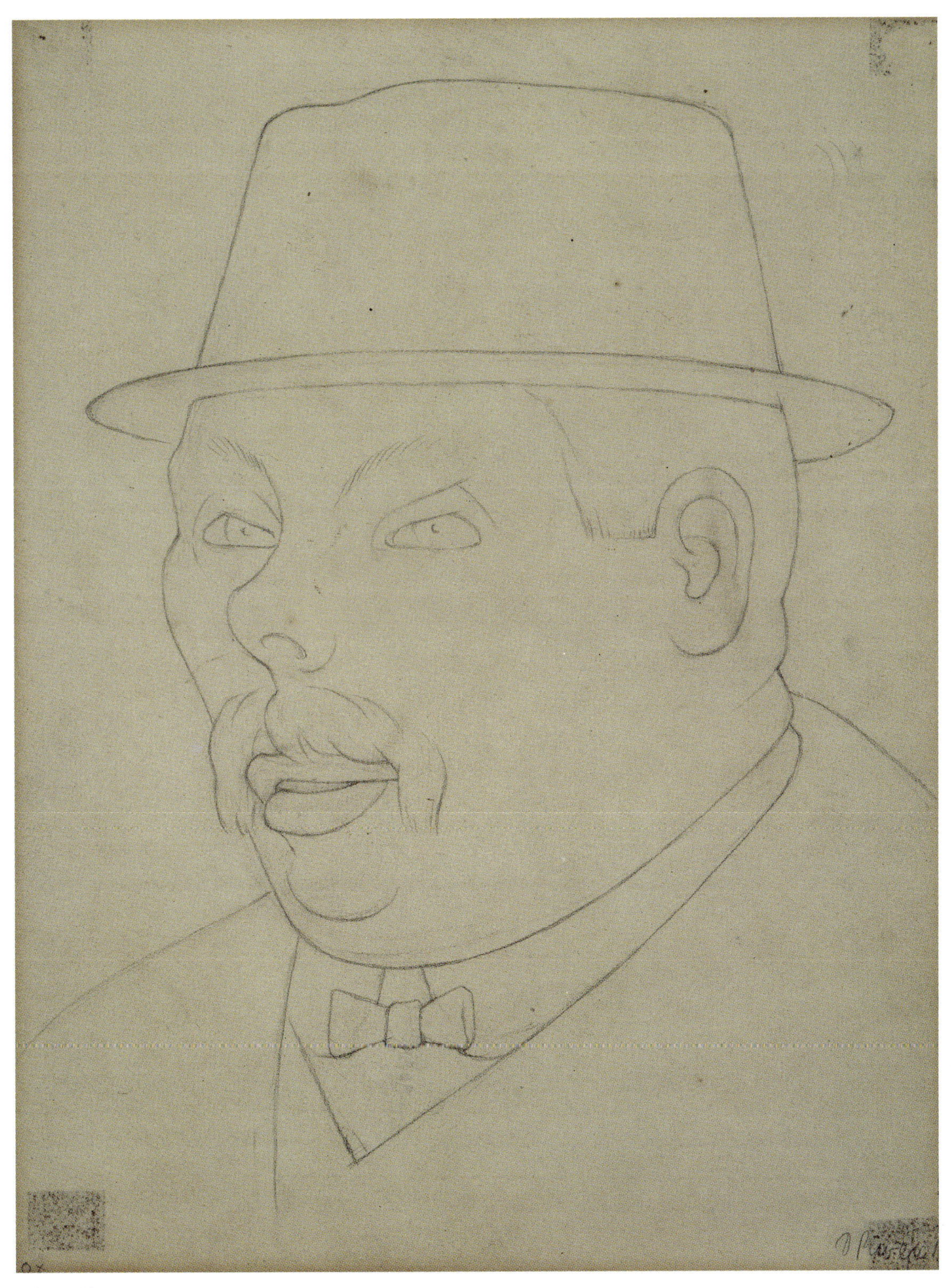

Diego Rivera
Untitled / *Sin título*, Undated/*Sin fecha*, Pencil on paper / *Lápiz sobre papel*, 31 x 23 cm, 12$^{1/4}$" x 19"

Jesús Reyes Ferreira

(1882-1977)

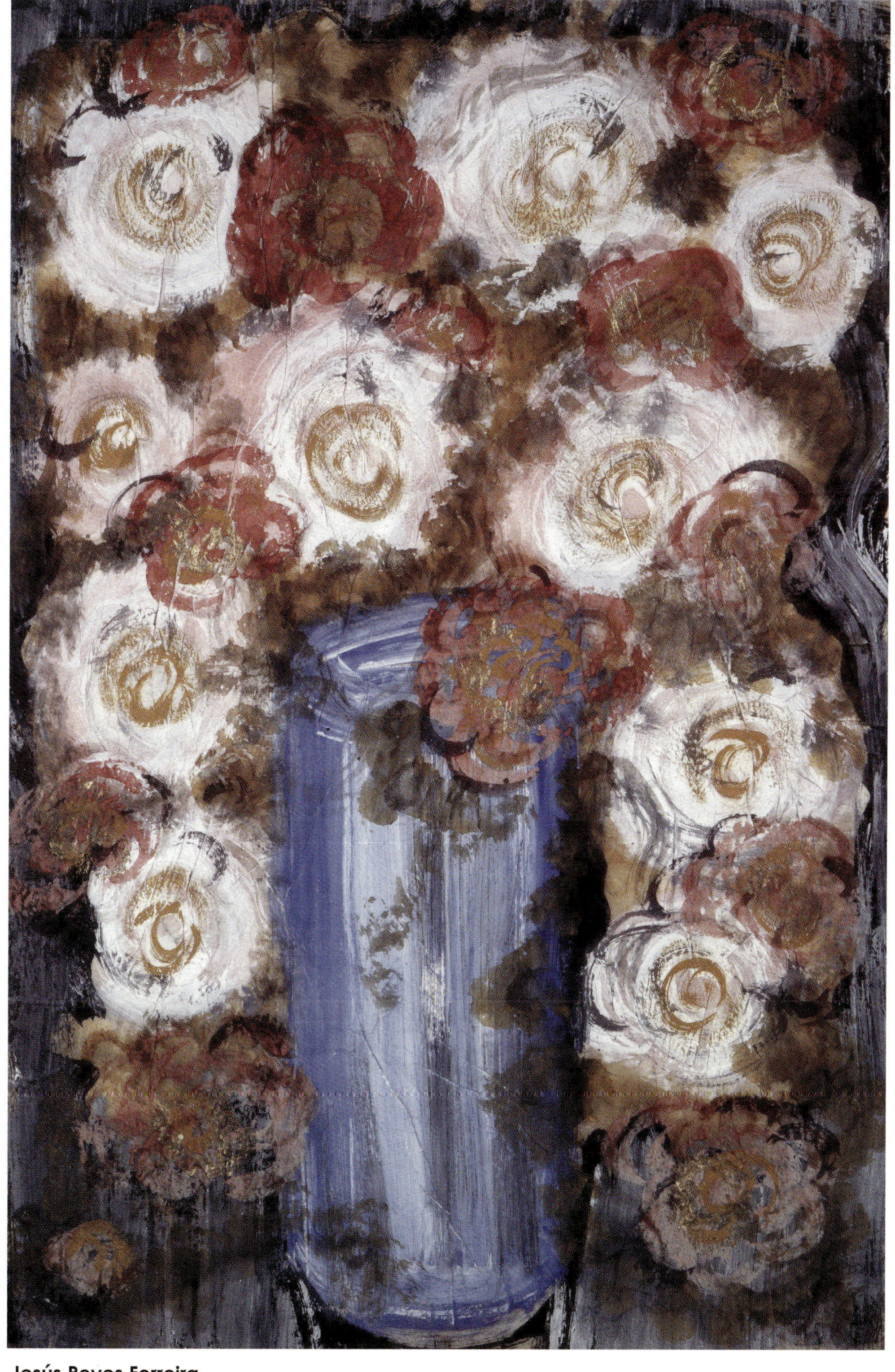

Jesús Reyes Ferreira
Flower Vase / *El florero*, Undated / *Sin fecha*, Tempera on china paper / *Temple sobre papel de china*, 74 x 48.5 cm, 29 1/8" x 19"

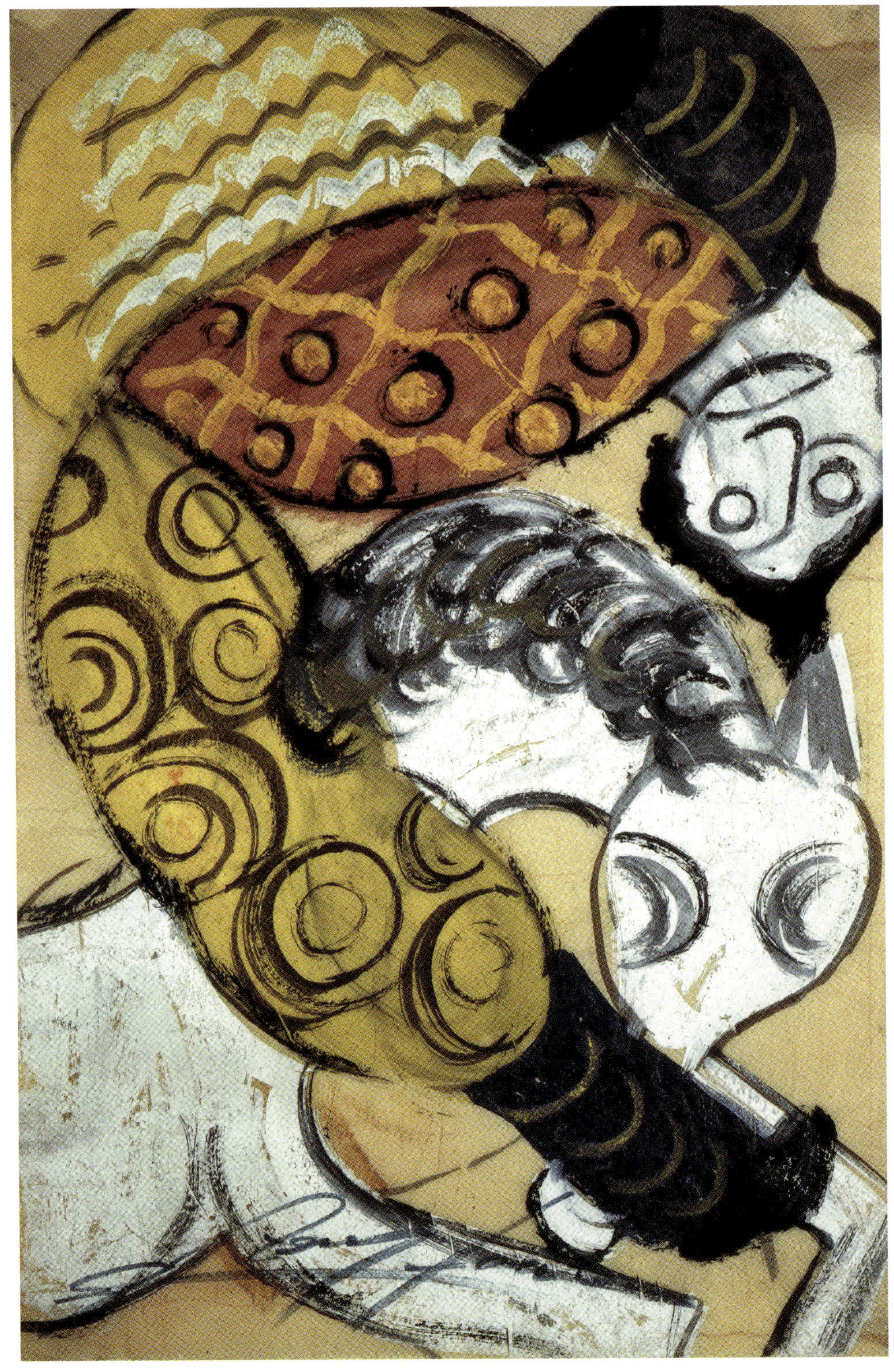

Jesús Reyes Ferreira
Untitled / *Sin título*, Undated / *Sin fecha*, Tempera on china paper / *Temple sobre papel de china*, 75 x 48.5 cm, $29^{1/9}$" x 19"

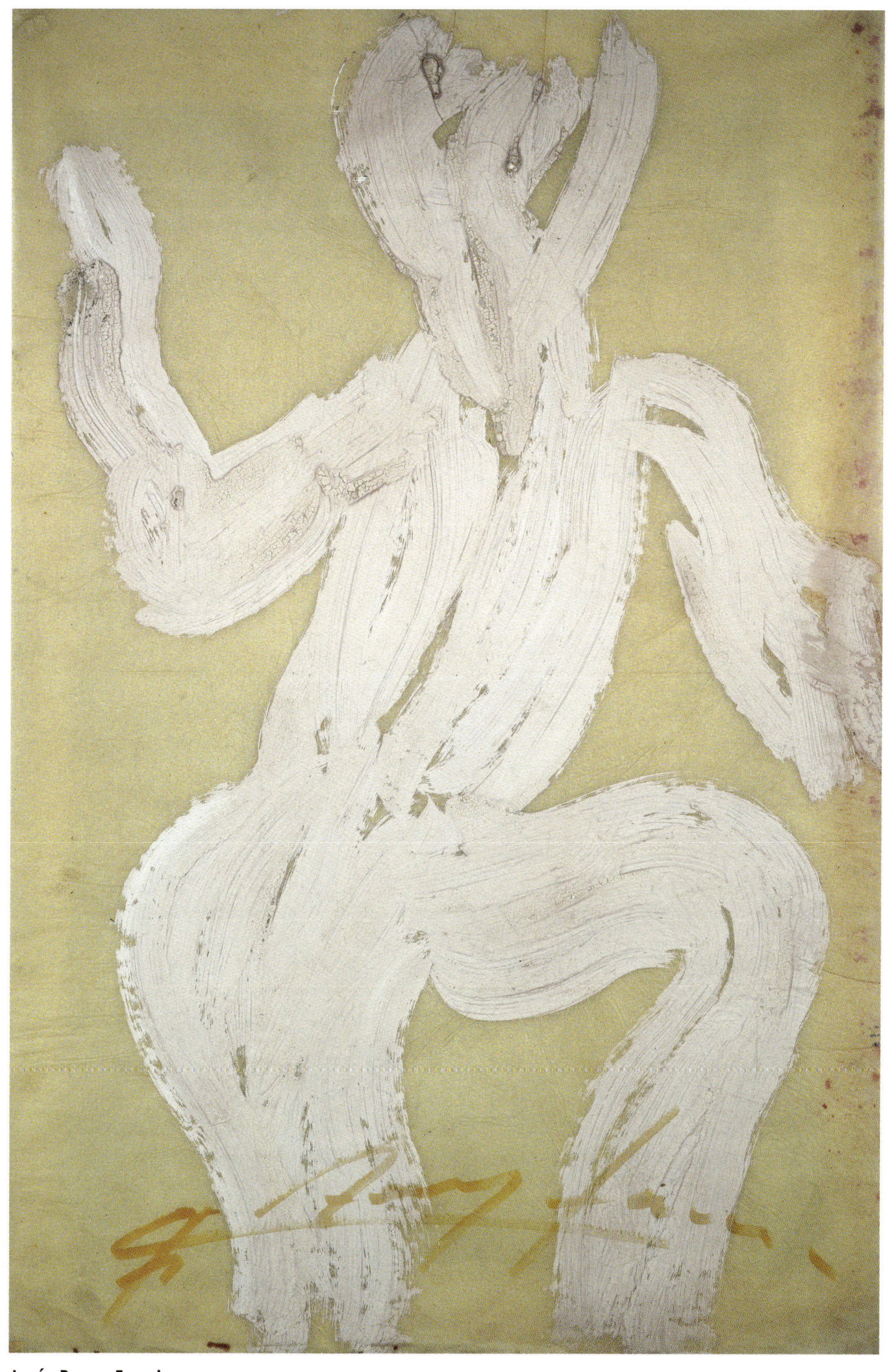

Jesús Reyes Ferreira
The Goodbye / *El adios*, Undated / *Sin fecha*, Tempera on china paper / *Temple sobre papel de china*, 75.5 x 49.5 cm, 29$^{3/9}$" x 19$^{1/2}$"

David Álfaro Siqueiros
(1896-1974)

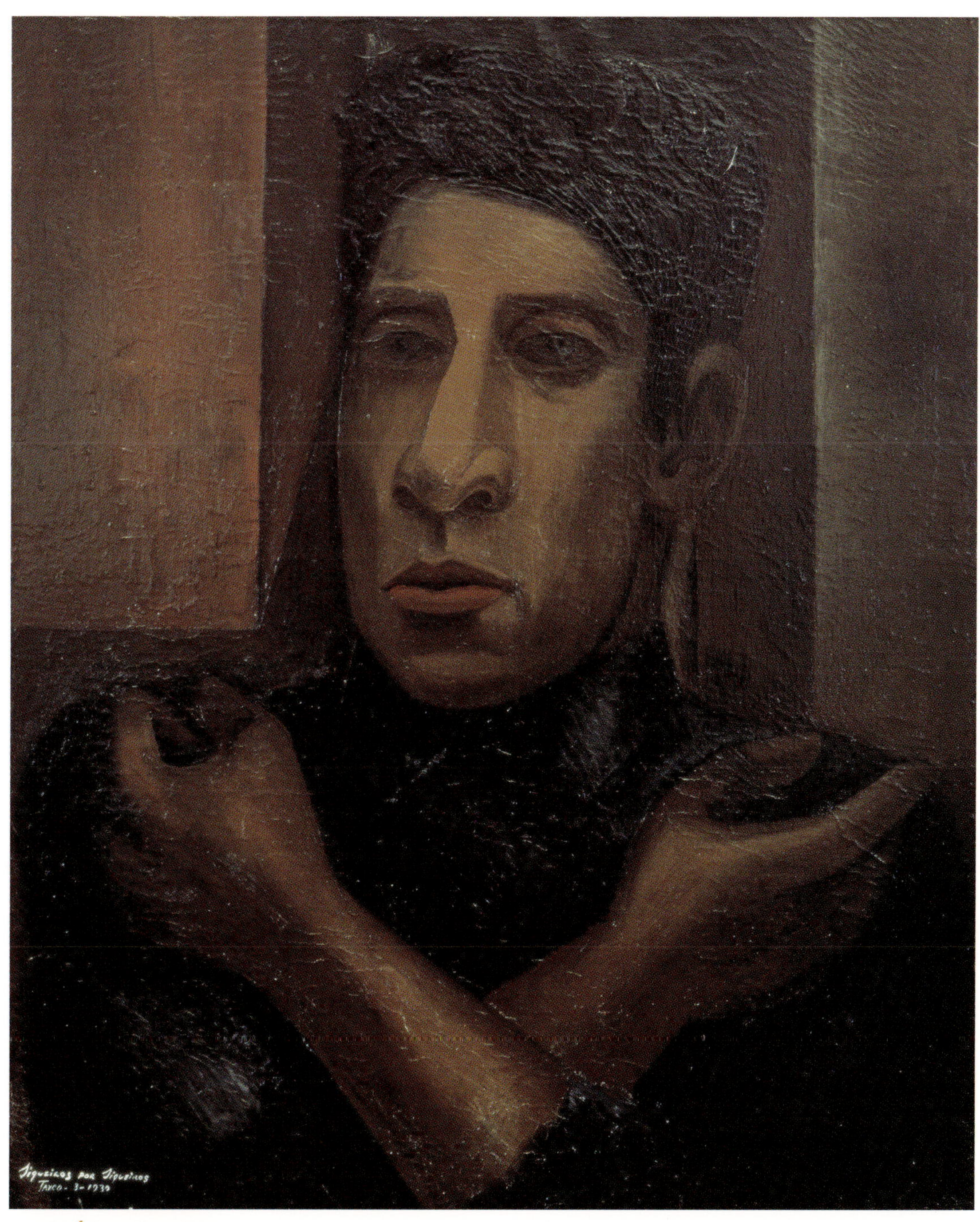

David Álfaro Siqueiros
Siqueiros by Siqueiros / *Siqueiros por Siqueiros* 1930, Oil on canvas / *Óleo sobre tela*, 99 x 79 cm, 39" x 31"

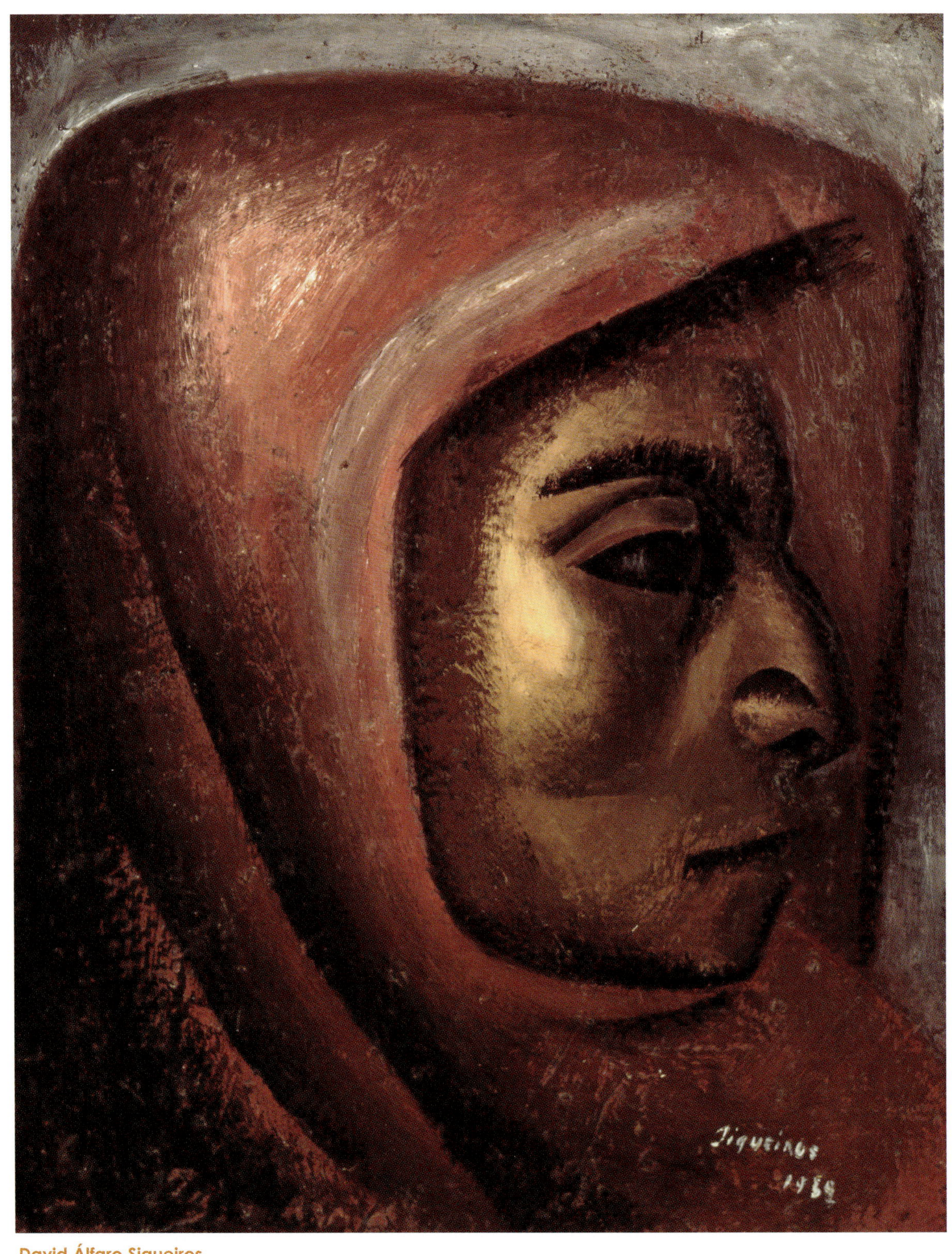

David Álfaro Siqueiros
Head of a Woman / *Cabeza de mujer*, 1939, Oil on canvas / *Óleo sobre tela*, 54.5 x 43 cm, 21 1/2" x 16 7/8"

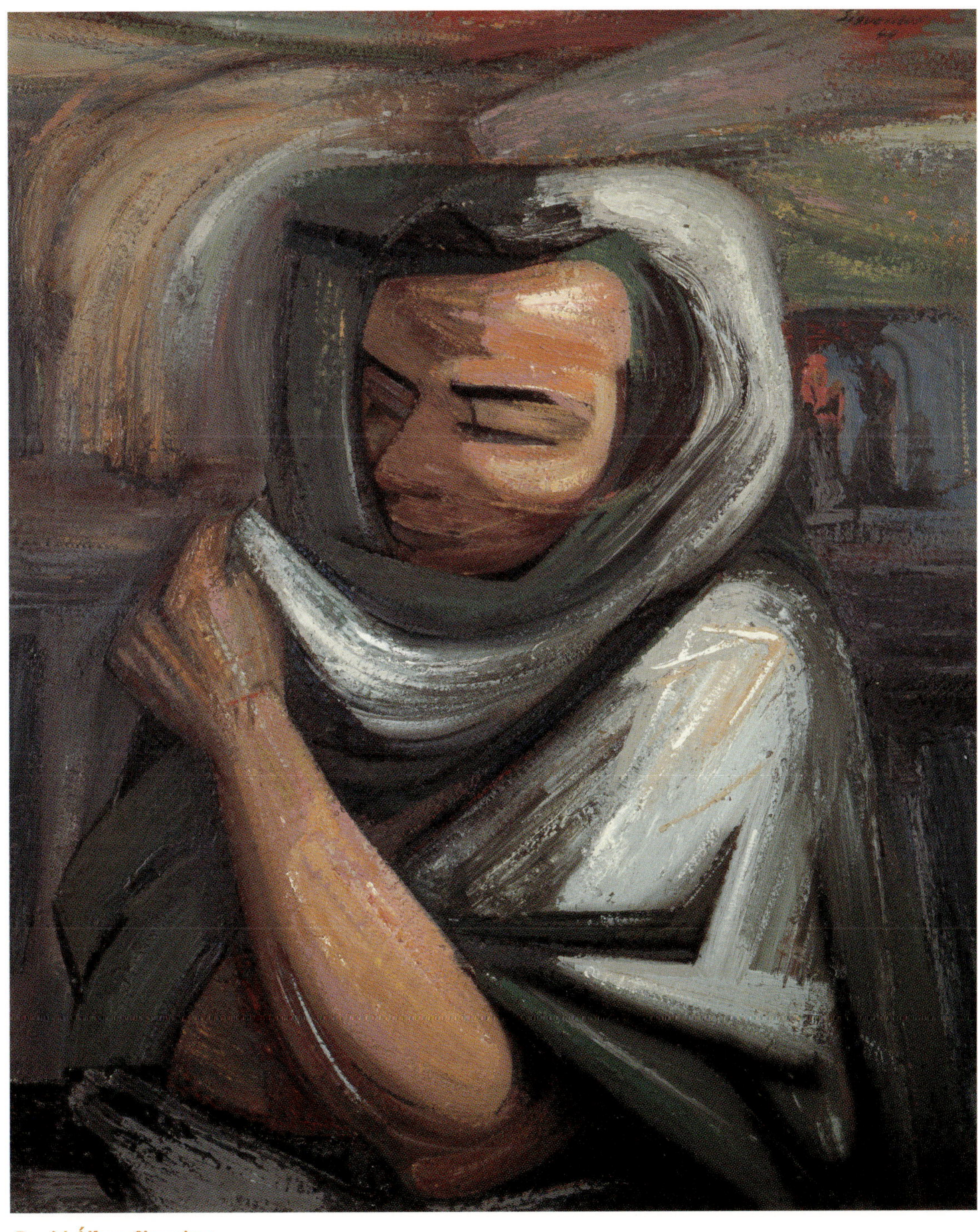

David Álfaro Siqueiros
Woman with Rebozo / *Mujer con rebozo*, 1949, Piroxiline on Masonite / *Piroxilina sobre Masonite*, 119.5 x 97 cm, 47" x $38^{1/8}$"

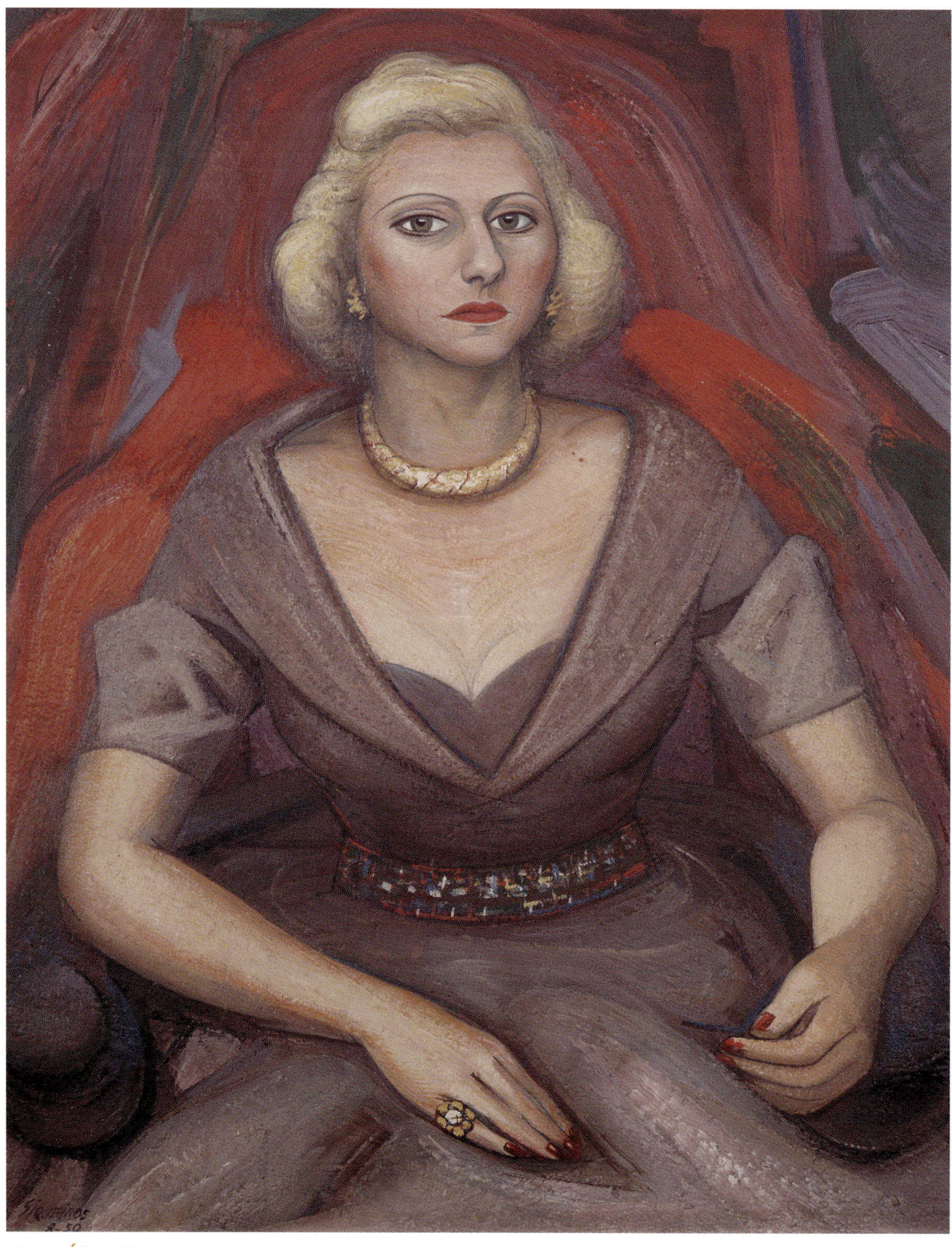

David Álfaro Siqueiros
Portrait of Mrs. Natasha Gelman / *Retrato de la Señora Natasha Gelman,* 1950, Piroxiline on Masonite / *Piroxilina sobre Masonite*, 120 x 100 cm, $47^{1/4}$" x $39^{3/8}$"

Juan Soriano

(1920-)

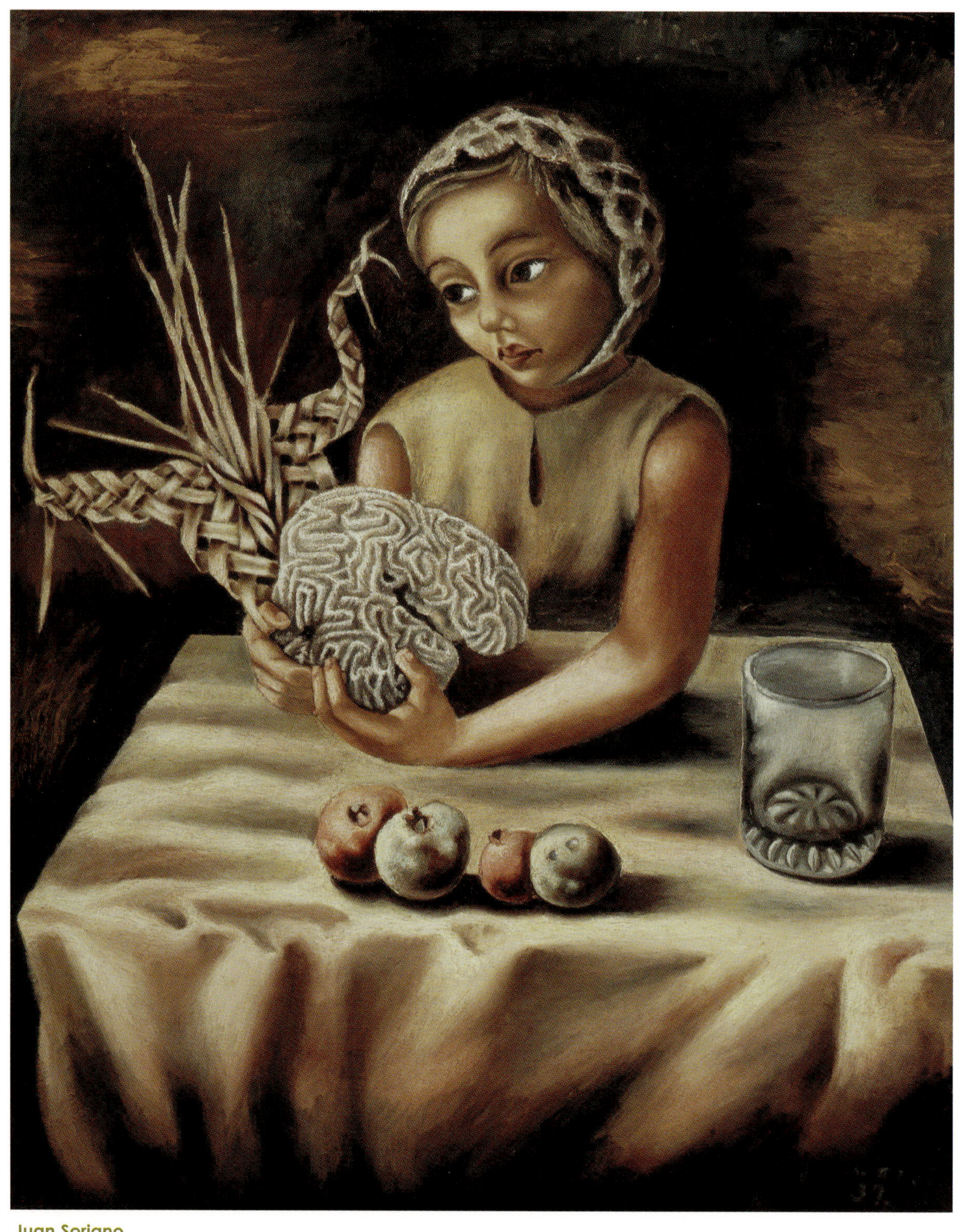

Juan Soriano
Girl with Still Life / *Niña con naturaleza muerta*, 1939, Oil on canvas / *Óleo sobre tela*, 81.3 x 65.2 cm, 32" x 25 5/8"

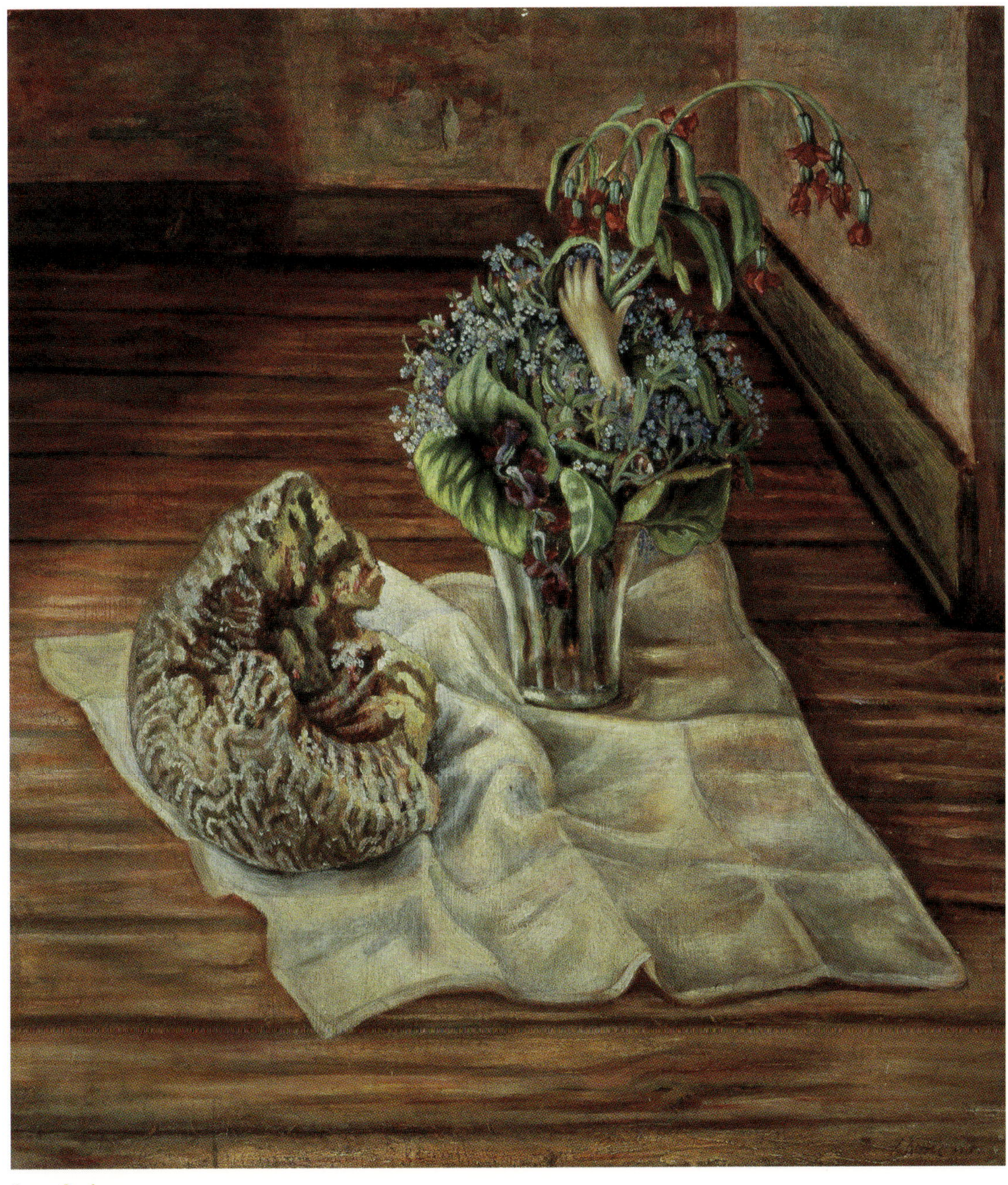

Juan Soriano
Still Life with Brain Coral / *Naturaleza muerta con madrepora,* 1944, Oil on Masonite / *Óleo sobre Masonite,* 60.3 x 51.9 cm, $23^{3/4}$" x $20^{1/2}$"

Rufino Tamayo

(1899-1991)

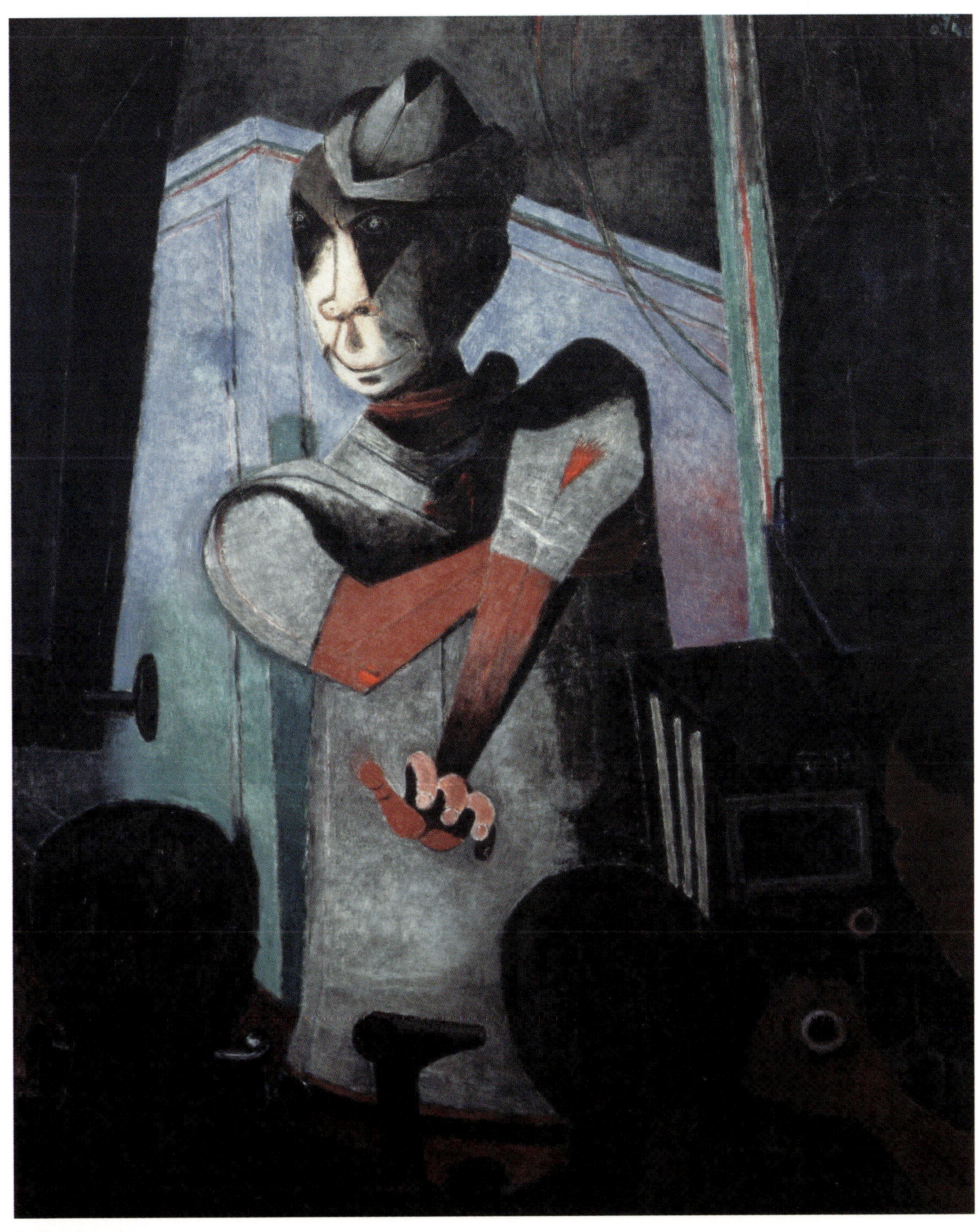

Rufino Tamayo
Portrait of Cantinflas / *Retrato de Cantinflas*, 1948, Oil on canvas / *Óleo sobre tela*, 100 x 80.5 cm, $39^{3/8}$" x $31^{3/4}$"

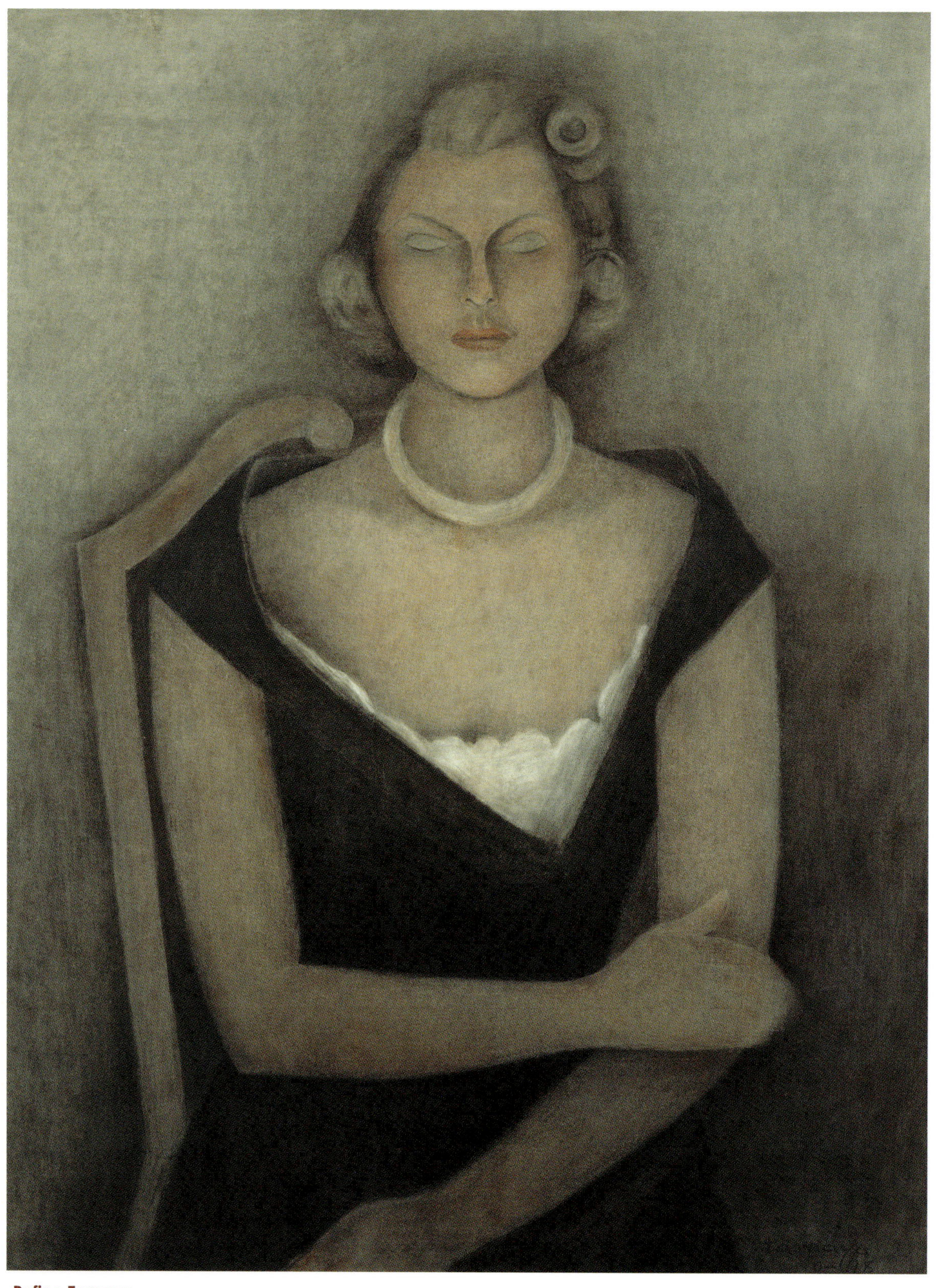

Rufino Tamayo
Portrait of Mrs. Natasha Gelman / *Retrato de la Señora Natasha Gelman,* 1948, Oil and charcoal on Masonite / *Óleo y carbón sobre Masonite*, 120 x 91 cm, 47 1/2" x 35 7/8"

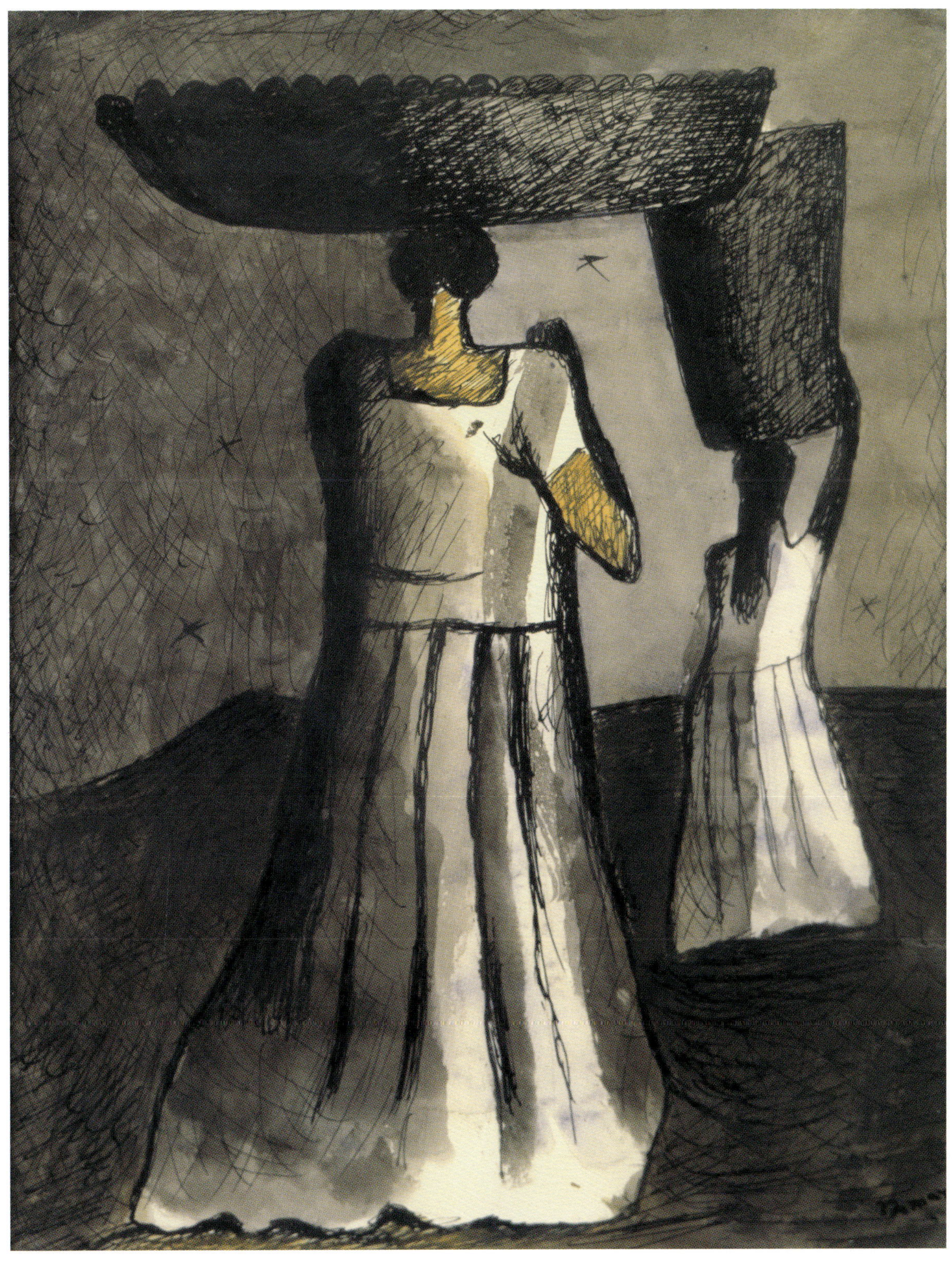

Rufino Tamayo
Untitled / *Sin título*, 1950, Watercolor and pastel on paper / *Acuarela y pastel sobre papel*, 23 x 17 cm, 9" x 6$^{3/4}$"

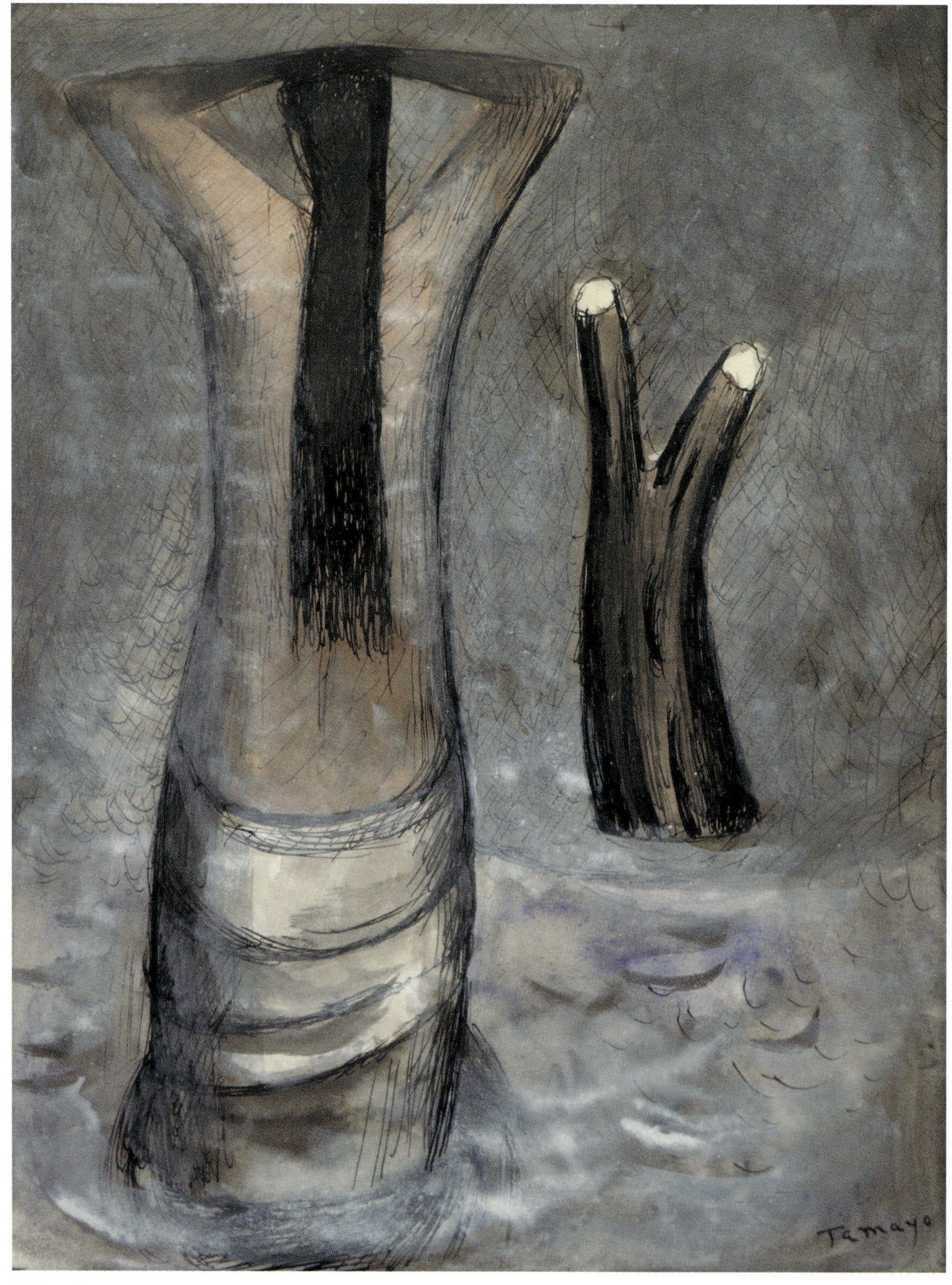

Rufino Tamayo
Untitled / *Sin título*, Undated / *Sin fecha*, Ink and watercolor on paper / *Tinta y acuarela sobre papel*, 28 x 21 cm, 11" x 8 1/4"

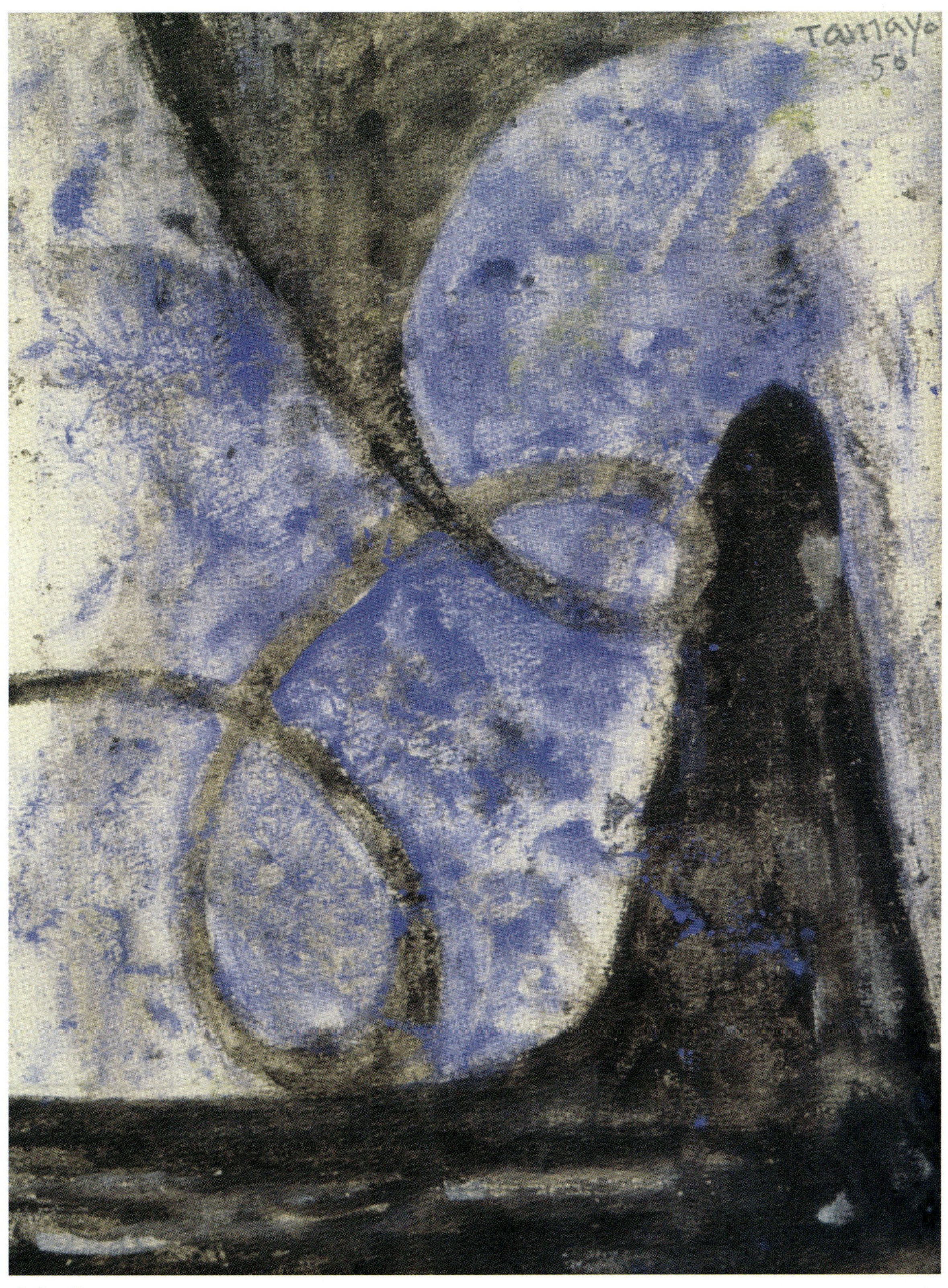

Rufino Tamayo
Untitled / *Sin título*, Undated / *Sin fecha*, Ink and watercolor on paper / *Tinta y acuarela sobre papel*, 28 x 21 cm, 11" x 8 1/4"

Francisco Toledo

(1940-)

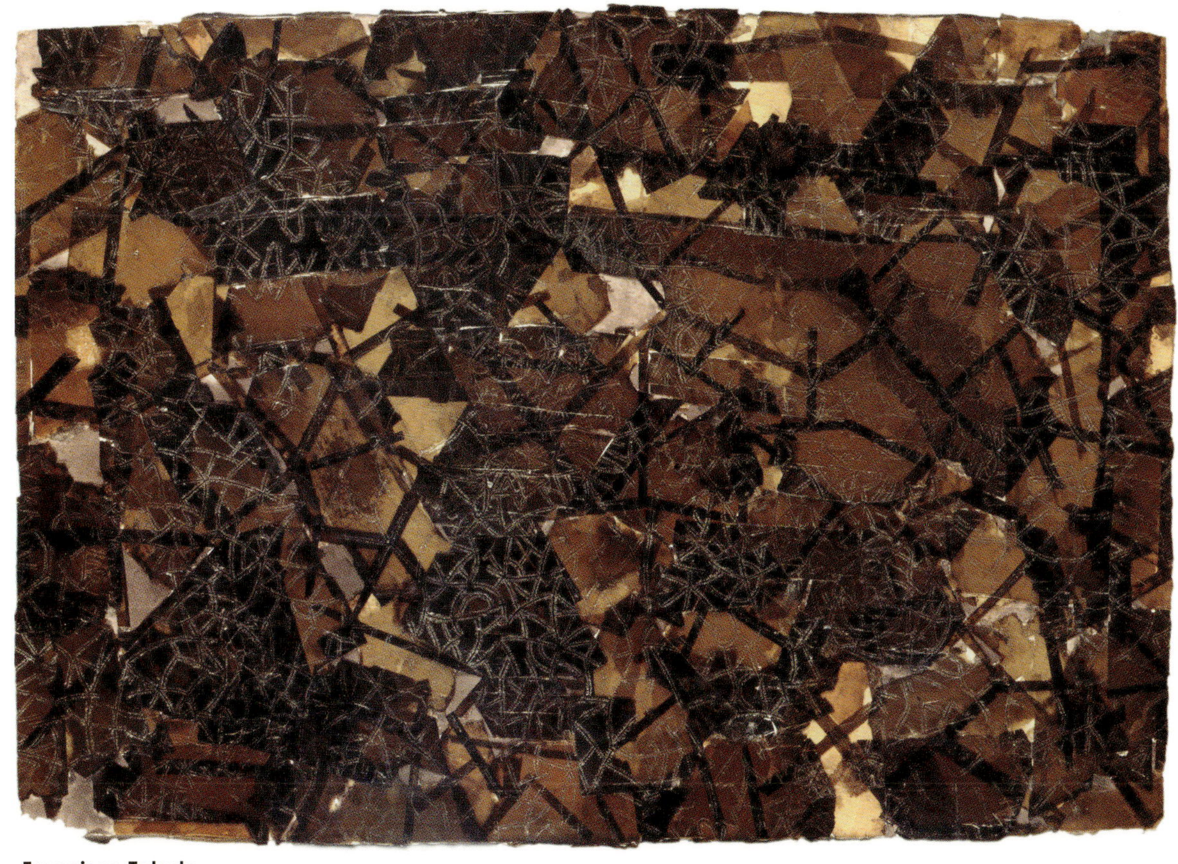

Francisco Toledo
Plan of Juchitan / *Plan de Juchitán*, 1972-73, Oil with sand on canvas / *Óleo sobre tela con carga arenosa*, 135 x 154 cm, 53$^{1/4}$" x 60"

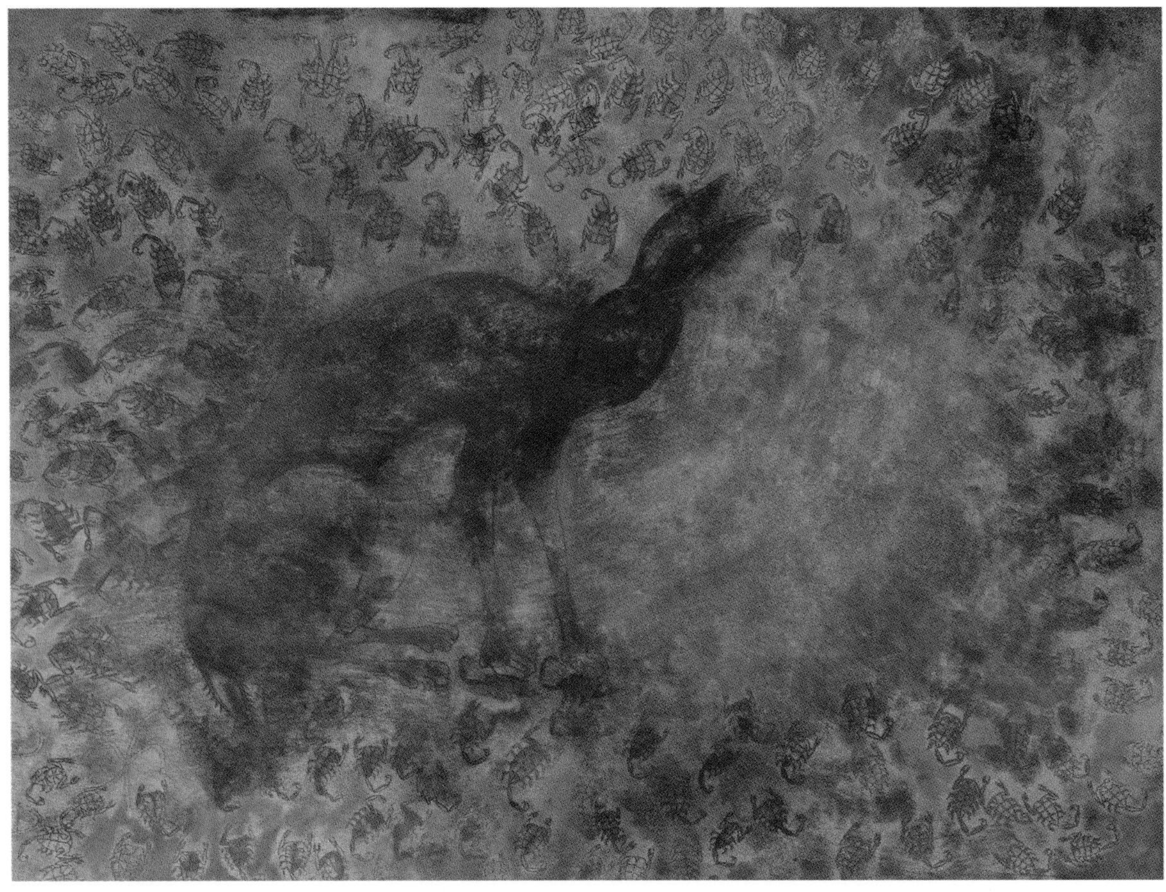

Francisco Toledo
Rabbit of the Scorpions / *Conejo de los escorpiones*, 1975, Oil on canvas with sand / *Óleo sobre tela con carga arenosa*, 100 x 129.5 cm, 39 3/8" x 51"

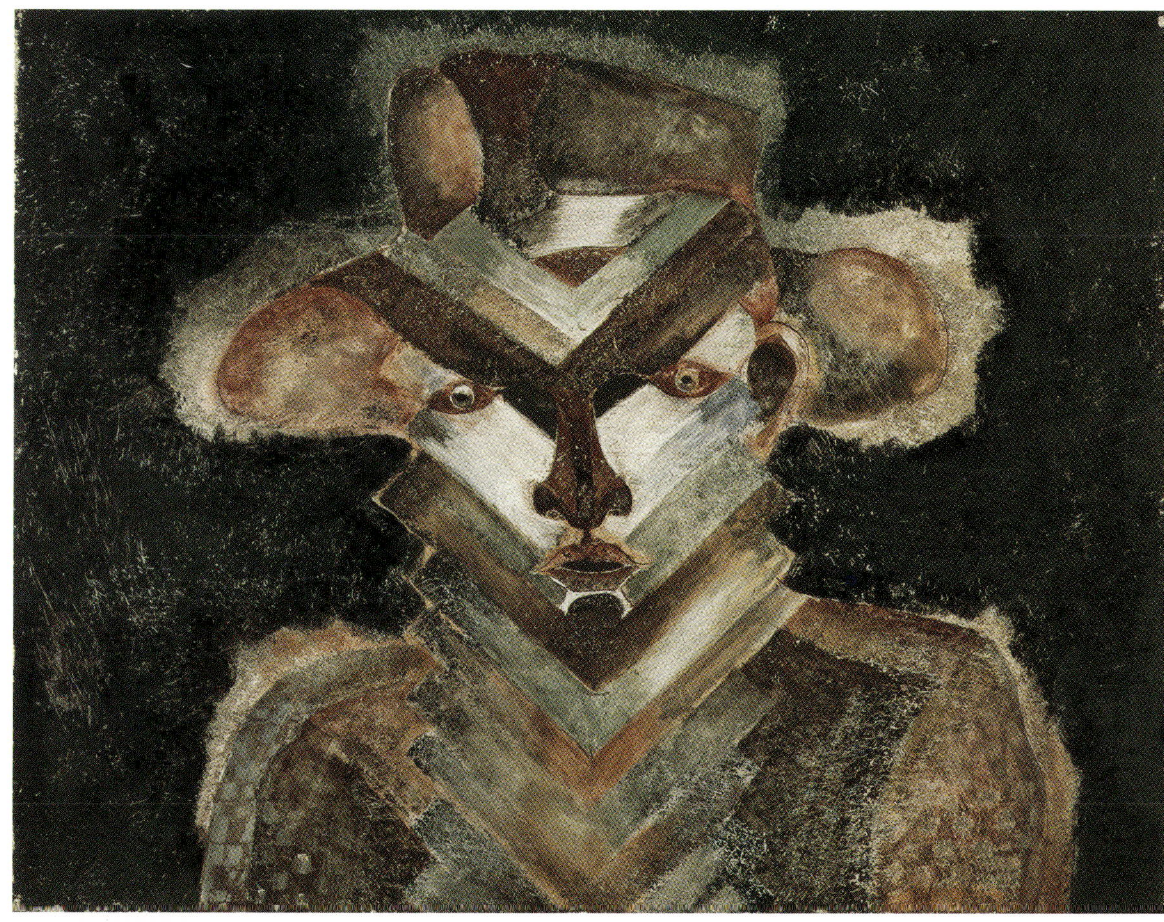

Francisco Toledo
Self-portrait with Hat / *Autorretrato con sombrero*, 1987, Oil and tempera on canvas on Masonite / *Óleo y temple sobre tela sobre Masonite*, 60 x 70 cm, $23^{5/8}$" x $27^{1/2}$"

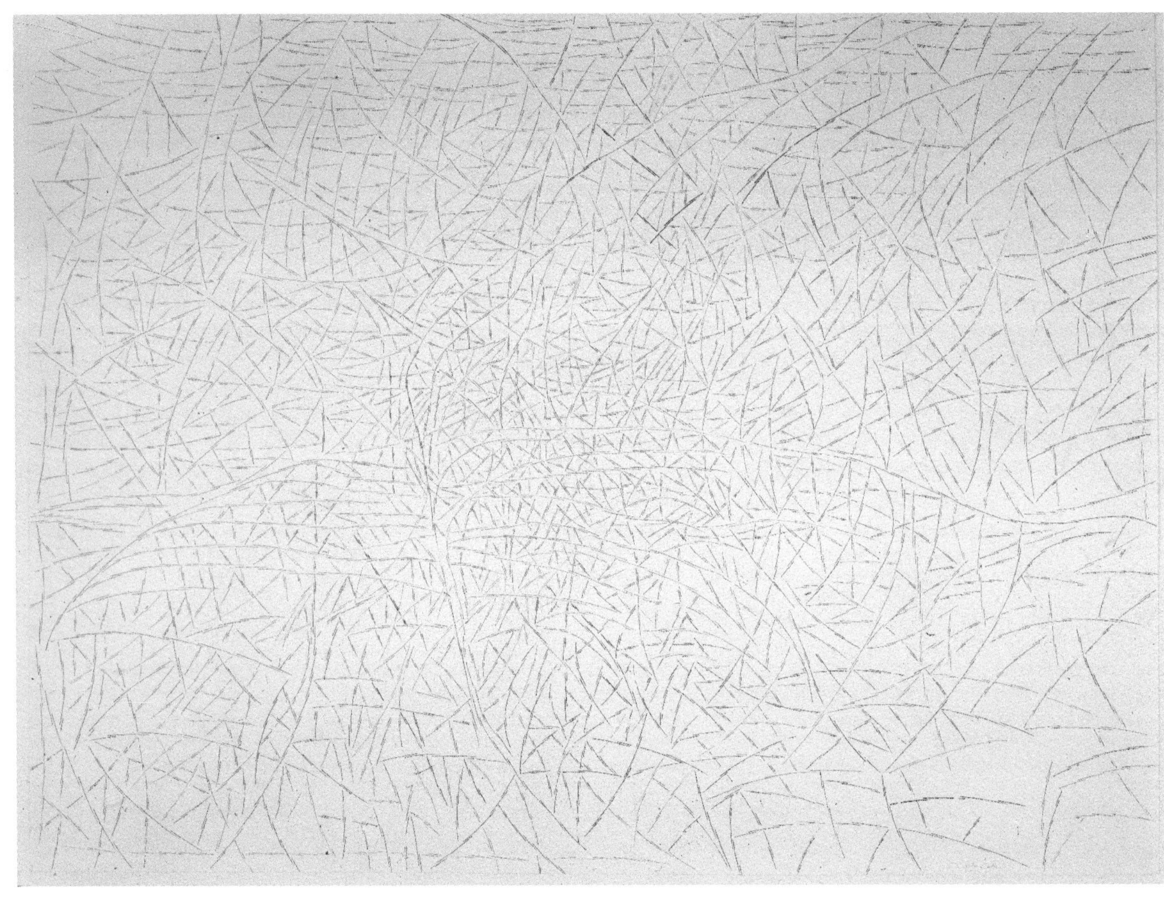

Francisco Toledo
Net / *Red*, 1988, Ink on paper / *Tinta sobre papel*, 49.5 x 65 cm, 19$^{1/2}$" x 25$^{5/8}$"

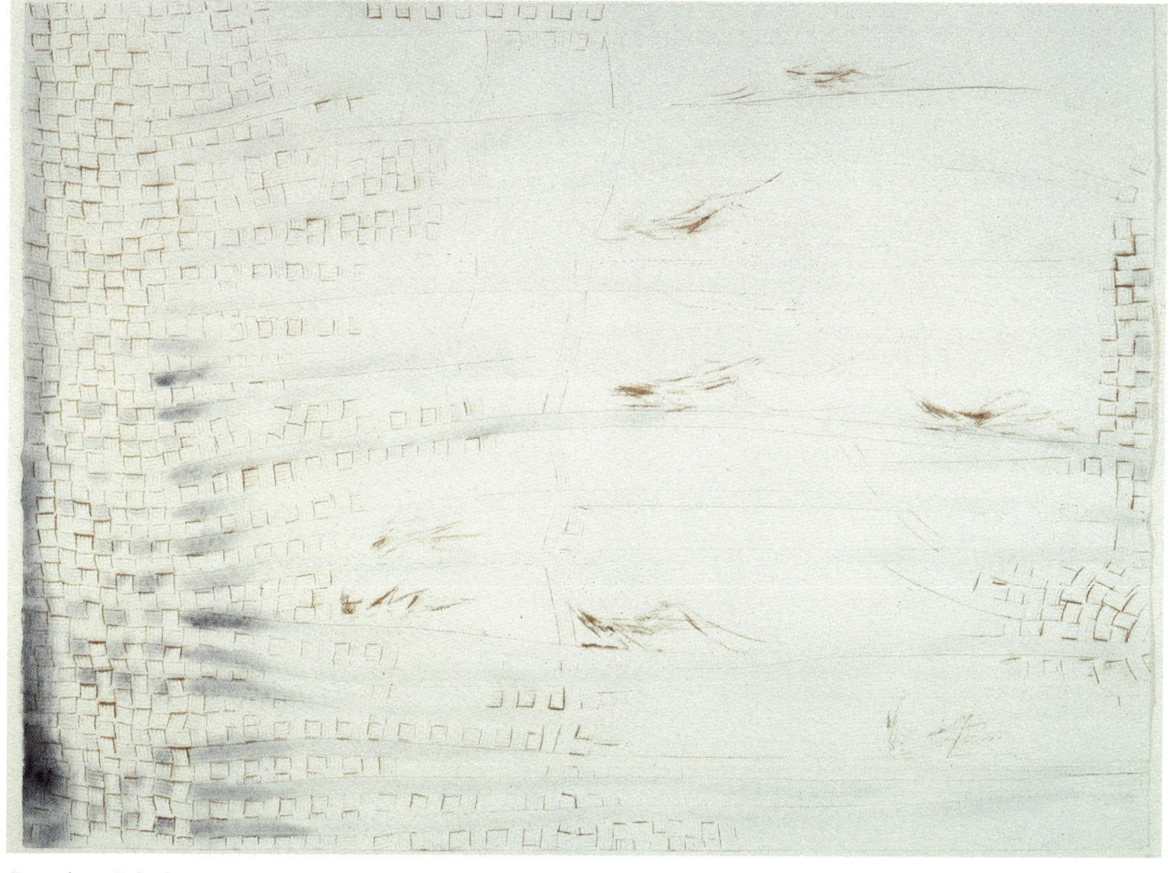

Francisco Toledo
Palm-rug of Grasshoppers / *El petate de los chapulines*, 1989, Pencil and ink on paper / *Lápiz y tinta sobre papel*, 49.5 x 65 cm, $19^{1/2}$" x $25^{5/8}$"

Angel Zárraga

(1886-1946)

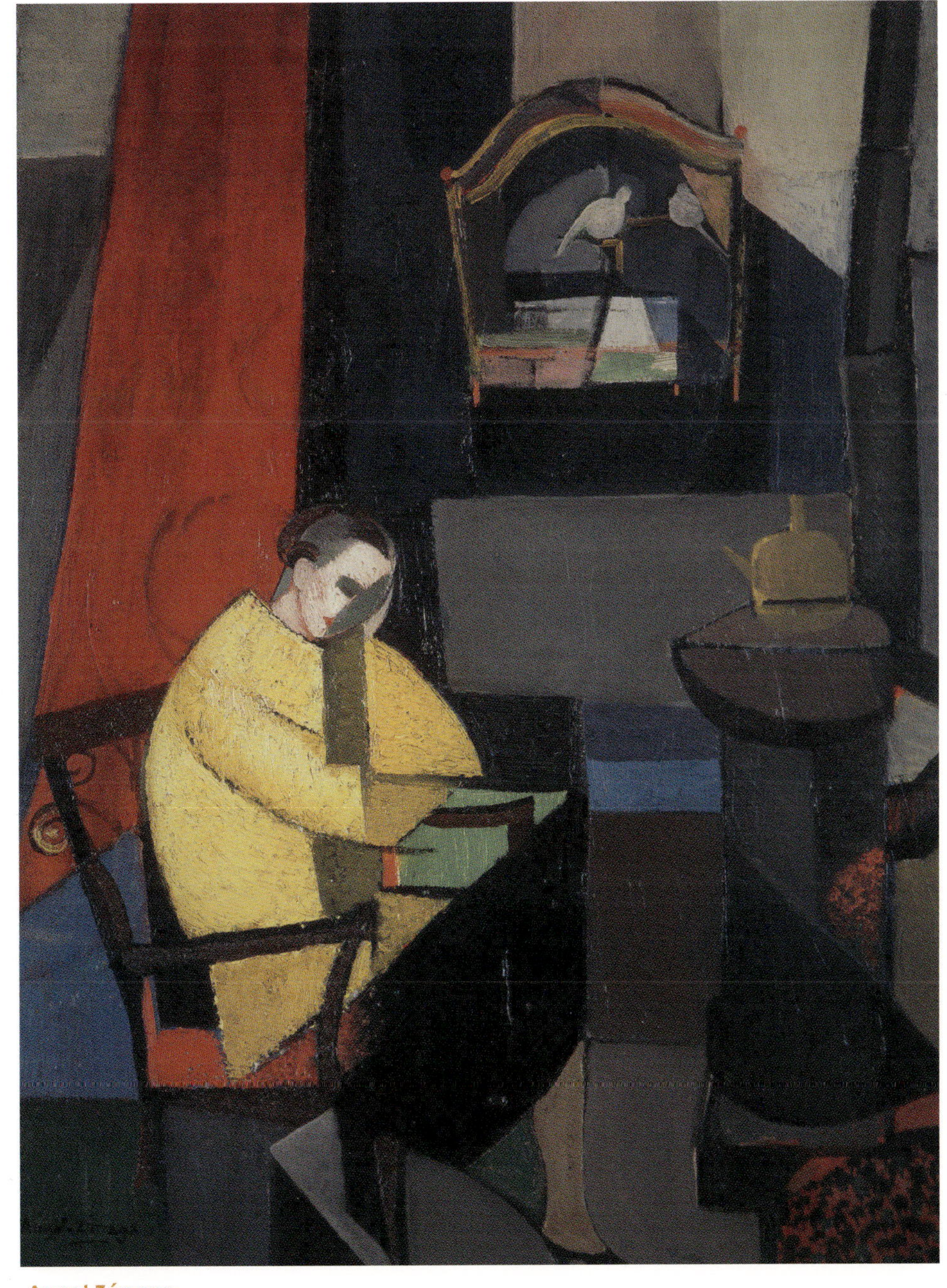

Angel Zárraga
Untitled / *Sin título*, ca. 1917, Oil on canvas / *Óleo sobre tela*, 46.5 x 33.5 cm, 18 1/4" x 13 1/2"

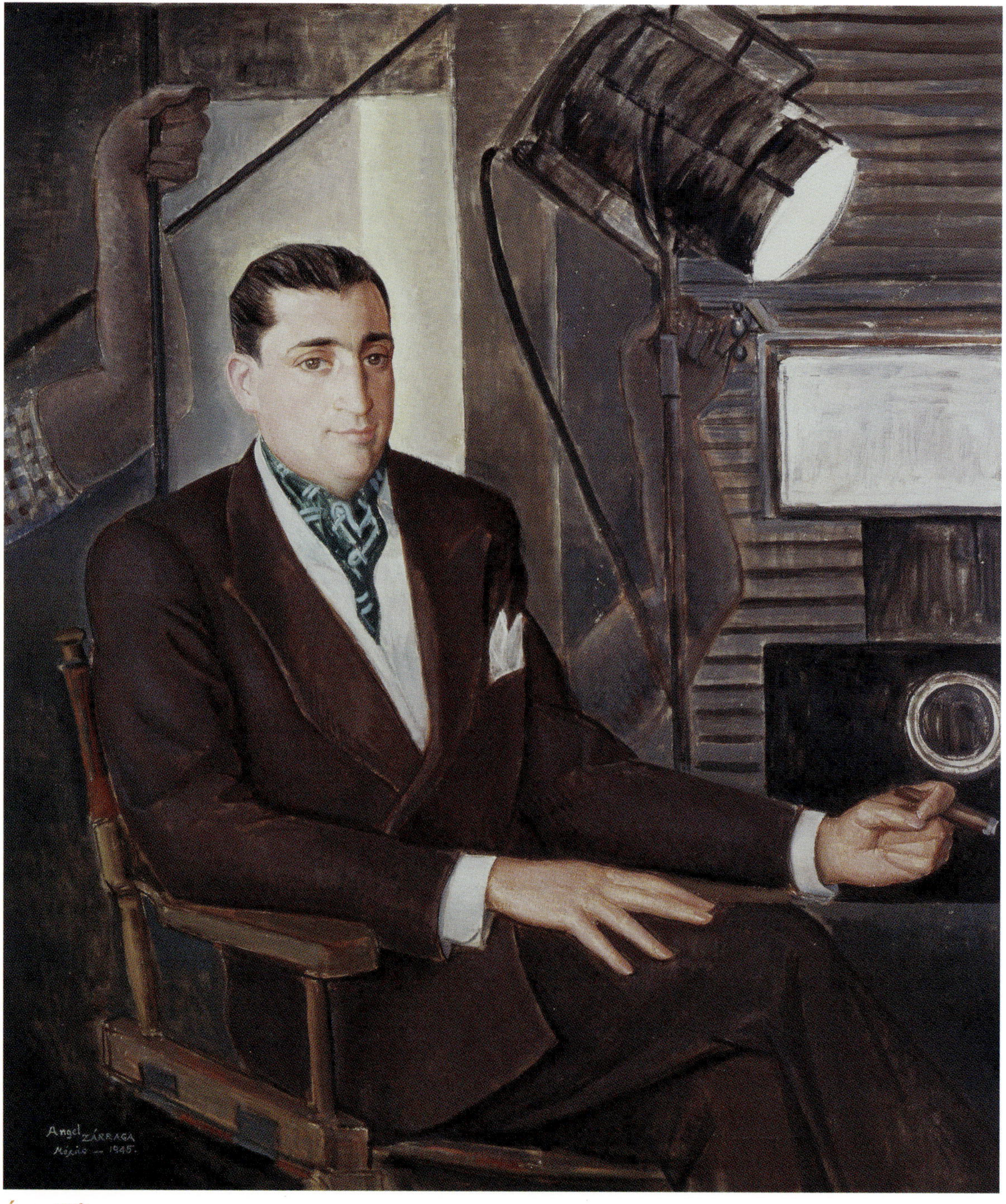

Ángel Zárraga
Portrait of Mr. Jacques Gelman / *Retrato del Señor Jacques Gelman*, 1945, Oil on canvas / *Óleo sobre tela*, 130.5 x 110.5 cm, $51^{3/8}$" x$43^{1/2}$"

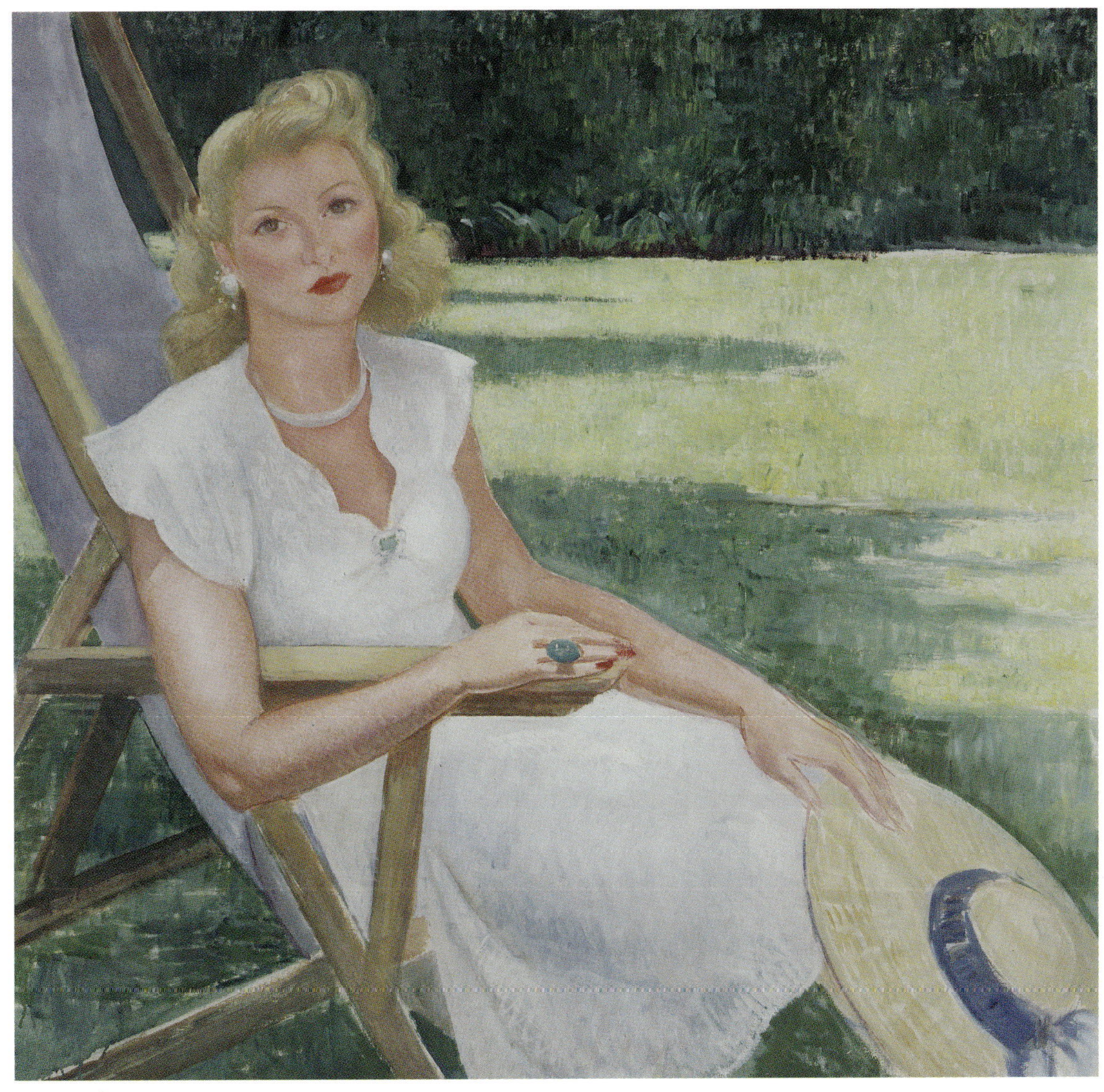

Angel Zárraga
Portrait of Mrs. Natasha Gelman / *Retrato de la Señora Natasha Gelman*, ca. 1946, Oil on canvas / *Óleo sobre tela*, 109 x 109 cm, 43" x 43"

Nahum Zenil

(1947-)

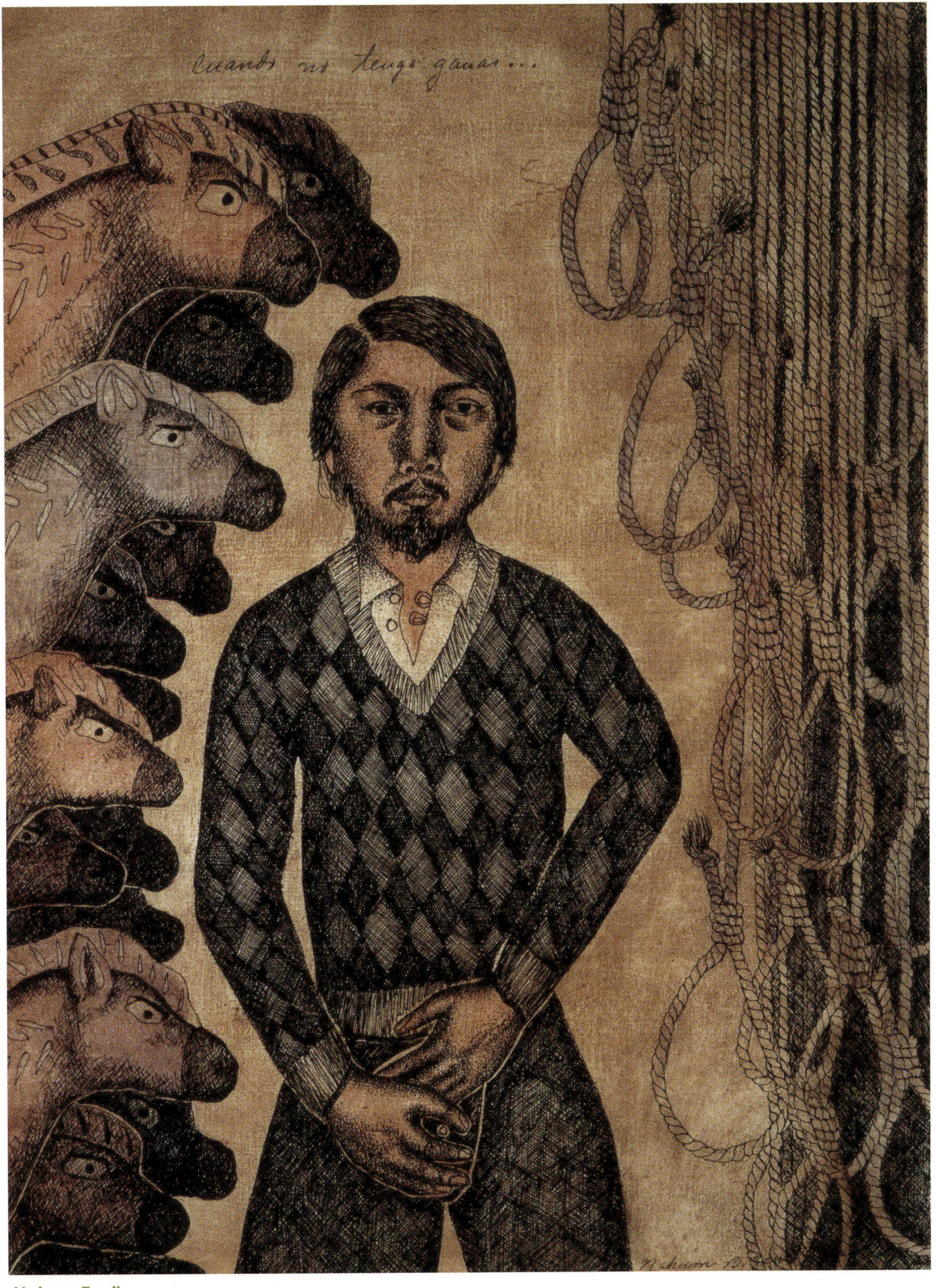

Nahum Zenil
When I Don't Feel Like It / *Cuando no tengo ganas*, 1984, Mixed media on paper / *Técnica mixta sobre papel*, 29.5 x 21.5 cm, 11$^{5/8}$" x 8$^{1/2}$"

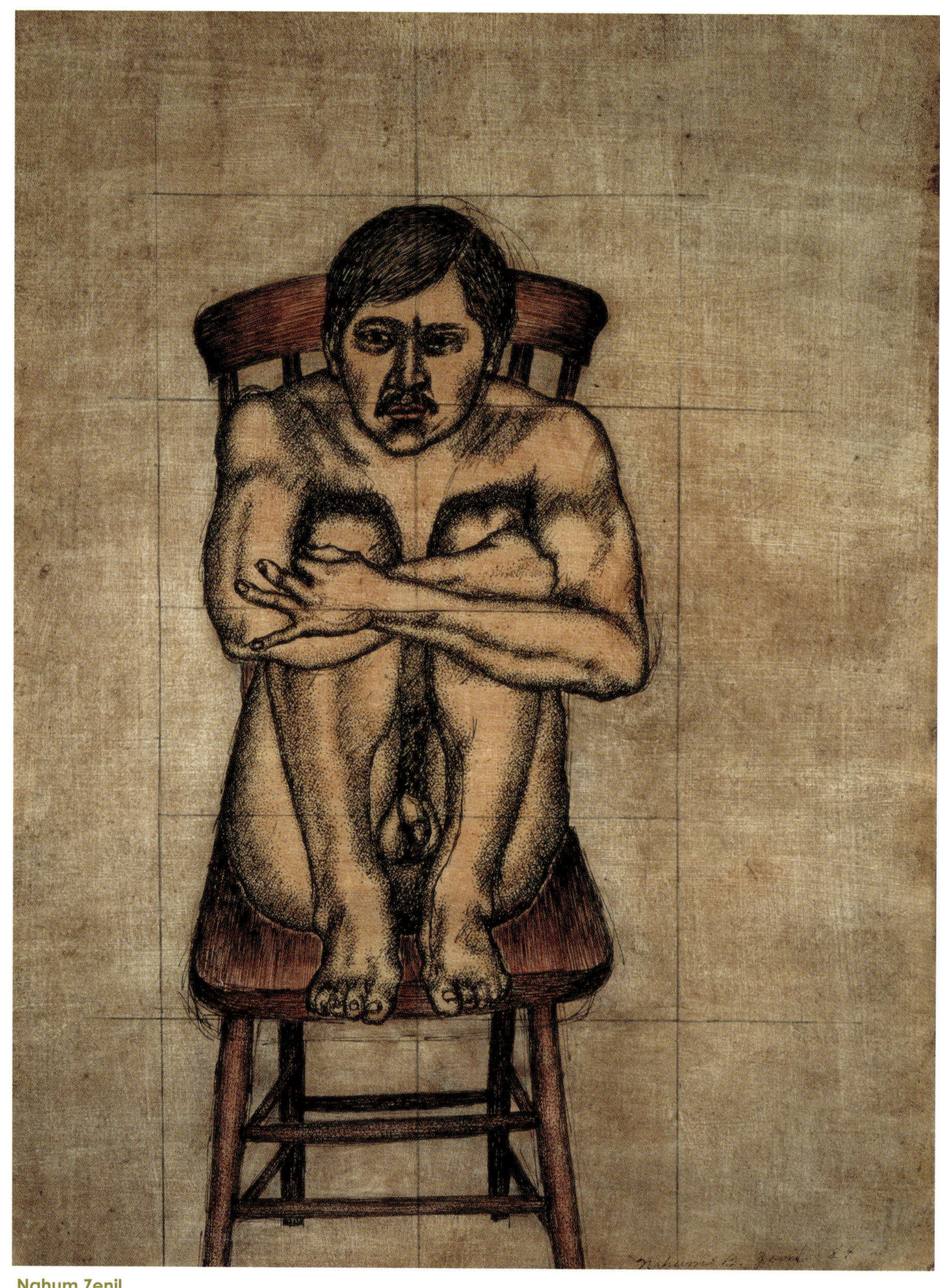

Nahum Zenil
Waiting / *Esperando*, 1984, Mixed media on paper / *Técnica mixta sobre papel*, 29.5 x 21.5 cm, 11[5/8]" x 8[1/2]"

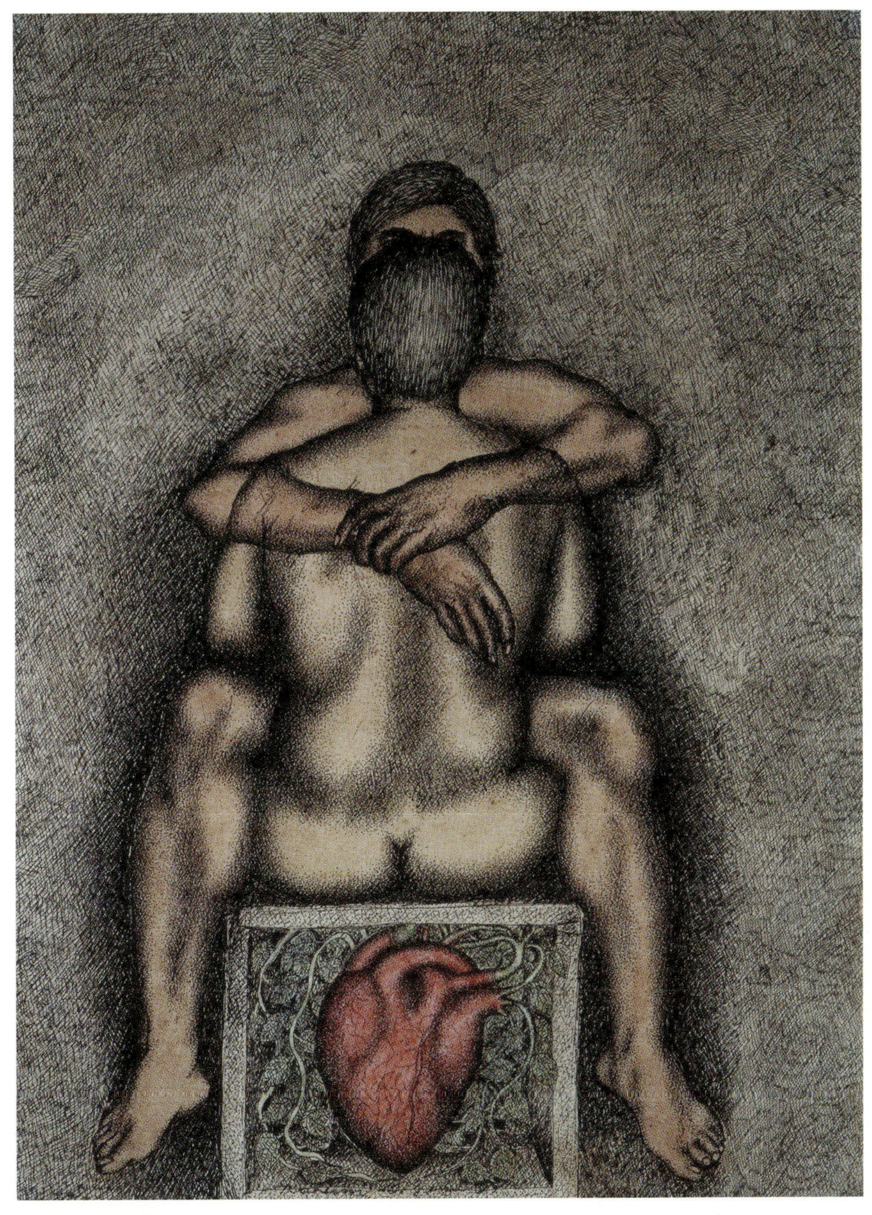

Nahum Zenil
Heart / *Corazón*, 1987, Mixed media on paper / *Técnica mixta sobre papel*, 29.5 x 21.5 cm, $11^{5/8}$" x $8^{1/2}$"

The Exhibition

Emilio Baz Viaud
Portrait of Margot Mac Inteyre / *Retrato de Margot Mac Inteyre*, 1950, watercolor and dry brush on cardboard / *acuarela y pincel seco sobre cartulina*, 91.5 x 61 cm, $35^{3/4}$" x 24"

Emilio Baz Viaud
Portrait of Nazario Chimez Barket / *Retrato de Nazario Chimez Barket*, 1952, watercolor and dry brush on cardboard / *acuarela y pincel seco sobre cartulina*, 74 x 53 cm, $29^{1/8}$" x 207/8"

Lola Alvarez Bravo
The Dream of the Drowned / *El sueño del ahogado*, ca. 1945, photo-collage (gelatin silver print, offset and ink) / *fotocollage (plata gelatina, offset y tinta)*, 26 x 22 cm, $10^{1/4}$" x $81^{1/16}$"

Lola Alvarez Bravo
The Hangover / *La cruda*, 1945, Veracruz, Mexico, gelatin silver print / *plata gelatina*, 25.4 x 20.32 cm, 8" x 10"

Lola Alvarez Bravo
Erongarícuaro, 1945, Michoacán, Mexico, gelatin silver print / *plata gelatina*, 17.78 x 24.13 cm, 7" x $9^{1/2}$"

Lola Alvarez Bravo
How Thirsty...! / *¡Que Sed...!*, 1945, Mexico City, Mexico, gelatin silver print / *plata gelatina*, 17.78 x 24.13 cm, 7" x $9^{1/2}$"

Lola Alvarez Bravo
The Vow / *La manda*, 1946, gelatin silver print / *plata gelatina*, 25.4 x 20.32 cm, 8" x 10"

Lola Alvarez Bravo
Burial at Yalalag / *Entierro en Yalalag*, 1946, Oaxaca, Mexico, gelatin silver print / *plata gelatina*, 17.78 x 24.13 cm, 7" x $9^{1/2}$"

Lola Alvarez Bravo
Other People's Guilt / *Por culpas afines*, 1948, Mexico City, Mexico, gelatin silver print / *plata gelatina* 17.78 x 22.86 cm, 7" x 9"

Lola Alvarez Bravo
Shark Hunters / *Los tiburoneros*, 1950, Acapulco, Gro., Mexico, gelatin silver print / *plata gelatina*, 17.78 x 22.86 cm, 7" x 9"

Lola Alvarez Bravo
Little Bull / *El torito*, Undated / *Sin fecha*, gelatin silver print/ *plata gelatina*, 17.78 x 24.13 cm, 7" x $9^{1/2}$"

Manuel Alvarez Bravo
Mattress / *Colchón*, 1927, platinum print / *platino*, 20.32 x 25.4 cm, 8" x 10"

Manuel Alvarez Bravo
Our Daily Bread / *Pan nuestro*, 1929, platinum print / *platino*, 20.32 x 25.4 cm, 8" x 10"

Manuel Alvarez Bravo
Obstacles / *Obstáculos*, 1929, platinum print / *platino*, 20.32 x 25.4 cm, 8" x 10"

Manuel Alvarez Bravo
Organ Pipe Cacti / *Cactus*, 1929, platinum print / *platino*, 25.4 x 20.32 cm, 10" x 8"

Manuel Alvarez Bravo
The Instruments / *El instrumental*, 1931, silver gelatin print / *plata gelatina*, 20.32 x 25.4 cm, 8" x 10"

Manuel Alvarez Bravo
The Implied Laundry Women / *Las Lavaderas Sobrentendidas*, 1932, platinum print / *platino* 25.4 x 20.32 cm, 10" x 8"

Manuel Alvarez Bravo
Large Ladder / *Escalera grande*, 1932, platinum print / *platino*, 25.4 x 20.32 cm, 10" x 8"

Manuel Alvarez Bravo
The Black Mirror / *El espejo negro*, 1947, platinum print / *platino*, 25.4 x 20.32 cm, 10" x 8"

Manuel Alvarez Bravo
The Bird Sings While the Branch Rustles / *El Pájaro canta mientras la rama cruje*, 1960, platinum print / *platino*, 20.32 x 25.4 cm, 8" x 10"

Manuel Alvarez Bravo
Sweethearts / *Novios de Usila*, 1964, platinum print / *platino*, 25.4 x 20.32 cm,10" x 8"

Manuel Alvarez Bravo
Forbidden Fruit / *Fruta prohibida*, 1976, platinum print / *platino*, 20.32 x 25.4 cm, 8" x 10"

Manuel Alvarez Bravo
In a Small Space / *En un pequeño espacio*, 1995 platinum print / *platino*, 25.4 x 20.32 cm, 10" x 8"

Leonora Carrington
The Powers of Madame Phoenicia / *Los poderes de Madame Phoenicia*, 1974, mixed media on silk / *técnica mixta sobre tela de seda*, 42.5 x 44.5 cm, $16^{3/4}$" x $17^{1/2}$"

Elena Climent
Blue Pail / *Cubeta azul*, 1990, oil on canvas / *óleo sobre tela*, 28.5 x 23 cm, $11^{1/4}$" x 9"

Elena Climent
Objects with Photo of Spanish Porch / *Objetos con foto en un pórtico español*, 1999, oil on canvas on board / *óleo sobre tela sobre Madera*, 21.6 x 27.9 cm, $8^{1/4}$" x $10^{3/4}$"

Miguel Covarrubias
Portrait of Diego Rivera / *Retrato de Diego Rivera*, 1920s, ink and watercolor on paper / *tinta y acuarela sobre papel*, 29 x 21 cm cm, $11^{7/16}$" x $8^{1/4}$"

Gabriel Figueroa
Figure, from the movie "The Fugitive" / *Silueta, de la película "El fugitivo"*, 1947, Palladium platinum print / *platino*, 20 x 25 cm, 8" x 10"

Gabriel Figueroa
Fishermen, from the movie "Maclovia" / *Pescadores, de la película "Maclovia"*, 1948, Palladium platinum print / *platino*, 20 x 25 cm, 8" x 10"

Gabriel Figueroa
Procession, from the movie "Hidden River" / *Procesión, de la película "Rio Escondido"*, 1947, Palladium Platinum print / *Platino*, 20 x 27.5 cm, 8" x 10"

Gabriel Figueroa
The Eyes of María, from the movie "Woman in Love" / *Los ojos de María, de la película " Enamorada"*, 1948 Palladium platinum print / *platino*, 20 x 25 cm, 8" x 10"

Gabriel Figueroa
Rails, from the movie "Victims of Sin" / *Rieles, de la película "Victimas del pecado"*, 1950, Palladium platinum print / *platino*, 20 x 25 cm, 8" x 10"

Gabriel Figueroa
Maguey, from the movie "A Love Date" / *Maguey, de la película "Una cita de amor"*, 1956, Palladium platinum print / *platino*, 20 x 25 cm, 8" x 10"

Gunther Gerzso
The Four Elements / *Los cuatro elementos*, 1953, Oil on canvas / *óleo sobe tela*, 100 x 65 cm, $39^{3/8}$" x $25^{5/8}$"

Gunther Gerzso
The Cat from London Street / *El gato de la calle Londres*, 1954, oil on canvas / *óleo sobre tela*, 64 x 80 cm
$25^{3/16}$" x $31^{1/2}$"

Gunther Gerzso
Archaic Landscape / *Paisaje arcaico*, 1956, oil on Masonite / *óleo sobre Masonite*, 80 x 53 cm , $31^{1/2}$" x $20^{7/8}$"

Gunther Gerzso
Portrait of Mr. Jacques Gelman / *Retrato del Señor Jacques Gelman*, 1957, oil on canvas / *óleo sobre tela*
72 x 60 cm, $28^{3/8}$" x $23^{5/8}$"

Gunther Gerzso
Figure in Red and Blue / *Personaje en rojo y azul*, 1964, oil on canvas / *óleo sobre tela*, 100 x 73 cm, $39^{3/8}$" x $28^{3/4}$"

María Izquierdo
Horses / *Los caballos*, 1938, watercolor on paper / *acuarela sobre papel*, 21 x 28 cm, $8^{1/4}$" x 11"

María Izquierdo
Circus Scene / *Escena de circo*, 1940, *gouache* on paper / *gouache sobre papel*, 42 x 54 cm, $16^{1/2}$" x $21^{1/4}$"

María Izquierdo
Circus Scene with Gypsy / *Escena de circo con gitanos*, 1940, *gouache* on paper / *gouache sobre papel*

Frida Kahlo
Self-portrait with Necklace / *Autorretrato con collar*, 1933, oil on metal / *óleo sobre lámina*, 35 x 29 cm
$13^{3/4}$" x $11^{7/16}$"

Frida Kahlo
Drawing of Nacho Aguirre / *Dibujo de Nacho Aguirre (anverso)*, 1935, pencil on paper / *lápiz sobre papel*
22 x 22 cm, $8^{3/4}$" x $8^{3/4}$"

Frida Kahlo
Drawing of Eyes / *Dibujo de ojos (reverso)*, 1935, pencil on Paper / *lápiz sobre papel*, 22 x 22 cm, $8^{3/4}$" x $8^{3/4}$"

Frida Kahlo
Portrait of Diego Rivera / *Retrato de Diego Rivera*, 1937, oil on Masonite / *óleo sobre Masonite*, 53 x 39 cm, $20^{7/8}$" x $15^{3/8}$"

Frida Kahlo
Self-portrait with Bed / *Autorretrato con cama*, 1937, oil on metal / *óleo sobre lámina*, 40 x 30 cm, $15^{3/4}$" x $11^{3/4}$"

Frida Kahlo
Self-portrait with Braid / *Autorretrato con trenza*, 1941, oil on canvas / *óleo sobre tela*, 51 x 38.5 cm, 20" x $15^{1/8}$"

Frida Kahlo
Self-portrait with Red and Gold Dress / *Autorretrato con vestido rojo y dorado*, 1941, oil on canvas / *óleo sobre tela*, 39 x 27.5 cm, $15^{3/8}$" x $10^{7/8}$"

Frida Kahlo
Portrait of Mrs. Natasha Gelman/*Retrato de la Señora Natasha Gelman*, 1943, oil on Masonite / *óleo sobre Masonite*, 30 x 23 cm, $11^{7/8}$" x 9"

Frida Kahlo
Diego on My Mind / *Diego en mi pensamiento*, 1943, oil on Masonite / *óleo sobre Masonite*, 76 x 61 cm, $29^{7/8}$" x 24"

Frida Kahlo
The Bride Who Became Frightened When She Saw Life Opened / *La novia que se espanta de ver la vida abierta*, 1943, oil on canvas / *óleo sobre tela*,
63 x 81.5 cm, $24^{7/8}$" x 32"

Frida Kahlo
Self-portrait with Monkeys / *Autorretrato con monos*, 1943, oil on canvas / *óleo sobre tela*, 81.5 x 63 cm, 32" x $24^{7/8}$"

Frida Kahlo
Karma I , 1946, sepia ink on paper / *tinta sepia sobre papel*, 18 x 27 cm, $7^{1/4}$" x $10^{3/4}$"

Frida Kahlo
Karma, 1946, sepia ink on paper / *tinta sepia sobre papel*, 21.3 x 27 cm, 8" x $10^{3/4}$"

Frida Kahlo
The Love Embrace of the Universe, the Earth (Mexico) Diego, I and Señor Xolotl / *El Abrazo de Amor del Universo, la Tierra (México), Diego, yo y el Señor Xolotl*, 1949, oil on Masonite / *óleo sobre Masonite*, 70 x 60.5 cm, $27^{1/2}$" x $23^{7/8}$"

Frida Kahlo
Collage with Two Flies / *Collage con dos moscas*
ca. 1953, Collage and watercolor on cardboard /
collage y acuarela sobre carton

Frida Kahlo
Drawing with Foot / *Dibujo con pie*, Undated / *Sin fecha*, Color pencil and graphite on paper / *lápiz de color y grafito sobre papel*, 21.3 x 27 cm, 8" x $10^{3/4}$"

Agustin Lazo
Execution by Firing Squad / *Fusilamento*, ca. 1930 – 1932, Gouache and ink on paper/*gouache y tinta sobre papel*, 24.6 x 33 cm, $9^{5/8}$" x 13"

Agustin Lazo
Dangerous Games / *Juegos peligrosos*, ca. 1930 – 1932, Gouache and china ink on paper/ *gouache y tinta china sobre papel*, 35 x 23.5 cm, $13^{3/4}$" x $9^{1/4}$"

Agustin Lazo
Bank Robbery / *Robo al banco*, ca. 1930 – 1932, Gouache and ink on paper / *gouache y tinta sobre papel*
24.6 x 33 cm, $9^{5/8}$" x 13"

Carlos Mérida
Festival of the Birds / *Fiesta de pájaros* , 1959, Polished board / *tablero pulido*, 50 x 40 cm, $19^{3/4}$" x $15^{3/4}$"

Carlos Mérida
The Message / *El mensaje*, 1960, Polished board / *tablero pulido*, 71 x 88 cm, 28" x $34^{5/8}$"

Carlos Mérida
Variation on an Old Theme / Variación a un viejo tema, 1960, Oil on canvas / *óleo sobre tela*, 89 x 69.5 cm
35" x $27^{3/8}$"

Carlos Mérida
Five Panels / *Cinco paneles*
1963
a)Watercolor and pencil on cardboard
b) *Gouache*, watercolor and pencil on cardboard
c) *Gouache*, watercolor and pencil on cardboard
d) *Gouache*, watercolor and pencil on cardboard
e) *Collage*, watercolor and pencil on cardboard
130 x 25 cm (cada panel), 511/4" x 93/4" (each panel)

José Clemente Orozco
Torso Study (Studio drawing for the murals of the National Preparatory School) / *Estudios de figura (para los murales de la Escuela Nacional Preparatoria)*, ca. 1926, Charcoal on *kraft* paper / *carboncillo sobre papel kraft*
61.5 x 96.5 cm, $24^{1/2}$" x 38"

José Clemente Orozco
Figure Study (Studio drawing for the murals of the National Preparatory School) / *Estudios de figura (para los murales de la Escuela Nacional Preparatoria)*, ca. 1926, charcoal on *kraft* paper / *carboncillo sobre papel kraft*, 95 x 71 cm, $37^{3/8}$" x 28"

José Clemente Orozco
Self-portrait / *Autorretrato*, 1932, watercolor and gouache on paper / *acuarela y gouache sobre papel* 37 x 30 cm, $14^{1/2}$" x $11^{7/8}$"

José Clemente Orozco
Untitled (Salon Mexico) / *Sin título (Salón México)*, 1940, gouache on paper / *gouache sobre papel* 49 x 67 cm, $19^{1/4}$" x $26^{3/8}$"

José Clemente Orozco
Painting / *Pintura*, 1942, oil on paper / *óleo sobre papel*, 37 x 25 cm, $14^{1/2}$" x $9^{7/8}$"

José Clemente Orozco
Liberty / *Libertad*, 1945, pencil and ink on paper / *lápiz y tinta sobre papel*, 37.5 x 28 cm, $15^{3/4}$" x 11"

José Clemente Orozco
Female Nude / *Desnudo femenino*, Undated / *Sin fecha*, ink and charcoal on paper / *tinta y carboncillo sobre papel*, 48 x 64 cm, $18^{7/8}$" x $25^{1/4}$"

Carlos Orozco Romero
Entrance to Infinity / *Entrada al infinito*, 1936, oil on canvas / *óleo sobre tela*, 75 x 55 cm, $29^{1/2}$" x $19^{3/4}$"

Carlos Orozco Romero
Protest / *Protesta*, 1939, oil, gouache and pencil on canvas / *aguada de óleo y lápiz sobre tela* 39 x 32 cm, $15^{3/8}$" x $12^{5/8}$"

Carlos Orozco Romero
The Bride / *La novia*, 1939, oil on canvas / *óleo sobre tela*, 41 x 31 cm, $16^{1/8}$" x $12^{1/8}$"

Carlos Orozco Romero
Dancers / *Danzantes*, Undated / *Sin fecha*, pencil and watercolor on paper / *lápiz y acuarela sobre papel* 48 x 59 cm, $18^{7/8}$" x $68^{1/4}$"

Diego Rivera
The Last Hour/*Última hora*, 1915, oil on canvas / *óleo sobre tela*, 92 x 73 cm, $36^{1/4}$" x $28^{3/4}$"

Diego Rivera
Landscape with Cactus / *Paisaje con cactus*, 1931, oil on canvas / *óleo sobre tela*, 125.5 x 150 cm, $49^{3/8}$" x 59"

Diego Rivera
Modesta, 1937, Oil on canvas / *óleo sobre tela*, 80 x 59 cm, $3^{11/2}$" x $23^{1/4}$"

Diego Rivera
Portrait of Mrs. Natasha Gelman / *Retrato de la Señora Natasha Gelman*, 1943, oil on canvas / *óleo sobre tela* 115 x 153 cm, $45^{1/4}$" x $60^{1/4}$"

Diego Rivera
Sunflowers / *Girasoles*, 1943, oil on wood / *óleo sobre madera*, 90 x 130 cm, $35^{1/2}$" x $51^{1/8}$"

Diego Rivera
Calla Lily Vendor / *Vendedora de alcatraces*, 1943, oil on Masonite / *óleo sobre Masonite*, 150 x 120 cm 59" x $47^{1/4}$"

Diego Rivera
Girl with gloves / *Niña con guantes*, 1943, watercolor on paper / *acuarela sobre papel*, 73 x 53 cm, $28^{3/4}$" x $20^{7/8}$"

Diego Rivera
The Healer / *El curandero*, 1943, gouache on paper / *gouche sobre papel*, 47 x 61 cm, $18^{1/2}$" x 24"

Diego Rivera
Untitled / *Sin título*, Undated / *Sin fecha*, pencil on paper / *lápiz sobre papel*, 31 x 23 cm, $12^{1/4}$" x 19"

Jesús Reyes Ferreira
Flower Vase / *El florero*, Undated / *Sin fecha*, tempera on china paper / *temple sobre papel de china* 74 x 48.5 cm, $29^{1/8}$" x 19"

Jesús Reyes Ferreira
Untitled / *Sin título*, Undated / *Sin fecha*, tempera on china paper / *temple sobre papel de china* 75 x 48.5 cm, $29^{1/9}$" x 19"

Jesús Reyes Ferreira
The Goodbye / *El adios*, Undated / *Sin fecha*, tempera on china paper / *temple sobre papel de china*, 75.5 x 49.5 cm, $29^{3/9}$" x $19^{1/2}$"

David Álfaro Siqueiros
Siqueiros by Siqueiros / *Siqueiros por Siqueiros* 1930, oil on canvas / *óleo sobre tela*, 99 x 79 cm, 39" x 31"

David Álfaro Siqueiros
Head of a Woman / *Cabeza de mujer*, 1939, oil on canvas / *óleo sobre tela*, 54.5 x 43 cm, $21^{1/2}$" x $16^{7/8}$"

David Álfaro Siqueiros
Woman with Rebozo / *Mujer con rebozo*, 1949, Piroxiline on Masonite / *Piroxilina sobre Masonite* 119.5 x 97 cm, 47" x $38^{1/8}$"

David Álfaro Siqueiros
Portrait of Mrs. Natasha Gelman / *Retrato de la Señora Natasha Gelman*, 1950, Piroxiline on Masonite / *Piroxilina sobre Masonite*, 120 x 100 cm, $47^{1/4}$" x $39^{3/8}$"

Juan Soriano
Girl with Still Life / *Niña con naturaleza muerta*, 1939, oil on canvas / *óleo sobre tela*, 81.3 x 65.2 cm, 32" x $25^{5/8}$"

Juan Soriano
Still Life with Brain Coral / *Naturaleza muerta con madrepora*, 1944, oil on Masonite / *óleo sobre Masonite* 60.3 x 51.9 cm, $23^{3/4}$" x $20^{1/2}$"

Rufino Tamayo
Portrait of Cantinflas / *Retrato de Cantinflas*, 1948, oil on canvas / *óleo sobre tela*, 100 x 80.5 cm, $39^{3/8}$" x $31^{3/4}$"

Rufino Tamayo
Portrait of Mrs. Natasha Gelman / *Retrato de la Señora Natasha Gelman*, 1948, oil and charcoal on Masonite / *óleo y carbón sobre Masonite*, 120 x 91 cm, $47^{1/2}$" x $35^{7/8}$"

Rufino Tamayo
Untitled / *Sin título*, 1950, watercolor and pastel on paper / *acuarela y pastel sobre papel*, 23 x 17 cm, 9" x $6^{3/4}$"

Rufino Tamayo
Untitled / *Sin título*, Undated / Sin fecha, ink and watercolor on paper / *tinta y acuarela sobre papel* 28 x 21 cm, 11" x $8^{1/4}$"

Rufino Tamayo
Untitled / *Sin título*, Undated / *Sin fecha*, ink and watercolor on paper / *tinta y acuarela sobre papel* 28 x 21 cm, 11" x $8^{1/4}$"

Francisco Toledo
Plan of Juchitan / *Plan de Juchitán*, 1972-73, oil with sand on canvas / *óleo sobre tela con carga arenosa* 135 x 154 cm, $53^{1/4}$" x 60"

Francisco Toledo
Rabbit of the Scorpions / *Conejo de los escorpiones*, 1975, oil on canvas with sand / *óleo sobre tela con carga arenosa*, 100 x 129.5 cm, 39$^{3/8}$" x 51"

Francisco Toledo
Self-portrait with Hat / *Autorretrato con sombrero*, 1987, oil and tempera on canvas on Masonite / *óleo y temple sobre tela sobre Masonite*, 60 x 70 cm, 23$^{5/8}$" x 27$^{1/2}$"

Francisco Toledo
Net / *Red*, 1988, ink on paper / *tinta sobre papel*, 49.5 x 65 cm, 19$^{1/2}$" x 25$^{5/8}$"

Francisco Toledo
Palm-rug of Grasshoppers / *El petate de los chapulines*, 1989, pencil and ink on paper / *lápiz y tinta sobre papel*, 49.5 x 65 cm, 19$^{1/2}$" x 25$^{5/8}$"

Angel Zárraga
Untitled / *Sin título*, ca. 1917, oil on canvas / *óleo sobre tela*, 46.5 x 33.5 cm, 18$^{1/4}$" x 13$^{1/2}$"

Angel Zárraga
Portrait of Mr. Jacques Gelman / *Retrato del Señor Jacques Gelman*, 1945, oil on canvas / *óleo sobre tela* 130.5 x 110.5 cm, 51$^{3/8}$" x43$^{1/2}$"

Angel Zárraga
Portrait of Mrs. Natasha Gelman / *Retrato de la Señora Natasha Gelman*, ca. 1946, oil on canvas / *óleo sobre tela*, 109 x 109 cm, 43" x 43"

Nahum Zenil
When I Don't Feel Like It / *Cuando no tengo ganas*, 1984, mixed media on paper / *técnica mixta sobre papel* 29.5 x 21.5 cm, 11$^{5/8}$" x 8$^{1/2}$"

Nahum Zenil
Waiting / *Esperando*, 1984, mixed media on paper / *técnica mixta sobre papel*, 29.5 x 21.5 cm 11$^{5/8}$" x 8$^{1/2}$"

Nahum Zenil
Heart / *Corazón*, 1987, mixed media on paper / *técnica mixta sobre papel*, 29.5 x 21.5 cm, 11$^{5/8}$" x 8$^{1/2}$"

Exhibition Credits

Exhibition Coordinators
Cesáreo Moreno
Rebecca Meyers

Exhibition Design
Cesáreo Moreno
Angelina Villanueva

Registration
Rebecca Meyers
Raquel Aguiñaga~Martinez
Cristina Carrera
Alicia Silva

Installation
Oscar Sanchez
Guillermo Aguiñaga
Cesáreo Moreno
Raquel Aguiñaga~Martinez
Rebecca Meyers
Cristina Carrera
James Perry
Alicia Silva
Luis Guzman
Aldo de Santiago
Luis Tubens
Miguel Zuniga
Walter Ornelas
Carlos Aguiñaga

Gallery Text
provided by the Seattle Art Museum
translated by Gretchen Sleicher

Labels
Cesáreo Moreno
Alicia Silva
Luis Ulloa
Luis A. Guzman
Angelina Villanueva

Special Thanks
Robert R. Littman
Magda Carranza de Akle
Lydia Huante

Mexican Fine Arts Center Museum

Staff

Administration
Carlos Tortolero – Executive Director
Juana Guzman – Associate Executive Director
Rachel Blanco – Administrative Office Manager
Sonia Gonzalez – Receptionist
Vanessa Puentes-Sanchez – Intern
Almadelia Hernandez – Intern

Business Office
Silvia Z. Cisneros – Business Director
Eimy Rosales – Assistant Business Director
Imelda Rodriguez – Intern

Development
Randy Adamsick – Development Director
Juan C. Hernandez – Associate Development Director
Aidé Rodriguez – Grants Officer
Edward Herrerias – Development Associate, Government Relations

Education
Lydia Huante – Education Director
Nancy Villafranca – School Programs Coordinator
Dolores Mercado – Arts Educator
Georgina Osuna-Diaz – Assistant Arts Educator
Noelia Salinas – Assistant Arts Educator

Tour Guides
Jonathan Aguilar
Aldo De Santiago
Luis A. Guzman
Montserrat Hernandez
Jesus Sanchez
Luis Tubens

Gift Shop
Raquel Rios – Retail Manager
Maria Tortolero – Assistant Retail Manager
Maria Luisa Estanislao – Gift Shop Assistant
Socorro Aguiñaga – Gift Shop Assistant

Graphic Arts
Angelina Villanueva – Graphic Arts Director

Performing Arts
Amber Da – Director of Performing Arts
Gabriel Perez - Intern

Permanent Collection
Rebecca Meyers – Registrar/ Permanent Collection Director
Cristina Carrera – Permanent Collection Assistant Director/ Associate Registrar

Public Relations
Eva Penar – Marketing / Media Director
Anel Marchan – Marketing / Media Intern

Visual Arts
Cesáreo Moreno – Visual Arts Director
Raquel Aguiñaga-Martinez – Visual Arts Assistant Director
Oscar Sanchez – Arts Preparator
Alicia Silva – Intern

Operations
Ignacio Guzman – Building Operations Consultant
Román Serrano – Director of Operations
Efrain Macias – Operations Assistant
Jose Aguilar – Operations Assistant
Luis Martin Gámez – Custodian
Lucas Martinez – Custodian

Gallery Attendants
Tony Adamiak
Yolanda Balenegro
Janet Bataz
Mirella Campos
Frank Garcia
Adriana Garcia
Maria Guzman
Lluvia Hernandez
Rudy Hernandez
Liz Hurtado
Juan Lopez
Leticia Lozano
Jesus Macias
Nancy Mendoza
Karla Ortiz
Salvador Ortiz
Joe Rodriguez
Denise Salinas
Luis Sandoval
Lucia Tapia
Martin Zamora

Yollocalli Youth Museum
Walter Ornelas – Director
William Estrada – Visual Arts Educator
Jaime Muñoz – Office Manager
Maria Gaspar – Youth Net Coordinator
Anthony Marcos Rea – Youth Net Coordinator

Radio Arte WRTE 90.5 FM
Yolanda Rodriguez-Pacheco – Station Director
Jorge Valdivia – Assistant Station Director
Monica Posada-Ferro – Marketing & Program Director
Jesus Echeverria – Special Programs Manager

Sponsors:

This exhibition has been made possible by
Esta exposición es presentada por cortesía de

The Vergel Foundation, New York
Secretaría de Relaciones Exteriores de México

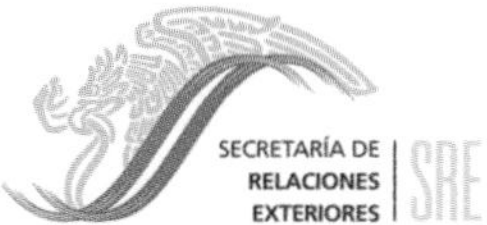

CONACULTA

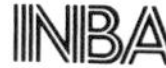

Instituto Nacional de Bellas Artes

Funders:

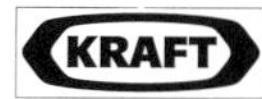

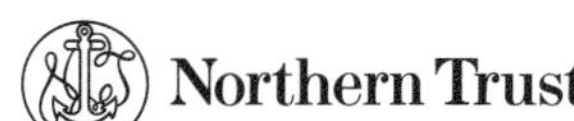

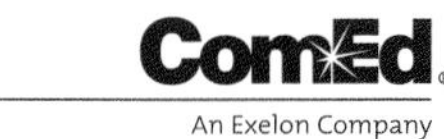

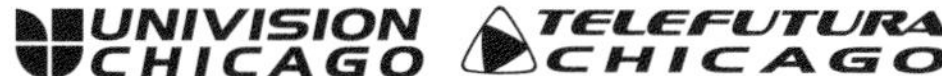

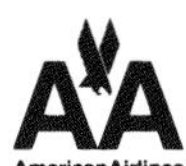

Transportation provided by American Airlines

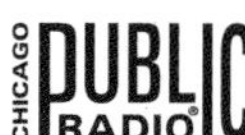

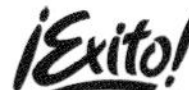

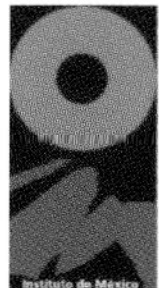

Instituto de Mexico Chicago

Additional Funders:

The Joyce Foundation
Chicago Park District
Chicago Department of Cultural Affairs
Illinois Arts Council
Accommodations provided by Lenox Suites

Exhibition Padrinos:

Maria Bechily & Scott Hodes
Pamela Crutchfield and Myron Szold
Flavia Hernandez
Ruth Horwich
Belen Jaquez
Daniel & Lucia Woods Lindley
Manuel Medina
Maria Medina
Clare Muñana
Erasmo Salgado
Rebecca Sive & Steve Tomashefsky
Univision Chicago
V&V Foods
Arthur R. & Joanne Velasquez
John & Dorianne Venator